COL. R. W. SIMPSON.

HISTORY

—of—

OLD PENDLETON DISTRICT

—with—

A GENEALOGY OF THE LEADING FAMILIES

OF THE DISTRICT

—by—

R. W. Simpson

1913
Oulla Printing & Binding Company
Anderson, S. C .

Facsimile Reprint

Published 1988 By
HERITAGE BOOKS, INC.
1540E Pointer Ridge Place, Bowie, Maryland 20716
(301)-390-7709

ISBN 1-55613-124-0

A Catalog listing Hundreds Of Titles On
Genealogy, History, And Americana
Available Free Upon Request

PREFACE

W E HAVE for quite a number of years felt the importance of preserving to some extent, at least, the history of Pendleton, as well as that of the County of Pendleton as much as possible. Many intervening years, the death and removal of some of the prominent citizens of the past as well as their descendants, have made this pleasant duty almost an impossibility. Our duties otherwise have also made this labor a burden instead of a pleasure. But, nevertheless, with the help of friends and neighbors, we have ventured upon the experiment.

A wise historian has said that history ought not to be written until one hundred years have elapsed since the event. Be this as it may, it appears to us to be the duty of all good citizens, in passing through life's toils and pleasures, to preserve the facts and circumstances of history, so that in the future the history of Pendleton may be presented accurately by the coming historian. We, therefore, present with some misgivings as well as pleasure, such facts and circumstances in the history of Pendleton as we have been able to trace them in the past.

R. W. SIMPSON.

Pendleton, S. C.

RICHARD WRIGHT SIMPSON

BY WILLIAM S. MORRISON, PROFESSOR OF HISTORY AND
POLITICAL ECONOMY, CLEMSON COLLEGE,
SOUTH CAROLINA.

R ICHARD WRIGHT SIMPSON was born on his
father's farm near Pendleton, Anderson County,
South Carolina, September 11, 1840.

His father was Richard F. Simpson, a native of
Laurens District, South Carolina, a graduate of the
South Carolina College, and for many years a lawyer at
Laurens Court House; a soldier with the rank of major
in the Florida war; a member of both branches of the
General Assembly of his native State; three terms
(1842-48) a member of the House of Representatives of
the Congress of the United States; and a signer of the
Ordinance of Secession of the State of South Carolina.

His mother was Margaret Taliaferro, a native of
Anderson District, South Carolina, whose parents were
Virginians by birth.

"Dick" Simpson enjoyed an ideal boyhood. He
was well and strong, the son of indulgent parents, living
a free country life. He enjoyed hunting and fishing
and was fond of work with tools. At home he read the
Bible, Shakespeare, and Scott's Novels. He attended
Pendleton Academy from which he went to Wofford
College. The late Dr. James H. Carlisle, at the time
the only surviving member of the Wofford Faculty of
the fifties, was asked a few years since, to write his re-
collections of the "Simpson Brothers" as students. The
following is a literal copy of his answer:

"The Simpson Brothers—this is the way in which

the survivors of the generation of Wofford students, 1857-1861—think of T. N. Simpson and R. W. Simpson, as the catalogues gave their names. Their brotherly affection was marked. Each might have said of the other what the late Robert W. Boyd said to me about his brother Charles: 'We were not only brothers—we were great friends.' They were gentlemanly, self-respecting young men, whose conduct represented the refined Christian home, which they had left. Joining different lit erary societies each gained the highest honor in the gift of his fellow-members. At the Anniversary the two brothers sat on the platform as presidents of the Calhoun and Preston Societies. In their Senior year (1860-61) the clouds of war gathered. The students formed a military company, 'The Southern Guards,' and T. N. Simpson was elected captain. Arrangements were made for the usual May exhibition. The program had these names and subjects:

T. N. Simpson—Vox Populi.

R. W. Simpson—Republican Institutions in North America—are they a failure?

Surely these were timely subjects, well fitted to draw out the feelings and convictions of the young patriots and orators. But when the time came these speakers were not on the platform. They were on the tented field. The bombardment of Fort Sumter, April 12, 13, 1861, seemed to the students as their mother's call to duty, and they answered at once.

Capt. T. N. Simpson was one of the unreturning braves. His sword is now among the valuable relics in Wofford College. His brother was spared for years of service with his fellow-citizens in carrying his native State through a great historical crisis."

R. W. Simpson served as a private in the Confederate army in Company A, Third Regiment South Carolina Volunteers, and in Adams' battallion of cavalry from April, 1861 to 1863, when, on account of disease

contracted in the service, he was detailed for special
duty until the close of the war.

From 1865 to 1874 Colonel Simpson farmed. Then
began his sympathy with the tillers of the soil. In the
fall of 1874 he was chosen a member of the State Legislature, and was re-elected in 1876—the year of Carolina's redemption from the hand of the alien and the
traitor—the "carpet bagger" and the "Scalawag." He
was made chairman of the Committee of Ways and
Means of the "Wallace House," always a position of
great responsibility, then one of peculiar dangers and
difficulties, as is well understood by all who remember
the struggles of that time and by every student of "Reconstruction." Colonel Simpson's friends claim for him
the credit of first suggesting the idea of the Democrats
of South Carolina breaking loose from the maternal
party—of securing control of the State and letting Til-
den's friends fight for their own cause—the plan of cut-
ting what Gen. M. W. Gary called the "gordion knot"—
a plan which resulted in President Hays withdrawing
the United States troops, and Governor Hampton securing undisputed possession of the State House and the
State.

Chairman Simpson's services in settling the dis-
ordered finances of the State were delicate and difficult,
but time proved the wisdom of his views. "He devised
the plan—and secured the adoption—which reduced the
debt of the State to its present small proportions."

It was while serving in the Legislature that R. W.
Simpson was appointed a member of the Governor's
Staff, with the rank of Colonel of Cavalry, by Governor
Wade Hampton.

During those days he became convinced that
changed conditions made necessary a change in our educational system. He became an earnest advocate of the
establishment of an agricultural college. He was the
confidential advisor of the Honorable Thos. G. Clemson—

wrote that gentleman's will, was made executor of that
instrument, and on the organization of the Board of Trustees of the Clemson Agricultural College of South Carolina
was elected chairman of that Board, which position he
resigned, on account of impaired health a few years before his death. His interest in, and his devotion to the
welfare of Clemson College are well known to all who
know anything of the history of that institution for the
first twenty years of its existence.

About the time he went into politics Colonel Simp-
son studied law, was admitted to the bar, practiced at
Anderson Court House, and was local attorney for the
Southern Rail Road flfteen years and for the Blue Ridge
Railway for eight years. He was also attorney for the
Bank of Pendleton.

Colonel Simpson was a life-long member of the
Methodist Episcopal Church, South. He loved its doc-
trines and polity and was many years a Sunday School
teacher and superintendent.

On February 10, 1863, R. W. Simpson was married
to Miss Maria Louise Garlington, of Laurens County, S.
C. Their beautiful home-life, their devotion to
each other are well known to all their friends. Of this
happy union ten children were born—of whom nine are
now living: Mrs. W. W. Watkins, Mrs. P. H. E. Sloan, Jr.,
Miss M. L. Simpson, Mrs. A. G. Holmes, Mrs. S. M. Martin, Mrs. W. W. Klugh, Messrs. R. W. Simpson, Jr., J. G.
Simpson and T. S. Simpson.

Colonel Simpson died in a hospital in Atlanta where
he had been taken for treatment a few days before, at
four o'clock in the morning of the 11th day of July,
1912. The afternoon of the next day his remains were
laid to rest by the new made grave of his wife, near the
resting place of his father and his mother and his soldier

boy brother, in the family burying ground at the old
home place near Pendleton, South Carolina.

"When a great man dies
For years beyond our ken
The light he leaves behind him lies
Upon the paths of men."

PENDLETON

PREVIOUS to the year 1768 the only court held in South Carolina was in the City of Charleston. In that year the State was divided into six districts, and Courts of General Sessions and Common Pleas were thereafter established and held in each of the said districts. The judges were authorized to build court houses and other necessary public buildings in some convenient place in each. A court house was established at Ninety-Six, at Cambridge, (See State Statutes, Vol. 7, p. 197.)

At the close of the Revolutionary War all the territory embraced in the present counties of Greenville, Anderson, Oconee and Pickens belonged to the Cherokee Indians, although embraced within the State lines. Many adventurous white people had founded settlements within this territory, and, for their protection from the Indians, the State had built forts in several places, and maintained garrisons therein. All of this territory, except the extreme upper portion of Oconee and Pickens counties was ceded to the State by the Cherokees shortly after the close of the war by a treaty negotiated by Gen. Andrew Pickens near his home on Seneca River. Tradition points out a large oak tree, near the banks of the Seneca River, under which General Pickens met the Cherokee chiefs and made with them the treaty by which the State secured the exclusive possession of this territory.

In 1816, General Statutes, Vol. U, p. 252, another treaty was concluded in the City of Washington by which the Cherokee Indians ceded to the State the remaining parts of the land lying above the old Indian boundary, and within the limits of the State lines as they now exist.

By Act of March 16, 1783, commissioners were appointed to divide the six judicial districts into counties of not more than forty miles square for the purpose of establishing county courts. Andrew Pickens, Richard Anderson, Thomas Brandon, Levi Keysey, Philemon Waters, Arthur Simpkins and Simon Berwick were appointed commissioners to divide the District of Ninety-Six, (Vol. 4, p. 561). By Act of 1785, Vol. 4, p. 661, the several districts were divided into counties. The District of Ninety-Six was divided into the counties of Abbeville, Edgefield, Newberry, Laurens, Union and Spartanburg; and the Justices of Peace were authorized to locate and build court houses and jails, and to levy taxes to pay for the same. And the lands ceded to the State by the Cherokee Indians, embracing the present counties of Anderson, Greenville, Pickens and Oconee were attached temporarily to the adjoining counties of Abbeville, Laurens and Spartanburg. Pendleton County, as afterwards established, was attached to Abbeville County, and for the time being was in the judicial district of Ninety-Six, which by the way explains why we find some of our land deeds styled Ninety-Six.

Acts of 1789, Vol. 7, p. 252, sets forth as follows: "Whereas, the people residing in that part of the lands ceded to the State by the Cherokee Indians, north of the Indian boundary and between the Seneca and Saluda rivers, have experienced many inconveniences by being attached to Abbeville County, which renders it necessary to establish it into a separate county. Therefore, be it enacted, That the same be laid off into a county to be called Pendleton County. The other part of the said ceded lands was laid off into a county to be called Greenville County.

Pendleton was named in honor of Judge Henry Pendleton, a native of Virginia, who rose to distinction in this State by reason of his great ability and patriotism.

By Act of 1789, Vol. V., p. 105, the new counties of Pendleton and Greenville were allowed representation in the legislature, each to have one senator and three members in the lower house. At the same session commissioners were appointed to locate a court house for the County of Pendleton. The commissioners were Andrew Pickens, John Miller, John Wilson, Benj. Cleveland, Wm. Halbert, Henry Clark, John Moffett and Robert Anderson. These commissioners purchased from Isaac Lynch a tract of land, about as near the center of the County of Pendleton as practicable, containing eight hundred and eighty-five acres. And the same was conveyed to the said commissioners in trust for the County of Pendleton, as appears by deed dated April 8, 1790, and recorded in book "A," page 1.

Upon this tract of land the Town of Pendleton is located. This tract of land, or a part of it, was laid out into streets and village lots, which were numbered, and the remainder of the tract was divided into what were called "out-lying" lots.

The first court house was located on what is called the Tanyard Branch, near the culvert under the big fill on the Blue Ridge Railroad which crosses the old public road leading from Pendleton to old Pickens Court House.

The first court held in Pendleton County was held by the magistrates on the second day of April, 1790. Andrew Rowe was employed to erect a temporary log court house, 18 feet by 25 feet. John Miller was elected clerk of the court. On the 10th day of May, 1790, the first quarterly court was held in the new court house. Present: Magistrates Robert Anderson, John Wilson and William Halbert. The following grand jury was drawn to serve at the next court, namely: David Hamilton, Lewis Daniel Martin, Jonathan Clarke, Thomas Garvin, William McCharles Yates, Robert Dowdle, Alex. Oliver, Benjamin Horsce, Isaac Lynch, John Polluck, Joseph Kennedy, Duncan Cameron, Joseph Brown, James Gates,

John Grisham, Sr., James Hamilton, William Mackey, Jacob Vance, and Samuel McCullom. At the same time the following petit jury was drawn to serve at the next court, namely: David Pruitt, James Davenport, Abel Anderson, John Dixon, Robert Stevenson, James Barton, John Martin, William Troop, Eli Kitchens, Elisha Gaillard, William Pilgrim, James Embree, Samuel Porter, Richard York, Andrew Riddle, Hamilton Montgomery, Benjamin Norton, Richard Lancaster, William Grant, John Burton, Philemon Hawkins, Alexander Ramsey, William Steele, William Lewis, John McCutchin. Alexander McCrery, John Tweety, O. Smith, Thomas Moss, and John Mayfield.

Samuel Lofton exhibited to the court his commission from the Governor as sheriff, which was ordered recorded. The county courts exercised a wide jurisdiction. Among other things they laid out all the public roads in the county.

By the Act of 1791, Vol. 7, p. 262, Gen. Andrew Pickens, Col. Robert Anderson, Capt. Robert Maxwell, John Bowen, James Harrison, Maj. John Ford and John Hallum were appointed to purchase land and superintend the building of a court house and jail for the district of Washington. Washington District was composed of the counties of Pendleton and Greenville. The court house was located at Pickensville, near the present Town of Easley.

By the Act of 1792, Vol. V, p. 210, it was enacted, that the village in Pendleton County where the court house and jail of Washington District have been located, shall be called Pickensville, so named in honor of General Pickens. Here were held the Courts of Common Pleas and General Sessions for a few years only.

By the Act of 1798, Vol. VII, p. 283, the name County was changed to District. And at the court house in each of the several districts there shall be held, after 1800, Courts of Sessions and Common Pleas, to possess and exercise the same powers and jurisdiction as is held by the district courts. By the same Act, it was enacted that the court for Pendleton District should be held at Pendleton Court House. And that the several courts of General Sessions of the Peace, Oyer and Terminer, Assizes, and General Jail Delivery, and Common Pleas, now established in this State, are hereby and forever abolished. The new courts established by this Act were called Courts of Sessions and Common Pleas. By the Act of 1799, Vol. VII, p. 291, county courts as they then existed, were also abolished.

By the Act of 1799, Vol. VII, p. 299, it was enacted, that all laws then of force relative to the district courts shall be construed to relate to the new districts and the courts thereof. By the Act of 1868, the name "District" was changed back to "County."

The first court house for the Courts of Sessions and Common Pleas for Pendleton District, was located in the present public square of the Town of Pendleton, in the hollow near the public well. The jail remains as it was then built. These two buildings were built of brick. In 1826, at the time when Pendleton District was divided into Pickens and Anderson, the commissioners were engaged in erecting a new court house, where the Farmers' Hall now stands. The Pendleton Farmers' Society purchased the old, and the new court house being built then erected, and with the material of the old, finished the new, which is still owned by the Pendleton Farmers' Society.

The records of the Court for Washington District, are said to be found in the Clerk's office at Greenville. The records of the Courts held at Pendleton may be found in the Clerk's office at Anderson.

The following are the names of some of the lawyers who practiced in the Courts at Pendleton, namely: Pickens and Farrar, Warren R. Davis and Lewis, Taylor and Harrison, Yancey and Whitfield, B. J. Earle, Geo.

W. Earle, Bowie and Bowie, Robert Anderson, Jr., Saxon, Yancey & Shanklin, Saxon & Trimmier, T. J. Earle, Z. Tal_ iaferro, Choice, Earle & Whitner, Thompson, Tillinghast, Norten, George McDuffie.   Doubtless there were others, these are all that can be found.

The Lynch tract of land, upon which the Town of Pendleton was located, at the time of its purchase, was bounded on all sides by lands still belonging to the State. But, it was located on the main thoroughfare or Indian trail, from Ninety-Six to Fort George, located further up in the lands formerly belonging to the Indians— Keowee being their chief town, and lying on the west bank of the beautiful river by that name.   The lands for many miles surrounding were slightly rolling and very rich and fertile, with numerous water courses traversing them.   As shown by the profile of the railroad, from Belton to Walhalla, Pendleton is situated in a basin, and in altitude above the sea, is considerably lower than Belton.   The Blue Ridge Mountains are distant about twenty-five miles, and the spectacle they present to the eye is grand and magnificent.   Lord Lowther of England was so much impressed with this mountain view that he caused a large dwelling house to be erected on the highest point in the town.   This dwelling is still in a good state of preservation, and is now owned and occupied by Mrs. William Henry Trescott and her daughters.

At the close of the Revolutionary War, many families from Pennsylvania, Maryland, Virginia, and North Carolina settled in Pendleton District.   Gen. Andrew Pickens, Col. Robert Anderson, Col. Benjamin Cleveland, Samuel Earle, Samuel Warren, and Horse Shoe Robertson were of this distinguished number.   They, and many others, were attracted by its salubrious climate and its rich and fertile soil.   The native forests were covered with a heavy growth of wild pea vine, which furnished a luxurious pasture winter and summer for horses, cattle and game.   Pendleton soon became from its location

the great trading center for a large and extensive territory, and very naturally, the business men of the town,
of all avocations, became rich.   The lands contiguous to
the town were in great demand, and were very early
purchased by men of means.   Their owners built large
and comfortable dwellings thus early and farmed with
great success.   These farmers practiced a generous mode
of living, satisfied with the increase of their slave population.

Early in the eighteenth century many of the wealthy residents of the low lands, along the sea coast, were
also attracted by the great advantages which the Town
of Pendleton afforded as a summer resort and came to
Pendleton to spend the summer.   They also purchased
farms and erected large, and some of them, very fine
residences for summer homes.   But many of them became permanent residents.   So it came about that all
the old citizens of Pendleton, in speaking of Pendleton,
called the country for miles around the "Town of
Pendleton.   It was quite natural that these low country gentlemen should bring with them the refined
customs and manners of the French Huguenots,
which took root and spread among the sturdy and cul-
tured residents from Virginia and other contiguous states,
until the very name of Pendleton became a synonym for
refined and beautiful women, and for elegant, high-toned
and chivalrous gentlemen.   The names of some of these
families who came from the low country to Pendleton
are given.   These names will speak for themselves:
Pinckneys, Elliotts, Bees, Stevens, Chevers, Haskels,
Smiths, Tunnor, Jennings, Porchers, Ravenels, Humes,
Boons, Norths, Adgers, Potters, Darts, DuPrees, Hamiltons, Haynes, Campbells, Wilsons, Warleys, Trescotts,
Cuthberts, Gibbes, Stuarts and Hugers.

Only a few of these families have descendants in
Pendleton at this time.

In addition to these immigrants from the low country, many other people from various sections of the State, many of them wealthy, also came to Pendleton to secure the benefit to be derived there in many ways. Among them were the Calhouns, Adams, Earles, Harrisons, Pickens, Andersons, Taliaferros, Lewis, Maxwell, Seaborns, Symmes, Kilpatricks, Rosses, Warleys, Lattas, Shanklins, Dicksons, Sloans, Smiths, Taylors, Bensons, Mavericks, Van Wycks, Whitners, Reeses, Cherrys, Simpsons, Hunters, Clemsons, Millers, Gilmans, Sittons,, Burts.

There were many wealthy and influential families scattered over the territory of Pendleton. Descendants of many of these families have been men known far and wide for their fine characters and great ability. Such men for instance as James L. Orr, Benj. F. Perry, Stephen D. Lee, Joseph E. Brown and others. It would have afforded us great pleasure to have reached out and embraced the many distinguished families and men in this little history, but to have done so would have extended it beyond all reasonable bounds. It is a well known fact that the descendants of these early settlers in Pendleton have produced more prominent men than perhaps any other portion of this or any other state of equal size— men who have left here for other states and have attained there high and important positions.

It might be well to pause here and inquire into the causes which produced noticeable results. The rules of society in Pendleton were for the protection of the women primarily. None but gentlemen were admitted into the family circle. No matter how rich he might be, he could not enter, and a poor man, if a gentleman, was always welcome. The standard was character and knowledge of how to conduct himself according to the code of a gentleman. It was as much as a man's life was worth to speak disrespectfully of a woman or to do or say anything not permitted by the best society. Consequently, the mothers, wives and sisters of this favored region were respected and honored, and as a natural result they shed an influence which in turn elevated the children, and produced a race of men that have shed lustre upon the State and our common country. It is a common maxim that there never was a great man unless he had a great mother. When women are pulled down by the tongue of slander, and by a lack of that veneration due them by the men, from the high and exalted position in which God in his Providence has placed them, we will look in vain for the coming of great men. There never was a breath of scandal connected with a woman in Pendleton. The men in their intercourse with other men, observed with profound respect the rules which a refined society established for the government of such intercourse. These observances, coupled with a free and generous hospitality from one and all, won for the Town of Pendleton, lying in the lap of the beautiful Blue Ridge Mountains, an extended reputation for elegance, refinement and hospitality second to very few places in the State.

When we look back fifty years ago, when Pendleton was in its highest degree of prosperity, we recall with what strikes us now with peculiar force, that there never was any jealousy or unfriendly feeling existing among the men and their families. But all seemed to live in perfect harmony one with the other. On account of the scattered condition cf the different homes there were but few entertainments given at night. Dinings were frequent between the various families, and such dinings as they were too. A very pretty custom was when a family invited another in the cool of the summer evening to tea, as it was then called. It was handed around on big waiters, out on the piazzas, and it was not tea alone either. Weddings were memorable occasions, everybody was invited, and a supper was served in the most lavish style. Often there was sufficient to feed not only the guests present, but the whole neighborhood besides.

The citizens of Pendleton always took an active interest in everything that looked to the uplifting of the people generally. They too were always zealous and watchful to preserve the liberties of the country, and especially those interests and rights that belong to every man and to the State and entire country as well.

During the days of Nullification the people of Pendleton were staunch supporters of Mr Calhoun, the leading spirit of that memorable movement. And were also earnest advocates of, and active participants in, those measures which culminated in the Secession of the State of South Carolina from the United States in 1860. When war was inevitable these people, almost to a man, volunteered in the army. The young men volunteered first, and unfortunately many of our young men were absent in college, or engaged in business in other places, and they joined the companies being raised at those places they were then at. This and other causes prevented the people of Pendleton from organizing local companies, thus showing their loyalty to the great cause at stake. But the companies of Capt. Daniels, Capt. Shanklin, Capt. Kilpatrick of Pickens, Capt. Garlington's company, of Laurens Capt. Trenholm's Squadron, Capt. Calhoun's company, of Pickens, the Butler Guards, and so on had numerous recruits of Pendleton boys. Before the end of the war every man in Pendleton who was at all able to bear arms, was in the service, gallantly fighting the battles of his country. As a result the town and surrounding country were almost entirely denuded of men. No part of the Confederacy suffered more perhaps than this section of the State. The teachings and the training that these people were so familiar with could have no other result than to create men who were more than willing to give their lives in defense of their country. Their religious training also manifested itself in the tender care bestowed by them upon the sick and wounded soldiers.

Very early after the Town of Pendleton became the county seat of Pendleton County the citizens became interested in educational matters.   In 1808, the legislature passed an act authorizing and directing the commissioner appointed to sell the lots into which the tract of land purchased from Isaac Lynch had been divided to turn over all the money in their hands to certain persons therein named for the purpose of establishing a circulating library.   By the same authority other moneys and lands were added to the library fund.   In 1811, the circulating library was incorporated and authority was given to the incorporation to buy and sell land, and all the remainder of the Lynch tract of land unsold was by said act vested in the said incorporation.   The circulating library continued in operation until 1825, when by act of the legislature the library was incorporated as the Pendleton Male Academy.   The brick academy was then built upon some of the land which the legislature had given to the library.   Afterwards, about 1835, another large school house was erected near the brick academy; which last was then turned into a dwelling for the teachers, and the school was held in the large wooden building.   Both these buildings still remain, and are in fair condition; and a large graded school is now held therein. The Pendleton Male Academy was for many years a celebrated school, and was always largely patronized, particularly by those citizens who resided within four or five miles of the town.

In 1827, there was also in Pendleton a Female Academy, in which year the trustees thereof were incorporated as the trustees of the Pendleton Female Academy.   In the year 1828, the trustees of thePendleton Female Academy purchased, at public sale, the large brick jail and had it improved and added to for an academy.   This Academy also became famous, and largely patronized both by residents and students from abroad.   The Farmers' Society owned the building adjoining the Female Academy lot, which they sold to the Academy to better accommodate the boarding students.   This building, many years after, the Academy sold to Col. D. S. Taylor.

There was still another school in town presided over by Miss Mary Hunter.   When established, no one now living knows.   Miss Mary had been teaching for many years before 1845, and she was then quite an old woman. To this school all the little tots, boys and girls, in the town and surrounding country went to learn the things Miss Mary taught, and I venture the assertion, not one of her scholars ever forgot the "Multiplication Table" to the very end of their days.   Those who attended this celebrated school can no doubt recall many laughable little incidents which happened therein.   The little boys and sometimes the little girls were sent to this school on horseback attended by an old Negro man, who returned in the afternoon and piloted them safely home.   When they arrived at the age of maturity, that is when they had grown so big Miss Mary could not whip them, they were promoted to the Male and Female Academy.   There was frequently more than a hundred children in each of these schools.   They came principally from the homes of parents who resided within the limits of Pendleton.   They came on foot, or on horse-back, in buggies, carriages, carryalls, hacks, and in every conceivable vehicle.   As the boys grew large enough they drove their sisters to the Female Academy, and they kept the vehicle and horses at their school, and in the afternoon the whole "lay-out" drove to the Female Academy, received their loads and returned home.

The men of Pendleton were ever noted for their high toned and chivalric characters.   They strictly observed all the courtesies and amenities of life, due from one gentleman to another, and any departure therefrom met with immediate condemnation—as with the parents, so with the boys.   There was no hazing at the Male Academy, but when a boy entered this school he had very soon to learn that he had to be a gentleman in his conduct. If he was not an apt student in learning the ways of a gentleman he had more fights on his hands than he could possibly attend to. And woe be to the boy who should make a remark reflecting upon the life or character of a lady. It made no difference what lady either. Thus were the boys trained in the ways of their fathers —to respect women, to honor the aged, and, in their intercourse with each other, to be honest, upright and gentlemanly. Their training was sometimes rough, yes, very rough, but in the end many honorable and noble men were turned out of this old Academy.

In 1834, the Pendleton Manual Labor School was incorporated. This school was under the direction of Rev. John L. Kennedy, who afterwards became famous as a teacher of the youth of the country. He afterwards taught most successfully at Pickens Court House, Thalian Academy, and other places. The labor school continued for a few years only. The reason given by Mr. Kennedy to the writer for its failure was two-fold. The boys could not stand being taken out of the school room to work in the sun. The sudden changes or other causes not determined, brought on an epidemic of typhoid fever, which caused the scheme to be abandoned.

It is somewhat peculiar that the citizens of Pendleton very shortly after the termination of the Confederate War attempted to establish a similar school but on a broader basis. Thos. G. Clemson, R. F. Simpson, W. H. Trescott, James W. Crawford, Dr. J. H. Maxwell, Maj. Benj. Sloan, Col. J. W. Livingston, Dr. H. C. Miller, and R. W. Simpson attempted, in an humble way, to establish an Agricultural School. And while their efforts failed there grew out of their efforts influences which culminated in the establishment of Clemson College, an institution far beyond the conception of those who first conceived the idea.

As early as 1815 the citizens of Pendleton began to

take an active interest in the improvement of their stock and the methods of farming. In the same year they organized a Farmers' Society. The officers were James C. Griffin, president; Josias Gaillard, vice-president; Robert Anderson, secretary and treasurer; and Joseph V. Shanklin, corresponding secretary. The resident members who first joined the Society were Thomas Pinckney, Jr., John L. North, Andrew Pickens, Benjamin Smith, John Miller, Sr., Charles Gaillard, John E. Calhoun, J. T. Lewis, Thomas L. Dart, J. B. Earle, William Hunter, Benjamin DuPre, Sr., Joseph Grisham, L. McGregor, Samuel Earle, Richard Harrison, Patrick Norris, J. C. Kilpatrick, Joseph B. Earle, T. W. Farrar, C. W. Miller, Samuel Cherry, John Taylor, Thomas Stribling, John Green. The next year the following names were added: John Maxwell, B. F. Perry, William Hubbard, E. B. Benson, George Reese, Sr., George W. Liddell, J. B. Perry, John Martin, T. Farrar, Warren R. Davis, William Gaston, Joseph Reed, Elam Sharpe, D. Sloan, Jr., Samuel Warren, Leonard Simpson, Major Lewis, Samuel Taylor.

In 1817, the following members were added to the Society: William Steele, James Laurence, Frances Burt, John Hunter, W. S. Adair, William Taylor, William Anderson, Joseph Mitchell, Thomas Lorton, Rev. James Hillhouse, Benjamin Dickson, Richard Lewis, J. T. Whitfield, J. B. Hammond, John Halbert, and Robert Lemon.

In 1818, the following members were added: John Hall, David Cherry, John Gaillard, Charles Stony, McKenzie Collins, George Taylor, Theodore Gaillard, Samuel Gassaway, R. A. Maxwell, J. P. Lewis, F. W. Symmes, George Reese, Jr., Joseph Whitner, James Faris, James O. Lewis, Thomas Sloan, Henry McCrary, David K. Hamilton.

Many addresses and reports of committees are still preserved in which are shown the great interest taken at that early date in the improvement of everything pertaining to agriculture. This society is the oldest of its kind in the United States, except the one organized in Philadelphia a year or two before this one. The Pendleton Farmers' Society, in 1828,, bought the old court house and the new one being then erected in Pendleton. And, with the material of the old court house, completed the new building for the Farmers' Society, which is still the property of the Society. For many years stock shows and fairs were annually held. Improved breeds of cattle and other kinds of stock were imported. Horses, cattle jacks, sheep and hogs in great numbers were put on exhibition. And thus these shows were kept up for years. Ever since the war some notable exhibition of stock has taken place. The Farmers' Society has maintained its organization to the present time.

John Miller, who assisted in the publication and circulation of the famous Junius' Letters in London, came to America. He published the first daily paper ever issued in Charleston. Afterwards he made Pendleton his home, and was elected Clerk of the County Court in 1790. Mr. Miller commenced the publication of a weekly newspaper in Pendleton early in the nineteenth century. The paper was first known as Miller's Weekly Messenger, and afterwards appeared as the Pendleton Messenger, with Dr. F. W. Symmes as editor. Dr. Symmes was a man of ability and wielded a controlling influence in the politics of this section of the State. He was a Democrat and a fearless advocate of Mr. Calhoun and his politics in his remarkable career in the country. In 1849 he sold the Messenger to Burt & Thompson, who conducted the paper for several years.

Major George Seaborn edited and published the Farmer and Planter at Pendleton for a number of years. Major Seaborn was a native of Greenville, and reared a large and interesting family. He took great interest in improving the methods of farming as he found them here. His paper was not only useful and ably edited, but it was very popular in the State.

Early in the history of Pendleton a Jockey Club was incorporated by the legislature. A number of good citizens engaged in the sport of racing, not because it was profitable as such, but because in that way the stock of the country could be improved. There was no betting or immorality in the mere act of racing. It was encouraged because it afforded amusement to the people at large.

One small event may be recorded without loss of temper or currency This was known as the worm Multicallus incident. Many trees were planted, and some silk was evolved by the silk worms. The fortunes to be made by the trees did not materialize, but quite a number of persons, including Mrs. Samuel Reid, of Pickens, were very successful in making silk and manufacturing it into beautiful cloth.

One of the great events in the history of Pendleton was the removal of Hon. John C. Calhoun, from Abbe ville, to Fort Hill in 1824. Incidentally, it connects his family with the origin of Clemson College, of which we desire to make brief mention. The great struggle, tne fierce "War between the sections," left the entire South barren in almost every respect. As an agricultural people we were bereft of labor and capital, and, to add to this, our political condition was rendered almost intolerable by the unrelenting disposition of the North in its hour of success. Our educational institutions went down in the general wreck. They had been too, mostly of a literary character. Something practical in this respect was a necessity. Col. Thomas G. Clemson, a son-in-law of Mr. Calhoun, was an eminently practical man, and had been very thoroughly educated in this respect. He was a scientist of very high character. Colonel Clemson was in the overthrow with his family, and saw his way clearly as to the necessities of the future. The education of the youth of the South must in a measure be of a practical character; and he, in his old age, gauged the future most successfully. He resided on a spot dear to every Southern man by its associations. Was the future of a great people to be made certain by the practical and scientific knowledge of Colonel Clemson? Let us see.

We have already seen that the people of Pendleton had at a very early period, become interested in the practical character of the "Labor School" established near town. They also redoubled their efforts after the war to establish a more effective institution. These gentlemen were the companions of Colonel Clemson, and his desire in this connection rekindled their efforts. This was especially true as to Col. R. W. Simpson. He had nobly discharged his duty as a private in the ranks of the Confederate Army. He was not only a successful farmer, but also a lawyer of distinction. He was often consulted by Colonel Clemson as to his business generally and especially as to the establishment of such an institution as Clemson College has proved to be. He wrote his will, giving in a marked degree, the directions of Colonel Clemson in this respect, and was his companion generally in the passing years of his useful and eventful life.

On one occasion, Colonel Simpson was requested by the Trustees of the College to prepare a sketch of the life of Colonel Clemson. This he did, and read the same before the authorities of the College.

This is a brief memorial of Colonel Simpson to his departed friend, and we have drawn largely from it in concluding this article.

"Col. Thomas G. Clemson was born in the City of Philadelpha, July, 1807, died at Fort Hill, S. C., April 6, 1888, and was buried at Pendleton, S. C. Colonel Clemson was six feet six inches tall. His features were handsome and his appearance commanding. His deportment and manner were dignified and polished. His intellect was of a high order, and he was gifted with fine conversational powers. His views and opinions were broad and liberal and there was nothing narrow or contracted about him.

"While possessed of ample means he had no disposition to spend more money upon himself than was actually necessary. His greatest desire was to take care of his property and increase it that he might the better carry out his promise to his wife, which was to found an Agricultural College upon Fort Hill, upon the very spot she herself had selected for the location of the main college building. How faithfully he redeemed his promise to his dear wife, let Clemson College as it stands today in all of its magnificence speak. Colonel Clemson well knew that the property donated for the purpose would not be sufficient to build and maintain such a college as he conceived of; but having a firm reliance upon the liberality of the State of South Carolina, he felt assured that when the necessities of the people, growing out of their changed conditions resulting from the effects of the war, were properly understood and appreciated, his efforts to benefit the farmers would be recognized, and that the State would supplement his donation by whatever amount might be necessary to establish the dream of his life. He reasoned wisely and correctly.

"Very early in life Colonel Clemson developed a great taste for the study of the sciences, especially chemistry, mineralogy and geology. In 1823, when hardly sixteen years old he ran off from home, not on account of any disagreement with his parents, but simply for adventure and to see the world. At that time, though so young, was six feet tall and exceedingly handsome, both in form and feature. He first went to England, but remained there only a short time and then visited Paris. At that time France was particularly friendly towards the United

States, and this handsome young American very soon attracted the attention of the young nobility of the great
City. Through these young men he also became acquainted with some of the leading officials of the City.
During his stay in Paris he shouldered a musket and
joined his young friends in several of the revolutions or
outbreaks for which that City has been famous. His
gallantry displayed on these occasions earned for him
the respect and esteem of the officials, who rewarded him
with a position in the celebrated School of the Mines.
He remained at the school for four years and graduated
with high honors. During his stay in Paris he also
found time to indulge his taste for painting, and had as
his teachers some of the celebrated artists of that time.
By these means he became acquainted with many painters
both in France and Germany, which enabled him in after
years to collect the many valuable and beautiful paintings
which now adorn the walls of John C. Calhoun's old
homestead at Fort Hill. During his stay in Europe his
father died and his large estate was divided in such a way
as to leave him no part of it, and just at the age of manhood found himself penniless; but he cheerfully set to
work in the practice of his profession and very soon
earned an enviable reputation. His services as mining
expert were particularly valuable, and though established
at Washington, his labors were not confined to this country alone, but extended to Cuba and South America also.
His fees were large and he soon after amassed a comfortable fortune. At Washington he was a conspicuous
and prominent person, and he had the entry into the most
exclusive families. Miss Floride, the eldest daughter of
John C. Calhoun, was in Washington on a visit to her
father, and there Colonel Clemson met her, and subsequently they were married at Fort Hill. Mrs. Clemson
was among women what her distinguished father was
among men. Her love for her home and country was
superb, and to this noble, generous and yet gentle woman,

South Carolina is as much indebted for Clemson College as to the distinguished husband, Thomas G. Clemson. Colonel Clemson was a great admirer of John C. Calhoun and earnestly supported his political views and opinions. During the administration of President Jackson he was appointed Minister to Belgium, but having very little taste for politics, at the expiration of his term, he returned to his home in Washington, and resumed the work of his profession. At the beginning of the war Colonel Clemson was residing at his home in Washington City with his family. which consisted of his wife and his son, John C. Clemson, and daughter, Floride Clemson —the son and daughter about grown. It was well known to the authorities that the sympathies of Colonel Clemson were with the South, and for this reason his movements were closely watched, and some time in 1862 his arrest was ordered, but being warned by a friend that he would be arrested the next day, he and his son escaped during the night, and crossed the Potomac in a row boat. Landing on Virginia soil they did not stop until they reached Richmond, having walked the entire distance. Upon arriving in Richmond they both tendered their services to President Davis. John C. was at once appointed a lieutenant in the army and assigned to duty. Colonel Clemson was assigned to the mining department of the trans- Mississippi. Here he remained in the service to the close of the war. At this time Mrs. John C. Calhoun resided at Pendleton, and here Colonel Clemson was reunited with his family, and here they resided until the death of Mrs. Calhoun in the latter part of 1866.

Previous to the war, Mrs. Calhoun had sold their old home—Fort Hill—and all her property thereon, to her son, Col. Andrew P. Calhoun, taking his bond and mortgage for the purchase money. Of this bond and mortgage Mrs. Calhoun willed three-fourths to her daughter Mrs. Thomas G. Clemson, and one-fourth to Mrs. Clemson's daughter, Miss Floride, who subse-

quently married Mr. Gideon Lee, of New York. The
mortgage of Col. A. P. Calhoun was foreclosed, and Mrs.
Clemson bought in Fort Hill, and divided it with her
daughter, Mrs. Lee, in proportion to the interest of each
under Mrs. Calhoun's will. In 1871, Mrs. Floride Lee
died, leaving one child, a daughter. Only seventeen days
after Mrs. Lee's death, John C. Clemson was
killed near Seneca by a collission of two trains on the
Blue Ridge Railroad. The loss of their only two children was a terrible shock to Mr. and Mrs. Clemson.
Desolate, they mourned—all the brightness had been
blotted out of their lives, but unsearchable are the Prov-
idences of God, for it was then that these two stricken
sorrowing parents determined to unite in so disposing
of all they had left of their property as to bring to their
fellowmen as much happiness and prosperity as they
could have wished for themselves. They agreed to make
wills to each other, and promised that the survivor would
make a will donating all of their joint property to erect an
Agricultural College at Fort Hill. In 1875, Mrs. Clemson died suddenly of heart disease, while Mr. Clemson
was absent from home. Many persons in Pendleton
remember the grief of this old and now desolate man at
the grave, when the remains of the devoted partner of
his life were being laid to rest. The remaining years
of his life Mr. Clemson spent desolate and alone, at Fort
Hill. After awhile he began to take more interest in
affairs. He was fond of reading and kept around him
the leading newspapers and standard magazines, by
which he was enabled to keep in touch with his fellowmen; otherwise he lived the life of a hermit, at least for
several years after the death of Mrs. Clemson. Eventually, however, his mind became fixed upon the one purpose of fulfilling the promise to his wife, and erecting
the College they had planned. Then he began again to
visit his friends, and many were the efforts he and his
friends made to interest others in this great work.

During this time he looked carefully after his finances, and tried to save all he could for the College. But still he provided generously for the faithful helpers who remained with him, and wished very much to help other poor friends in distress and did so. It was the privilege of the writer to visit him frequently during the last two years of his life, and during this time he talked freely of his life and experiences. He portrayed in a manner never to be forgotten, the condition the South was sure to be plunged into if something was not done to arrest the destructive tendencies of the times. Education, such as we had before our conditions were changed by the war, was all right, but not enough. To become successful the Southern people had to become practical, and a practical education was necessary to meet the people's necessities. During the latter part of his life he talked a great deal about religious matters and became very much concerned about the salvation of his soul. He requested the ministers to visit him. One good 'man who was with him to the last, said that beyond a doubt he had made his peace with his God, and his last words were in behalf of the poor and suffering. Can the people of South Carolina ever forget Thomas G. Clemson and the great work he helped to accomplish for them? If this is possible visit Fort Hill and look around you!"

This is the faithful tribute of Colonel Simpson to his friend, Thomas G. Clemson.

Clemson College has been partly burned, and has been rebuilt. Additions have been made from time to time. Recently large additions have been planned, and very soon more than eight hundred young men can be educated at this College along practical lines. The College is in a very prosperous condition.

REV. SAMUEL FENNER WARREN.

Rev. Samuel Fenner Warren was the father of Col.

Samuel Warren, the subject of this sketch. He officiated as the faithful pastor of old Eutaw Church for 31 years and died in 1789, and was buried in the church yard at old Eutaw church. A relative of the family furnishes the following inscription on the family tombstone at this sacred place.

"Beneath this marble is deposited the remains of the Rev. Samuel Fenner Warren. * * * * Col. Samuel Warren, his son, is buried in the same grave. He was born near the spot where his mortal remains repose, and at an early age was sent to England for his education, under the care of his uncle, John Warren, Bishop of Bangor, but when war ravaged his native State, his gallant spirit impelled him to fly to her rescue. Breaking through all restraints and the influence of dignified relatives, he returned and immediately took up arms in her defense. At the age of 18, when leading his command against the British lines, he received a bullet in his leg, but supporting himself upon his sword until another struck him on the knee, and shattered the thigh bone, he fell, was taken up from the field in Savannah; his thigh was amputated, he survived and continued to perform staff duties in the army until the establishment of national independence and the restoration of peace."

"Col. Warren was a true friend of the children of his early associations, most of whom he served, directing their education, and faithfully discharging the duties of educator and guardian. He was distinguished by South Carolina with many high and honorable trusts. Serving long in each branch of the Legislature, was made President of the Senate and was offered the appointment of governor, which he declined. Late in life he removed to the district of Pendleton, and there died suddenly on the last day of December, 1841, in the 79th year of his age, honored and respected as a patriot, a man of probity and a friend. This monumental slab bears testimony of the esteem and gratitude of many who honored him in life and revere his memory."

Col. Warren was a member of the Constitutional Convention of 1832, and voted for the Ordinance of Nullification.

Col. Warren resided on the Three and Twenty Mile Creek below Pendleton Factory. He was a gentleman of considerable means, and lived the life of a bachelor. His household consisted of himself and Lydia Ann Perdreau, his ward and adopted daughter, whom he educated and reared most tenderly. This young lady married John Miller, a son of John Miller, the Englishman, and who was the editor and proprietor of "Miller's Weekly Messenger," and afterwards the "Pendleton Messnger." Col. Warren gave all his property by will to Samuel Fenner Warren Miller, a son of the above first named John Miller.

At the recent session of the General Assembly of South Carolina, the descendants of Col. Warren presented to the State a very striking portrait of this distinguished patriot. This portrait was received in a formal manner, by both houses of the legislature, and now graces the walls of the Senate Chamber, a body over which Colonel Warren presided as president many years ago.

A history of Pendleton would be incomplete without honorable mention is made of the "Old Stone Church," where many citizens of Pendleton worshipped and were afterwards buried. This church, Presbyterian, was organized in 1789, and was then known as Hopewell-Keowee. The first house of worship was erected in 1790 of logs, about forty rods east side of the late Ezekiel Pickens' residence, on the north side of the road. The spot is grown over with trees. The second house of worship was completed in 1800. It was built of rock and is now known as the "Old Stone Church." Gen. Andrew Pickens, Gen. Robert Anderson and —— Dick-

son were the first elders. Rev. Thomas Reese, D. D.,
was the first pastor. He died in 1796, and was the first
person buried there. He was a graduate of Princeton
College. The name of the church—Hopewell-Keowee—
is taken from the residence of Gen. Andrew Pickens
near by. After the rock building was erected, it was
called the "Stone Meeting House." It was erected by
John R. Rusk, a Revolutionary soldier, and father of
Gen. Thos. J. Rusk, a U. S. Senator from Texas. Dr.
Frierson says that, "Meeting House is the precise mean-
ing of the word synagogue, the time-honored name of
the house in which Jesus Christ preached." Among the
members of this church were some prominent names:
Andrew Pickens, and Robert Anderson, men of great
influence in the State at that time. The present counties
of Anderson, Pickens and Oconee were then known as
Pendleton, a section of the country ceded some years
before by the Chickasaw, Choctaw, Cherokee and Creek
tribes of Indians, assembled in four different camps at
the residence of Gen. Andrew Pickens. This section of
the State, on account of its fertility, varied resources,
and salubrious climate, drew settlers from many quarters. After the treaty of Hopewell, which was coucluded
in 1783, and concluded between the belligerent powers
of the old Revolution, it was found by government census
to contain 9,500 persons." From 1824, the church at
Hopewell-Keowee began to decline. At that period a
church was built at the the Town of Pendleton, known
as Hopewell-Pendleton, and began to grow and prosper.
The interest for many years at the "Old Stone Church"
has centered mainly in the preservation and protection
of the old burying ground around the church. A rock wall
has encircled the sacred spot, and more attention is being
given to beautifying the grounds. The church building
is in fairly good condition, and services are held there
occasionally. This sacred spot is the resting place of
General Pickens' family, the Reeses, Cherrys, Whitners,

Maxwells, Lewises, Sloans, Calhouns, Bensons, Millers, Kilpatricks, Storeys, Symmes, Rosses, Dicksons, Doyles, Ramsays, Steeles, McElroys, Alexanders, Andersons, Breazeales, Crawfords, Greshams, Harris, Henrys, Hunters, Laniers, Livingstones, Lortons, McElhannys, Rusks, Sharpes, Walkers, and many others. Printer John Miller gave the land, something over sixteen acres, whereon to build the "Old Stone Church."

In 1832, when the State was greatly excited over the subject of Nullification, the people generally took an active part in advocating Nullification. Mr. Calhoun was the absolute leader of public thought, and, as is well known, strongly advocated the right of the State to nullify any act of Congress injurious to the interests of the State. Benj. F. Perry, a bold and fearless man, was then editing the Greenville Mountaineer, at Greenville, S. C. He dared to oppose Mr. Calhoun, and by his vigorous articles, began to win quite a number to his way of thinking. The friends of Mr. Calhoun became alarmed and were determined to break the force of the growing Union sentiment, and to put an end to Mr. Perry's opposition. With this end in view, Turner Bynum, Esq., a brilliant writer and fearless man, was induced to go to Greenville and become editor of the Greenville Sentinel, a spirited nullification journal. Mr. Bynum spent a good deal of his time at Pendleton, where he had many personal and political friends. It was expected that Messrs. Bynum and Perry advocating such opposite views, would sooner or later, meet each other in mortal combat. And so it happened. A challenge was passed and the principals and their friends met on the "field of honor" to settle their difficulties. The field was an island in Tugaloo River, in 1832. Mr. Bynum was mortally wounded and died the next day. His body was buried at the "Old Stone Church." There had been a heavy rain, the streams were swollen, and much difficulty was experienced by those in charge of the body, and they did

not reach the grave yard until about mid-night, at which
gloomy hour the mortal remains of this brilliant young
man were lowered into a grave half filled with water.
The two pine poles, cut to place across the grave upon
which to rest the body, after the burial were stuck in the
ground, the one at the head and the other at the foot of
the grave to mark the same.   These two pine poles
grew   and   became   large   pine   trees,   standing   as
faithful sentinels to keep watch over the sacred
spot.   Mr. A. C. Campbell was present at the
burial of Bynum and resided within a mile of the
spot.   He described the scene as above described, and
said that the statement in regard to the two pine poles
was true of his own knowledge.   The result of the election throughout the State for delegates to the convention
was largely in favor of nullification.   The vote in Pendleton District was two to one on the same side.   The
following gentlemen were elected members of the convention from Pendleton: Col. Samuel Warren, Dr. F. W.
Symmes, John T. Whitfield, Robert Anderson, Frank
Burt, Barnard E. Bee, Bailey A. Barton, Armistead Burt.
The Burts were brothers.

   There has been a number of duels in Pendleton.
The last one was fought between Col. W. Ransom Calhoun and Colonel Rhett ,of Charleston, during the war.
Colonel Calhoun was killed.   It was only twenty-eight
years from the date of the Nullification struggle to 1860,
when the people were nearly unanimous for war.   And
this has been the experience of mankind from the earliest
times.

   The   following   gentlemen, citizens of Pendleton,
have represented this Congressional District and the
State in the United States Senate and House of Repre-
sentatves up to 1860, to-wit:

   Third Congress.—Andrew Pickens, Representative.
   Fourth Congress.—Samuel Earle, Representative.

Seventh Congress.—John Ewing Calhoun, U. S. Senate.

Eighth Congress..—John B. Earle, Representative.

Eighth Congress.—John Gaillard, U. S. Senate.

Ninth Congress.—Elias Earle, Representative.

Ninth Congress.—John Gaillard, U. S. Senate.

Tenth Congress.—Joseph Calhoun, Representative.

Tenth Congress.—John Taylor, Representative.

Tenth Congress.—John Gaillard U. S. Senate.

Eleventh Congress—Joseph Calhoun, Representative.

Eleventh Congress.—John Gaillard, U. S. Senate.

Twelfth Congress.—John C. Calhoun, Representative.

Twelfth Congress.—Elias Earle, Representative.

Twelfth Congress.—John Gaillard, U. S. Senate.

Thirteenth Congress.—John C. Calhoun, Representative.

Thirteenth Congress.—Elias Earle, Representative.

Thirteenth Congress.—John Gaillard, U. S. Senate.

Fourteenth Congress.—John Gaillard, U. S. Senate.

Fourteenth Congress.—John C. Calhoun, Representative.

Fourteenth Congress.—John Taylor, Representative.

Fifteenth Congress.—Elias Earle.

Fifteenth Congress.—John Gaillard, U. S. Senate.

Sixteenth Congress.—Elias Earle, Representative.

Sixteenth Congress.—John Gaillard, U. S. Senate.

Seventeenth Congress.—John Gaillard, U. S. Senate.

Eighteenth Congress.—John Gaillard, U. S. Senate.

Nineteenth Congress.—John Gaillard, U. S. Senate.

Twentieth Congress.—Warren R. Davis, Representative.

Twenty-first Congress.—Warren R. Davis, Representative.

Twenty-second.—John C. Calhoun, U. S. Senate.

Twenty-second Congress.—Warren R. Davis, Representative.

Twenty-third Congress.—John C. Calhoun, U. S. Senate.

Twenty-third Congress.—Warren R. Davis, Representative.

Twenty-fourth Congress.—John C. Calhoun, U. S. Senate.

Twenty-fifth Congress.—John C. Calhoun, U. S. Senate.

Twenty-sixth Congress.—John C. Calhoun, U. S. Senate.

Twenty-seventh Congress.—John C. Calhoun, U. S. Senate.

Twenty-eighth Congress.—Richard F. Simpson, Representative.

Twenty-ninth Congress.—John C. Calhoun, U. S. Senate.

Twenty-ninth Congress.—Richard F. Simpson, Representative.

Thirtieth Congress.—John C. Calhoun, U. S. Senate.

Thirtieth Congress.—Richard F. Simpson, Representative.

Thirty-first Congress.—John C. Calhoun, U. S. Senate.

Thirty-first Congress.—James L. Orr, Representative.

Thirty-second Congress.—James L. Orr, Representative.

Thirty-third Congress.—James L. Orr, Representative.

Thirty-fourth Congress.—James L. Orr, Representative.

Thirty-fifth Congress.—James L. Orr, Representative.

The following gentlemen, citizens of Pendleton, have held the high positions given below:

From March, 1813, John Gaillard was not only a

member of the United States Senate, but was also President pro. tem. of that body from this date and also including the 11th, 12th, 13th, 14th, 15th, 16th, 17th and 18th Congresses.

From 1817 to 1821—John C. Calhoun, Secretary of war.

From 1821 to 1825—John C. Calhoun, Secretary of war.

From 1825 to 1829—John C. Calhoun, Vice-President of the United States.

From 1829 to 1833—John C. Calhoun, Vice-President, resigned in 1831.

1845 to 1849—John C. Calhoun, Secretary of war.

John C. Calhoun was U. S. Senator, March, 1850, when he died.

James L. Orr was Speaker of the House of Representatives, Senator of the Confederate State Congress, Envoy Extraordinary and Minister Plenipotentiary to Russia, and Governor of South Carolina.

Andrew Pickens, son of Gen. Andrew Pickens, was Governor of South Carolina in 1816.

Francis Burt was territorial Governor of Nebraska.

Dear old Pendleton! says a correspondent of the Keowee Courier, in May, 1891.   He writes brilliantly and enthusiastically when he states what hallowed associations does the name of this dear old town conjure up. How often in thought do we wander back there!   Old landmarks and many reminders are still to be seen, but the kindly faces and precious souls have nearly all gone across the bourne.   We hope to meet them again in the better land if admitted into the eternal realms of bliss; and, as time rolls on in her endless cycle, we feel that now and then we should feel constrained to spare a moment to peep down upon the old familiar spot, where our first fond hopes of earth aspired and indulged in many bright anticipations which have never been realized.   Fifty years ago old Pendleton was the fairest town in upper South Carolina, a community of wealth, intelligence, refinement and religion, and the home of the best people it has ever fallen to our lot to know—a resort of giant minds who would do honor to any age of the world's history. Such men as John C. Calhoun, Langdon Cheves, Daniel E. Huger, George McDuffie, Warren R. Davis, John Taylot, David K. Hamilton, the Pinckneys, Haynes, Hamiltons, Earles; the Generals Pickens, Andersons, Blasingames, the Colonels Warren, Alston and Barton, and the home of Barnard E. Bee, the Stevens brothers, Clement and Peter of Charleston gun boat fame, of Confederate times, home of John and Pat Calhoun, the well known young financiers of today; and from these old hills came the astute senator, Joseph E. Brown, Atlanta's brainest man, Dr. H. V. M. Miller, General Rusk of Texas, a power in his day; Governors Perry and Orr; Commander Stribling of the Navy, and hundreds who have left their impress upon this new world, and in their day and times helped to lay the foundation and build up this great country; and a host of others whose honorable names and useful citizenship would challenge the world for comparison. Such was the status of Old Pendleton fifty years ago, when in the full tide of her prosperity, a splendid Piedmont climate with fertile lands under the old slave regime, and when the wealth resided in the country and agricultural pur suits were regarded second to none other as an occupation of honor and profit; and were conducted with an intelligence and advancement scarcely surpassed today in the South.

Old Pendleton was famed for the beauty and gentleness of her women as well as for the high-tone and pluck of her men. Old Pendleton District was then about the size of the State of Rhode Island, and the good old town was the grand center of both society and trade, and, indeed was one of the foremost pioneer towns in the South.

It was in the streets of old Pendleton that her indignant citizens kindled the first bonfire that consumed in its flames the first incendiary papers and letters sent South by the abolitionists to stir strife and discord among a happy people.

One of the first female high schools in the South was conducted by the Misses Bates and Billings, from Vermont, who taught the young ladies etiquette and French, graceful attitudes and high-falutin notions, modern manners, to walk daintily and to scream fashionably at a bug or mouse.

One of the first military academies was here, where the boys were drilled daily, wore gray uniforms and brass buttons.

One of the first cotton spinning factories was established there and met with great success and profit. It was operated for many years and up to his death, by Maj. B. F. Sloan, and is still in successful operation by Mr. A. J. Sitton.

Pendleton and her Agricultural Society, fair grounds and race track, and some of her exhibitions, would put to blush some of the fairs of the present day.

Pendleton had four prosperous churches, two hotels, and who of her old citizens does not remember the long-ball-room in the old Tom Cherry Hotel, and the beautiful young girls who once skimmed like swallows over those well waxed floors, and the stately matrons, who as chaperones, patronized with their presence those delightful occasions, and gave dignity and respectability to the ball-room? The old Debating Society held in the old Farmers'Hall and ever graced by a full attendance of the fair sex? The fine coaches and the beautiful pairs of horses that whirled up the dust in the streets of the old town? What old citizen's heart is not made to throb at the recollection of thrilling notes from the stage horn over the hills to notify of its coming? How the people would gather around the hotels and the postoffice as the

great rocking, ponderous vehicle came rolling and swing-
ing over the rocks, drawn by four or six horses, dash-
ing in at a gallop into the center of the old town with its
passengers and mail.   And with what eager excitement
the citizens sought to welcome friends and visitors and
receive the tardy news.

Who does not remember the old "Pendleton Messenger" and Dr. F. W. Symmes, its able editor; and the "Farmer and Planter," and Maj. George Seaborn, editor and
proprietor; Mr. E. B. Benson, the long time merchant;
old Billy Hubbard, the jolly landlord; the old English
dancing master, Walon; rich Sam Manerick, the ec-
centric old man; Sid Cherry, the batchelor; Tommy
Christian, the town marshall, and many others we have
not space to mention.

Since the days of which we have been speaking, the
second and third generations are passing from the stage
of action, rapidly losing their grip on life and falling
off into the sea of time.   Of the second, Col. Tom Pickens,
Mr Dickson and John Sitton alone remain.   Mr. Wm.
H. D. Gaillard died but recently, and but a remnant of
the third generation is left.   Clemson Agricultural College is now being erected at Fort Hill, the old home of
John C. Calhoun and the old town is looking up somewhat.
May the Lord bless the faithful old spot, and may she
become once more as she was, in the days of yore, as
"a city set upon a hill."

NAMES OF MEMBERS OF SECESSION
CONVENTION.

Anderson—Joseph N. Whitner, James L. Orr, Richard F. Simpson, Jacob P. Reed, Benj. F. Mauldin.

Pickens—Andrew F. Lewis, William Hunter, Robert A. Thompson, William S. Gresham, John Maxwell.

FORT HILL GUARDS.

The following is a list of the names of the men who

composed the first company organized at Pendleton,
South Carolina, for service in the Confederate Army,
which afterwards became Company "I", of the Fourth
Regiment of South Carolina Volunteer Infantry, was
commanded by Capt. Julius L. Shanklin, and was known
as the "Fort Hill Guards."

Officers—Julius L. Shanklin, Captain; John C. Cherry, first lieutenant; John W. Daniels, second lieutenant;
Michael A. Belotte, third lieutenant; Gustavus H. Symmes, orderly sergeant; Augustus J. Sitton, second sergeant; J. Waddill Hillhouse, third sergeant; Richard W.
Grubbs, fourth sergeant; Daniel Magill, fifth sergeant;
J. O. Skelton, corporal; John A. Harris, corporal; T. Edward Maxwell, corporal; William G. Jenkins, corporal;
John M. Jolly, corporal.

Privates—John A. Amick, James O. Beard, John
Brooks, Samuel L. Bowden, William M. Belotte, L. M.
Bolt, Newton J. Browning, Joseph N. Chastain, John W.
Cox, Patrick Clifford, Thomas Crow, Samuel H. Cro-
mer, John C. Caminade, Joseph A. Crocker, N. Pickens
Carroll, James L. Dickson, Columbus A. Daniels, George
W. Dodd, Theodore Darricott, James M. Duke, Jacob
Eskew, Edward Fant, William W. Graham, W. Thompson
Grubbs, Thomas H. Gerard, John C. Gantt, William W.
Hamilton, Leonard S. Hamilton, S. Porter Hillhouse,
Edward M. Hall, John W. Hopkins, C. R. Hix, Robert
Hackett, David C. Keasler, Newton King, John T. Lewis,
David H. Lee, Thomas Massey, J. Sidney Marshall, Sam-
uel Mays, Dannett Mays, George W. Mackey, John W.
Morris, Newton T. Martin, William McClesky, Henry
Osgood, Turner Osborne, W. R. Pickerell, C. Milton R.
Palmer, Chandler Palmer, Roger Pinckney, Crayton L.
Reid, William Reams, Edward B. Stephens, James L.
Smith, J. Laurens N. Smith, Charles S. Steele, William
Steele, H. Frank Suber, William H. Stevenson, George
P. Sears, J. Richard Simpson, William C. Smith, W. R.

Sims, Samuel J. Taylor, L. R. Tribble, J. Edward Wilson, David A. Wells, P. Edward Werner, A. Frank White, Elias White, James White. Total 90.

Reconstruction in South Carolina, the Campaign of 1876 and the Wallace House

BY R. W. SIMPSON.

Ex-Governor D. H. Chamberlain wrote an article on Reconstruction in South Carolina, which was published in the Atlantic Monthly Magazine some time ago. This article attracted much attention, coming as it did from one who participated in that memorable drama. Mr. Chamberlain stated the facts as they appeared to him from his standpoint very frankly, but if his account of this, one of the most important eras in the history of South Carolina is to be accepted as the true and only history of that period, then the outrages, oppression and wrongs cruelly inflicted upon the white people of the State after their surrender by the Radical leaders in Congress will never be understood or appreciated by their children.

No Governor of the Radical party during the dark days of Reconstruction in South Carolina, elected to office by Negro votes, can describe the heroism and patience displayed by the white people during this dark period, or the conditions which influenced them to take the course they did in 1876, or what it was that sustained them in that final conflict for life and the preservation of the white race.

We think the time has come when the people of South Carolina should write their own history. Mr. Chamberlain's article will be handed down to future gen-

erations as an honest, fair account of the facts that trans-,
pired during reconstruction.   Mr. Chamberlain belonged
to that party that so cruelly oppressed the white people
of the State, and no matter how fair and honest he evidently intended to be, it was impossible for him to describe the feelings of the people whom he opposed.   The
man with his heel upon the neck of another cannot re-
alize the feelings of the one under the heel.   If the white
man's side of this history is ever written he must write
it himself.   This I propose to do briefly, stating only such
facts as were personally known to myself, or of such
common notoriety as were accepted as true by all.

To properly explain the motives which influenced the
people of South Carolina (we will hereafter call them
Democrats) to enter upon the campaign of 1876 and immediately subsequent thereto, it will be necessary to describe the condition in which they were placed at the
time.   It is not wise for the Democrats in South Carolina
to look back and recall the cruel wrongs inflicted upon
them after the surrender, and during the period of reconstruction, and reference is made thereto now, only to
explain and vindicate the course they pursued during this
memorable conflict.

Shortly before the close of the war Sherman marched
through South Carolina, then impoverished by four years
of war, and left behind him a burnt and blackened trail of
ruin and desolation.   In a tract running entirely through
the State, perhaps fifty miles wide, the lone chimneys of
once happy homes standing like tomb stones over the
graves of the dead, were all that was left to mark these
sacred spots.   Columbia, the State capital, was burned to
the ground, and thousands of old men, widows and or-
phans made so by the war, were cast out, homeless and
without a place to cover their heads, and destitute of
clothing or the necessities of life.   Huddled together in
shanties, they subsisted for a time on the scraps of food
thrown away by the soldiers.   Imagine if you can the

feelings of the ragged and half starved heroes when returning from Appomattox to what were once happy homes to find their dear ones surrounded by such harrowing conditions.

Notwithstanding the ruin and desolation which surrounded them, these brave and heroic men at once peaceably set to work to build new homes for themselves and families. Although they had lost all of their property, and dire poverty universally prevailed, yet they were not embittered thereby. The negroes too suffered like their former masters, and the kindest feelings continued to exist between the two races. The white people honestly accepted the results of the war and the freedom of the negroes, and had they been left alone there is scarcely a doubt but that the relations of the two races would have been happily and satisfactorily adjusted. But the Republican party was then in absolute control of the Federal Government and actuated by hatred for the South and with cruel disregard for the lives and safety of the white men, women and children, they inaugurated and put in operation the reconstruction measures, a scheme more heartless and heathenish than was ever before or since told of in history. The prime purpose of these measures was, through the negroes, to perpetuate the Republican party, and to place the South in such a position it could never again oppose its policy. To accomplish this purpose it was deliberately attempted to enslave the refined and chivalrous people of South Carolina and place them in bondage to their recently emancipated slaves. This is no fiction—the speeches in Congress on reconstruction openly avowed this purpose, and the administrative measures put in force by the Radical party then in power in the State proves the statement beyond controversy.

The first step taken was to place a garrison of Federal troops in nearly every town in the State. The white men were then disarmed and disfranchised, and universal suffrage was conferred upon the negroes. Then fearful that the whites might still be able to exert some influence upon the negroes, and to prevent it, their agents organized the negroes into secret societies, and to forever destroy the friendly relations then existing between the two races, they taught the negroes behind closed doors that the whites were their bitterest enemies, and only wanted the opportunity to re-enslave them—and thus inflamed them until this once happy and friendly race was converted into a howling mob ready to do any act of outrage which these agents in the accomplishment of their purpose might wish done.

The State government was then organized and the offices in the State were filled by ignorant negroes, and camp followers. Then to uphold their government they organized the negroes into militia companies and supplied them with both arms and ammunition, refusing at the same time to permit the white people to participate in the militia organization. Not content with his, carpet-bag and negro speakers were sent all over the State to still further inflame the negroes to insult and outrage the white people.

Backed by numbers and with arms in their hands· the negroes soon reached the conclusion that they were the masters in fact and in truth hence they very soon worked themselves into such a state of lawlessness and committed such deeds of outrage if now repeated could hardly be believed by their bitterest opponents. The white people were scattered over the country, and as there were but few white men in proportion to the negroes, and these few were very poorly armed or as was generally the case without any arms at all, there was very little protection for the women and children. Then when these negro militiamen with arms in their hands congregated in the country districts it was a fearful time for the whites. Gangs of these armed negroes would parade over the country cursing and abusing the whites and practiced by shooting into dwelling houses where the white families were congregated, and into churches where the whites were engaged in religious worship. They talked openly of their intention to kill the white men and take the white women for their wives. Imagine if you can what must have been the awful fear and dread of the refined and virtuous women of the State during this fearful time, conscious as they were that their protectors were but few in number, and many of these few were being chased and hunted down by the United States troops upon false charges brought against them by negroes and designing carpetbaggers. Many white men had to leave their unprotected families and seek safety by hiding in the swamps, and some who felt compelled to labor and support their families when they went to their fields to plow, the first thing they did was to let down gaps in the fences surrounding their fields so they could fly at a moment's warning and then plowed with a saddle on their horse's back.

Some may ask how and why did the veterans of the Confederate war submit to so many and outrageous insults—The answer is simple and easy—They had surrendered in good faith, and were bound by their parols Then the Federal troops were stationed all over the State for the express purpose of upholding the infamous government foisted upon the State. Nor were the white women and children as unprotected as they appeared to be. Secret organizations were effected among the whites, and arms and ammunition were quietly acquired. In some parts of the State the whites were driven to organize the Ku Klux,—an organization famous in the judicial history of the United States Courts in the State. While these outrages were being enacted in the country districts, the negroes and carpetbaggers in the cities and towns were giving their attention to politics. Unresisted they elected each other to be members of the General Assemby, and very soon, supported by Federal troops, they took possession of every office in the State. They

then began such a saturnalia of stealing and oppression
as was never before equaled in a civilized State   (See the
report of the Committee on Corruption commonly spok-
en of as the Cochran Peport.)   They issued millions of
Bonds upon the State's credit, every dollar of which they
unblushingly stole.   And when the credit of the State
was exhausted they laid heavy taxes on the almost impoverished white people (the negroes paid no taxes), the
proceeds of which they stole also.

The white people for some years could do nothing to
protect either their property or the credit of the State.
They were simply stunned.   About 1874 a mass meeting
of tax payers was held in Columbia but no relief was secured thereby.

The whites then began to take some interest in politics, with the hope that thereby their condition could be
improved.   In that year about thirty white men   were
elected to the legislature.   Imagine if you can the feelings of these thirty white men when they assembled in
the State House and saw before them a prostrated State,
a State absolutely under the control of the recently emancipated slaves.   These few white Democrats when assembled in the legislative halls of the once proud State constituted one little white spot in the dark black mass of
African ignorance.   They had no part in shaping legis-
lation, and were viewed with suspicion by the negroes,
but they constituted an object lesson to the thousands of
Northern tourists who visited Columbia during the sessions of the legislature to view for themselves the prostrate State.   They saw South Carolina, the once proud
and respected State—the leader always in the struggle for self government, for liberty and right—one of
the original thirteen states that contributed all she had
to secure the independence of America, and because she
dared maintain her construction of the Constitution, and
because she was then powerless, having submitted   her
cause to the arbitrament of arms, and surrendered, this

proud and still glorious State was subjected to the most
degraded position to which any people on earth had ever
been reduced. These Northern tourists saw what their
politicians had done to subdue a sister state, and through
them when they returned home the truth began to dawn
upon the minds of the real North, and eventually prepared them to understand the awful conditions existing
in the State, when the revolution of 1876 wrenched the
covering off, and exposed lying beneath the vile, stinking,
putrid mass of corruption.

And is it not true that the extreme degredation
sought to be imposed upon the people of South Carolina
was the highest tribute its oppressors could bestow upon
them—brave and patriotric, the only way to subdue them
was to exterminate them.   During the years of 1874 and
1875 there was a breach in the Republican or negro party
What produced this breach or what were the effects of it,
it is unnecessary to say, further than that Gov. Chamberlain saw the handwriting on the wall and was convinced that the negroes were totally unfit to govern.   He
therefore proposed to the white people that they unite
with the better element of the negro party, and many
good men in those sections of the State where the negroes were in the majority looked with favor upon the
proposition.   So completely were those sections under
the rule and dominion of the negroes they could see no
hope of relief except it come in that way.   In the latter part of 1875 great interest began to be taken in the
all important question, "What was best to be done."
The leading citizens of the State went to Columbia and
counseled together.   In these conferences some advocated an alliance with Chamberlain, and others counseled
a straightout movement,—upon the ground that the
white race was in danger, and any alliance with the negroes would of necessity endanger the civilization of the
white race to a greater degree by laying down the foundation for social equality.

It was determined at length to let the matter be decided by a convention of white men called to meet in Columbia during the summer of 1876. In this convention the question was earnestly debated and it was finally agreed that the white man would make no alliance with the negroes but would place a full white man's ticket in the field. There were no candidates, men were chosen for the several State offices because of their unblemished characters and fitness for the positions for which they were chosen. Gen. Wade Hampton was nominated for Governor, Col. W. D. Simpson for Lieutenant Governor, Gen. James Conner for Attorney General, Gen. Johnson Hagood for Comptroller General, R. M. Sims for Secretary of State, Hugh S. Thompson for Commissioner of Education and E. W. Moise for Adjutant and Inspector General.

The people were in earnest and when a definite policy was agreed upon, every one united heart and soul in the one great purpose,—the salvation of the white race. In this convention was born the policy which to this day governs the entire South—that is that the white people of the Southern States will never permit the white race to be pulled down from its high state of civilization by social intercourse or amalgamation with the negro. God made our race to differ from another race, as he made one star to differ from another in glory. They must obey the laws of God, if we wish to preserve the integrity of the white race.

But no people ever entered upon a political contest where there was more at stake, or had to face greater difficulties and dangers. The Government of the State, with all of the election machinery was in the possession of the negroes and their carpet bag leaders, which was held up and supported by the United States Courts, Judges, Marshals, and troops, together with a large number of State Constables.

The National Democratic Party regarding the State

safely Republican, and believing that the white men of the State, goaded to frenzy by the wrongs heaped upon them, would commit some rash acts which would endanger the success of the party, refused to render the State any assistance, and advised that they should tamely submit and not attempt to secure relief.

Under all these difficulties many regarded it as a strange proceeding to refuse to associate with Chamberlain and his so called reform faction of the negro party, and to risk their all upon what appeared a hopeless undertaking, and there are some even at this time who fail to appreciate the purposes of the white people in determining upon the course they did.

It should be remembered first that the white people fully realized their condition—they had reached a point when they could stand no more if there was any legal means to avoid it—they had no friends, and only themselves to rely upon. The Republican party was seeking to perpetuate itself in the State through the negro vote which largely outnumbered the whites. To accomplish this end the entire State government had been subverted.

Chamberlain on the other hand was equally Republican, associating with them, and elected by them to office, he was then as anxious and willing to perpetuate the Republican party as any of his party, but he had learned by experience that a government founded upon such material was a miserable failure, therefore to accomplish the same end he proposed to the whites to join with the better element of his party and in this way secure reform, his object of course was the perpetuation of the Republican party.

But the white people did not see how any good thing could come out of Nazareth. Suppose they did unite with Chamberlain could he control his followers? What was to prevent them at any time to leave the whites and go back to the other faction of their party and thus united, again control? They realized that this negro government could not exist much longer, but they saw supreme danger in Mr. Chamberlain's effort to strengthen the failing negro government with the native whites. Could he but accomplish his purpose and induce the whites to join in his Republican reform movement, the whites being in the minority would become suppliants to the Negro, a species of slavery which they could not voluntarily bring upon themselves. They could not see how two races of unequal social standing, such as existed between the whites and blacks, the blacks largely predominating, could be so united into a political party to control the State, so as to exclude a part of the lower and predominant race unless the whites recognized the social rights of those they were allied with. Social equality was all the whites had to offer in exchange for a share in the government. Simply this the whites were not willing to do—they were not prepared to go into partnership with the Negro when they owned only a minority of the stock. The campaign of 1876 was not a fight for liberty, but rather a desperate struggle for self preservation.

For a while after the convention there was a calm all over the State, then the towns, villages and neighborhoods began to organize clubs. There was no general plan of organization, nor was there apparently any concert of action between them, but each club organized according to its own ideas. In the meanwhile General Hampton after planning out his campaign announced that the first meetings would be held at Anderson C. H. on the —— day of ————, 1876. This day as well as we now remember came on Tuesday. On Saturday previous it was intended to organize a club at Pendleton preparatory for the meeting next week. During the morning of that day several gentlemen in Pendleton were discussing the best method of organizing the proposed club—one of them suggested that to make these clubs effective they should be uniformed, and that the uniform should be both cheap and conspicuous and suggested a red flannel shirt. The suggestion was immediately taken up, and they proceeded to interview the merchants to see if a supply of the material was on hand. One of the gentlemen bought the stuff and had a shirt made and when the club was organized that evening exhibited the shirt and proposed it as the uniform of the club. This was adopted and the members proceeded to secure their shirts for the big Hampton meeting next week. There were several gentlemen present that evening from the neighboring town of Central in Pickens county, who caught the uniform idea and secured uniforms for their company also. Another nearby club also wished to do the same, but the supply of material was exhausted. This club determined to appear in uniforms of white shirts. By agreement these three clubs numbering together about three hundred, were to march to Anderson in a body and were to be accompanied by the Pendleton brass band.

On the day of the great meeting these three clubs were late in getting to Anderson. Gen. Hampton with the other candidates for State offices, distinguished gentlemen from many other counties, and a great number of clubs from every part of the county were gathered at the fair grounds ready to start the procession which was to precede the speaking. Just about this time the Pendleton contingent came in sight, the band in front, the band wagon was painted red, the musicians were dressed in red, the instruments were wrapped with red, red flags were floating from the heads of the four horses, and from the wagon itself, and the harness was also wrapped in red. Behind the band came the three clubs all dressed in uniform and on horse back. The thrill of enthusiasm which surged through the other clubs assembled in the fair grounds as these uniformed clubs rode into their midst cannot be described, the very earth shook with the wildest yells—the effect upon them was as shaking a red cloth in the face of a bull to excite him to battle. The red shirt, the insignia of the campaign of 1876 was universally adopted without a vote, and telegrams went flashing all over the State for the clubs to uniform. This, the first campaign was a grand success, and created a wave of enthusiasm which swept over the State toward the sea, gathering force and strength as it went. The negroes did not believe there were as many white men on earth, and no wonder they were intimidated by this concentrated array of power and force. Uniformed and on horse back and in concentrated bodies they had the effect of magnifying their numbers in the negroes' eyes. This simple exhibition constituted the greater part of intimidation with which the whites were charged in that campaign.

We have been particular to describe this first Hampton meeting for to describe one is to describe them all. It is impossible to describe the rides of the red shirts by day and by night. These red shirt companies were careful, however, during the campaign not to violate the law. No ill treatment of the negro was permitted, instead by every means possible they tried to show the negroes that the white people were their only friends. Many negroes openly donned the red shirt and voted with their white friends. Towards the scalawag and the carpet bagger they showed no mercy—these were the men who received the lion's share in the stealings secured by the negroes' votes—they held the negro in their grip, and could safely expect to continue to grow rich as long as they continued to control them. These people were made to quail at many of their public meetings by the demands of the red shirts. These people were seeking to make or secure money and it was but human nature for them to want to save what they

had already stolen, rather than lose their lives as they
feared they would do. It was on election day, however, the excitement was greatest. Both sides were
early at the polls, ready if need be, at least so far as the
whites were concerned, for a resort to force.
But force was not necessary, finesse answered better.
Considering all things the election was remarkably fair.
There was some election trickery as usual practiced in
some quarters, but the presence of white men at the
polls in numbers sufficient to back up their demand for
a fair vote and a fair count, and their watchfulness
until the votes were counted is what carried the day.
Hampton and his ticket were elected by several thousand majority. There were perhaps several thousands
of native Northern men then residing in the State,
bona fide citizens, all of whom unhesitatingly cast their
votes for the State democrats, they were as much disgusted with negro rule as were the native whites.

For the House of Representatives the following
results were published by the returning board, a board
composed entirely of radicals.

From Abbeville—R. R. Hemphill, T. L. Moore, W.
K. Bradley, Wm. Hood and F. A. Connor.

Aiken—C. E. Sawyer, J. J. Woodward, John G.
Guignard, L. M. Asbill.

Anderson—W. C. Brown, R. W. Simpson, James L.
Orr, H. R. Vandiver.

Barnwell—Isaac S. Bamberg, J. W. Holmes, L. W.
Youmans, M. A. Rountree, Robert Aldrich.

Colleton—H. E. Bissell, Wm. Maree, J. M. Cummings, L. E. Parler, R. Jones.

Chesterfield—J. C. Coit, D. T. Redfearn.

Greenville—J. W. Gray, J. F. Donnald, J. T. Austin, J. L. Westmoreland.

Horry—L. D. Bryan, J. R. Cooper.

Lancaster—J. B. Erwin, J. C. Blakeney.

Lexington—G. Muller, G. Leaphart.

Marion—J. G. Blue, James McRae, R. H. Rogers, J. P. Davis.

Marlboro—P. M. Hamer, T. N. Edens.

Oconee—B. Frank Sloan, J. S. Verner.

Orangeburg—W. H. Reedish.

Pickens—D. F. Bradley, E. H. Bates.

Spartanburg—W. P. Compton, J. W. Wofford, E. S. Allen, C. Petty.

Sumter—J. H. Westberry.

Union—W. H. Wallace, G. D. Peake, William Jefferies.

York—A. E. Hutchison, W. B. Byers, B. H. Massey, J. A. Deal.

The Returning Board threw out many of the white votes in the counties of Edgefield and Laurens and declared the Radical candidates elected therein. But the Democrats carried the case to the Supreme Court, which Court after hearing the matter ordered the Returning Board to issue certificates to the Democratic candidates from those two counties—and upon their refusal to do so, had them put in jail for contempt. But the United States Court quickly had them released. The Supreme Court then ordered its clerk to issue to the Democrats certificates of election which he did as follows:

Edgefield—W. S. Allen, J. C. Sheppard, James Callison, T. E. Jennings, H. A. Shaw.

Laurens—J. B. Humbert, J. W. Watts, D. W. Anderson.

These representatives elect on November 28th, 1876, assembled in Carolina Hall elected W. H. Wallace of Union, Speaker, and the following communication was sent to the Senate:

Mr. President and Gentlemen of the Senate:

The House of Representatives respectfully informs your body that, pursuant to the provisions of the Constitution of the State of South Carolina, the members elect of the House of Representatives assembled in Carolina Hall this day at 8 o'clock P. M. when the following named gentlemen, sixty-six in number (given above) being a quorum of the whole representation of the House of Representatives, appeared, produced their credentials and were sworn in by the Hon. Judge Thompson H. Cook, and have organized by the election of Mr. W. H. Wallace, a member from Union, Speaker, and John T. Sloan, Sr., Clerk, and are ready to proceed to business.

Very respectfully,

W. H. Wallace,
Speaker of the House of Representatives.

To this communication to the Senate there was no reply. This body was composed of a large majority of Radicals and only eleven Democrats. One-half of the Senators held over, consequently the Democrats failed to carry the Senate at the election.

In the mean while, and on the same day, the Radicals assembled in the hall of Representatives in the State House. Refusing to recognize the mandate of the Court (which was Radical) they, by counting out the Democratic members from Edgefield and Laurens, eight in number, and recognizing the Radical members instead organized the House by electing E. W. M. Mackey, Speaker. This body was protected by a large number of negro constables appointed by D. H. Chamberlain, Governor, so-called, who were in turn supported by United States soldiers under the orders of Gen. Ruger.

On the 29th day of November, 1876, the Democratic House (hereafter will be called the Wallace House) formed and marched from Carolina Hall to the State House. On arriving at the outer door they found it

closed and guarded by a lieutenant and a squad of
United States troops. The Edgefield and Laurens
members were purposely placed in front, for fear if
they came last that they would be refused admission,
while the other members already in might be caught in
a trap and forced to unite with the Radicals in organizing the House. The lieutenant in command of the door
refused to permit it to enter, whereupon Mr. Sheppard
standing upon the steps of the State House began to
read a prepared protest to the large concourse of people and to the world against this unwarranted assumption of authority by the United States soldiers. The
Radical leaders, evidently fearful of a riot, ran up and
said we could enter. The soldiers disarming the members, opened the door, and the Democratic members
then proceeded to go forward, but were again stopped at
the door to the Hall of Representatives, and admission
into the Hall refused. The Democrats then quietly left
the State House and returned to Carolina Hall.

December 4th.—It was determined on this day to
enter the Hall of Representatives by force if necessary.
A committee of members was appointed to go before
and open the way for the others, who were to follow in
small sections so as not to attract a crowd. When
about to start Col. Alex, afterwards Judge Alex Haskell, asked that he and three others be appointed Assistant Sergeants at Arms and be allowed to accompany
the committee. The committee started at once, about
11 o'clock A. M. At the corner of the State House
grounds next to the Episcopal Church they halted in order to agree upon the course to pursue—and it was there
ascertained that there were present Judge Haskell and
five members, and J. S. Verner who asked to be permitted to go with us, making seven in all. Let me here
describe the conditions in the State House when we entered. In the long hall on the first floor, there was

drawn up a regiment of United States troops with fixed bayonets and all of the outside lower doors were guarded by troops. Upstairs in the large lobby was a large crowd of negro roughs brought there as suppo: :s. The committee rooms were filled with State constables, appointed by Chamberlain. A notorious character brought from New Orleans for the purpose was doorkeeper,—he had some fifteen assistants. The Mackey House was assembled and only waiting for the Speaker, and this House had as we were told at least a hundred Assistant Sergeants at Arms. For some reason not explained Gen. Ruger had promised Gov. Hampton to allow the Wallace House to enter the door over which he had control, hence there was no fear of a conflict with the troops, unless there was a fight.

The committee of seven knocked at the front door (outside) which was opened by an officer. We immediately entered and made a dash up the steps to the door of the Hall of Representatives. But the doorkeepers, who were lolling in the lobby, saw us, and broke for the door and drew up in line with their backs to the door, just as we ran up. We showed the doorkeeper our certificates of election as members of the House, and demanded that he open the door. This he refused to do and barred our way. Judge Haskell then said "Come men let's get at it," and at the same time seized the doorkeeper. The members of the committee also took hold of the man in front of him and there began a struggle which I cannot describe, for I was too busy to see anything but the thing I had immediately in hand. During this struggle the door, which was a large one divided in the middle, was pulled a little open and Verner slipped through. Bradley, D. F. either followed or preceded, I cannot say which, but when jerked open again I slipped in. All this took place quicker than it takes to tell it. We took one sweeping look at the scared and

amazed Mackey members, who were all standing up
looking at us with distended eyes and wide opened
mouths, and then turned to pushing against the door
(it opened outward.) Pushing from within and without the half of the door was raised off its hinges and fell
to the floor and the way was clear. Just as the door
fell Judge Wallace, followed by the other members,
came up, and marched immediately to the Speaker's
stand, and seated himself in the Speaker's chair. The
members, all but those who stood around Speaker Wallace, took seats on the Speaker's right, the negroes giving way and taking the seats on his left. Scarcely had
Speaker Wallace taken his seat and called the House to
order, when so-called Speaker Mackey came in and
ordered Wallace to vacate his seat. Wallace ordered
Mackey to leave the stand and take his place on the
floor. Several more commands and counter commands
were issued by these two, both of whom were supported by their armed supports. Finally Mackey took another chair and seated himself on the stand also. Two
Speakers, two Clerks on the stand at the same time—
and two opposing bodies occupying the Hall at the
same time. Then arose a scene perhaps never before
witnessed in any legislative body. It cannot be described. The central figure, Speaker Wallace, with his
fine commanding presence sat upon the stand calm and
undismayed while all around him raged, from 11 o'clock
A. M. until 12 o'clock that night, the wildest confusion
and danger. The Democrats had no dinner and no
supper, and although is was intensely cold, no fire on
their side of the house—until after mid-night fires were
lighted in the stoves. From mid-night to sun up the next
morning there was comparative calm. The Radicals
could go out and take some rest, but not so with the
whites they were in and there they had to stay—day
and night. It was the intention that the gentlemen ap-

pointed Assistant Sergeants at Arms to accompany the committee, should be charged with holding the door after it was opened, but for some reason, possibly they were never notified of their appointment, the door was left in possession of the Radicals, as soon as the Democrats entered. Hence there was but little going out and coming in. On the morning of the second day it was evident that the Radicals had begun to recover from their surprise of the day previous. Their friends gathered in the Hall and the negroes especially became very noisy and insulting in their manner, and frequently during the day both sides jumped upon their feet and drew their pistols. This was kept up until night. When night came on the negro members retired and placed other negroes in their places, who sang and caroused nearly the whole night. On the third day Hamilton and Myers, two intelligent and respectable negro members from Beaufort, requested to be sworn in as members of the Wallace House. The Republicans swore if they did so they would shoot them on the floor of the House, therefore the excitement was intense when they stepped to the Speaker's stand and asked to be sworn in. All during that day the wildest shouting, yelling and rowdyism prevailed which was kept up until near midnight. This night the Democrats secured blankets and lay upon the floor and got some sleep. At sun up next morning the uproar began again, and this day more than ever it seemed impossible to avoid a collision. So near did it come that Mackey ran over to the side of the Speaker's stand next to the Democratic side and held down his head to receive the shots he felt sure of receiving. The Republican leaders injected rowdies into the places of the negro members, who tried in every way possible to bring on a conflict, and repeatedly both sides stood ready for it. This exciting state of affairs with the close contact of the opposing parties, could not

continue much longer, every one felt some decisive result was sure soon to take place. In the afternoon of
this day it became known that the Radicals intended to
massacre the whites that night. They telegraphed for
the Hunkedory Club of Charleston (which started but
the engine broke down in the swamps.) Large numbers of State constables were appointed, armed and
placed in the nearby rooms. And it was said that even
the penitentiary convicts were brought over and placed
in the committee rooms and were promised their free-
doom if they would do the deed. Besides these a large
number of negro roughs were congregated into the
State House ready for the devilish deed. Some one
made known to Gov. Hampton the hellish purpose the
Radicals intended to perpetrate that night. He immediately notified Gen. Ruger, and at the same time said
to him if such a purpose as that was attempted he
would not insure the safety of his command, nor would
he guarantee the life of a negro in the State. Runners
were sent out to the nearby clubs of red shirts. By
dark these clubs began to arrive on horse back. The
City Hook and Ladder Company was ready to scale the
windows to reach the Democrats. The Company of
Artillery with guns loaded were kept ready to blow
open the outer doors. Some twenty young men got in
some how and guarded the entrance to the gallery, two
with sledge hammers to burst the door open at the first
intimation of a fight, and some thirty young men got
into the Hall. Under these conditions the night was
passed, the Democrats at least ready for the fray when
it came. We can only conjecture what prevented the
Radicals from carrying out their purpose. The next
morning we received official notice that President Grant
had ordered the Democrats to be ejected from the State
House. We had then been locked up, as it were, for
four days and nights with the Radical horde. About 11

o'clock A. M. Speaker Wallace addressed his House. He said he had been officially informed that at 12 o'clock M. that day the United States troops in obedience to orders received from President Grant would eject the Democratic members from the State House—that in obedience to the power and authority of the Federal Government, and uninfluenced by any power Chamberlain could bring against us, the Democrats or rather the white people would vacate their State House. He then delivered an earnest, manly protest against this unwarranted assumption of authority by the General Government, and then adjourned the House to meet immediately in Carolina Hall. There was no thought of surrender, we all knew the fight would go on, but right then as the members threw their blankets over their shoulders and marched out, things appeared very gloomy indeed. In the mean while word had been sent out for the red shirts to assemble immediately in Columbia, and they poured in all that night and the next day. So when the Wallace House left the State House such a scene as greeted our eyes is seldom seen. Standing at the State House door and looking up Main Street one could see nothing but one mass of white men. They were apparently unarmed and quiet. But when their legislature left the State House, a great wave of excitement swept over that portion next to and nearest the members,—seeing which Gov. Hampton jumped upon a rock and in a few words restored quiet. Quietly the Wallace House marched up the street, two and two—the crowd looking on in silence. At the Carolina Hall the House had to adjourn at once, because of the excessive coughing of the members. The crowd of white men assembled has been variously estimated, some placed the number present as high as thirty thousand. During the time they remained in Columbia there was no noise or rowdyism. But not a negro was seen on the streets.

Had these men seen the negro members and office holders
strutting up and down the streets as they did when they
were in possession, it is hard to say what would   have
been the result, but fortunately the negroes hid out.   After a day or two they dispersed to their homes, having
seen Gov. Hampton inaugurated and heard him assert
that he and he alone was Governor of South Carolina.
Governor Hampton and Lieutenant Governor Simpson
were inaugurated outside of and in front of Carolina
Hall' Gov. Hampton's ,address was received by the
people with great gladness for it revived hopes and con-
firmed the white people to do or die in this effort to
redeem themselves from the blight of negro domina-
tion.

The Democrats remained in session   until   near
Christmas.   During this time some seven or eight ne-
gro members who held certificates of election from the
Secretary of State were induced to join the Wallace
House.   As soon as these were all gathered in   (this
gave the Wallace House a majority of members declared elected by the returning Board) the Committee on
Privileges and Elections reported and recommended the
seating of the Democratic members from Laurens and
Edgefield counties.   Then whether the Radical allies remained with us or not (and they did not remain)   the
Wallace House had a constitutional majority of members.   The House as then organized elected Gen. M.
C. Butler United States Senator—passed a resolution
asking the tax payers not to pay any taxes to the Chamberlain authorities, and instead to pay 25 per cent of
their taxes to agents appointed by Gov. Hampton and
adjourned subject to the call of Gov. Hampton.

This brief historical sketch would be incomplete
without incorporating herein a copy of Gov. Hampton's
inaugural address, delivered on the street   December
14th, 1876—but space forbids, and any one interested may

find this address in the Journals of the House of Representatives, Regular Session of 1876—and Special Session 1877.

In pursuance of a proclamation of Gov. Hampton the General Assembly convened in Special April 24th, 1877. President Hayes had recognized the Hampton Government in South Carolina. The House was composed of the same members as organized in Carolina Hall, December, 1876—to these were added such Radical members as came before the bar of the House and purged themselves of their contempt. In the Senate the Radicals still had a majority. All the State offices were turned over to the Democrats elected thereto. No legislative body ever had graver responsibilities placed upon them. Gov. Hampton in his first message to the legislature, April 26th, 1877, said: "A great work— the greatest to which a patriotic people can be called —is before us, and a heavy responsibility rests upon us. We have to create anew a State which can of right demand and take the proud and honorable position in the Sisterhood of the great Republic. We have to restore her credit—to bring back her good name—to develop her boundless resources—to heal her wounds—to secure equal and exact justice to all of her children— to establish and maintain the supremacy of law—to diffuse the blessings of education, and to strive to bind all classes of both races in the bonds of peace." * * *

These were some of the duties which devolved upon the Wallace House. Were they equal to the trust? Read carefully the statutes of this Special Session of 1877, and the regular Session of 1877 and 1878. They did build anew a State. How and in what way this was done may be told hereafter in a separate chapter.

The State of South Carolina has always maintained among the other states of the Union a conspicuous and honorable position, both in war and in the halls of legis-

lation.   But if her history is ever hereafter written   it
will be found that in that period embraced within   the
years of 1865 and 1878 she wrought out the grandest
achievements in all of her glorious history.   With all of
her property swept away, attempted by force to be
placed under the rule of their former slaves—disarmed
—disfranchised, opposed by overwhelming negro majori-
ties then in possession of every department of the State
government, including of course the election machinery,
opposed also by the United States government, its troops
and its courts, and also by a State government as tyran-
nical and infamous as ever existed, harried down like
wild beasts, and driven to seek safety in flight, forsaken
by her friends and without help, she yet through it all
patiently endured until at last unable to endure more
she rose in her might, and by the strength of her own
right arm wrenched the State from the hands of the
robber—built anew a prostrate State—restored its credit, and secured again the blessings of liberty and safety.
For these achievements South Carolina is entitled to
take a higher position than she ever before   occupied
among the great and noble of this earth.

In trying to write up and preserve the genealogies
of the families of the early settlers of Pendleton, it has
been impossible to obtain the necessary information unless some of their descendants were living and were willing to help get up the data.   Some to whom when ap-
plication for information was made, failed to furnish it,
which no one regretted more than the writer.   It will
be our purpose to consider every family, and if any one
should be overlooked or not mentioned it will be owing
to the fact that they had passed entirely out of the
knowledge of the writer, and of those who aided and assisted him in this work.

JOSEPH D. SCOTT.

Was a soldier in the Revolution of 1776. He was engaged in the battle of King's Mountain, and was a witness to the hand to hand conflict between Col. Washington and Col. Tarlton. Washington in this fight cut off some of the fingers of Col. Tarlton, which caused him to drop his sword. Mr. Scott picked it up and handed it to Col. Washington, who told him to keep it. This sword is now in the hands of his nephew, Mr. T. E. Dickson. He had a son, Joseph D. Scott, who came to Pendleton from Abbeville County and married Narcissa Griffin, a daughter of Capt. James Griffin.

Joseph D. Scott and Narcissa (Griffin) Scott had three children:

A. E. Scott, James G. Scott and Julia K. Scott.

A. E. Scott married a Miss Reams· The other two never married.

DICKSON FAMILY.

The Dicksons came from Ireland in the early history of this country and settled in Virginia. Thomas Dickson with his brother, Michael Calvin Dickson, who was a distinguished divine of the Presbyterian faith came from Virginia and settled in Abbeville until 1841, when Thomas Dickson came to Anderson County and bought up a large estate on the waters of Three and Twenty, three miles east of Pendleton. He owned a large number of valuable slaves and during the war contributed largely of his means to support the government. He was one of the charter members of the Pendleton Farmer's Society. He married Nancy Young Scott, daughter of William Scott, who was a brave soldier in the war of the Revolution. They were blessed with five children, viz: Mary Montgomery Dickson

married Samuel McElroy.   Henry Franks married Ruth
Cannon of Anniston, Ala.   No issue.   Michael Calvin
married Addie A. Gilkerson of Laurens.   Thomas Eugene married Ella Jones, Anderson, S. C., Florence Scott
married George   Russell of   Anderson, S. C.   Mary
Montgomery Dickson and her husband Samuel McElroy
had the following children: William H. McElroy moved west.   James D. McElroy married Carolina   Watkins, no issue.   Antoinette McElroy married John L.
Gilkerson of Laurens, S. C., no issue.   Martha E. Mc-
Elroy married William Milan of Laurens, S. C.   Samuel M. McElroy moved west—resides in Oregon.   Thomas Eugene Dickson and his wife Ella (Jones) Dickson had the following children: Henry Frank died at
the age of 16 years.   Christine married Albert Adams
of Thomaston, Ga.   Inez   Dickson,   Columbia,   S. C.
Thomas Eugene, Jr., Columbia, S. C.

Micheal Calvin Dickson and his wife Addie (Gilkerson) Dickson had the following children:

Mary Dickson married W. Rufus Burriss of Anderson, S. C.

Thomas Paul Dickson, Anderson, S. C.

Michael Calvin Dickson, Jr., Anderson, S. C.

Nancy Eugenia Dickson died at the age of 10 years.

John Calhoun Dickson, Anderson, S. C.

MICHAEL CALVIN DICKSON.

One who knew him after he had passed through the
Civil War says—too much cannot be said of him—words
cannot do him justice, only those who saw him in   the
fierce conflict—only those who saw the gallant charges
that he made leading his fellow soldiers in the battle,
and ever standing the fury of the conflict, with invinci-
ble courage that drew forth the admiration of all who
beheld him.   Yes, only those could measure his strength

and rise up to take in his unselfish and lofty patriotism in defense of his country. Unflinchingly with a grand heroic spirit did he bear the hardships of war, and ever ready with a cordial greeting to cheer his comrades and brighten the monotony of camp-life with his natural witticism that always drew a circle around him. And when the end came, when the last roll was called and the brave soldier boys turned their faces homeward feeling "What is it all when all is done." His unconquered spirit—submitted to the inevitable with the conscious feeling that he had done his duty, his whole duty under the Confederate flag. Years afterward when he lay in the sleep of death friends gathered around him, and one who knew him best, with eyes fixed on his handsome, striking face—exclaimed, he looks like a warrior taking his rest and all knowing his record, there was an echo in the hearts of all who stood around his brier.

JACOB BELLOTTE.

Jacob Belotte married Sarah Dickson. (See Dickson family.) They had the following children:
I.   John E. Bellotte married Susanna DuPree.
II. Sarah Bellotte married Archie McElroy.
III. Thomas Bellotte—killed in Confederate War.
IV. Wm. Bellotte—killed in Confederate War.
V.   Michael Bellotte—killed in Confederate War.

I.   John E. Bellotte and wife Susanna (DuPree) Bellotte had the following children:
1. Sam Bellotte married Mary Milam.
2. Thomas Bellotte.
3. Wm. Bellotte married Mary Knight.
4. David Bellotte married Sarah Tillinghast.
5. Eliza Bellotte.

6.   Mary Bellotte married John E. Breazeale.

7.   Dickson Bellotte married Kate Rowland.

6.   Mary Bellotte and her husband J. E. Breazeale had the following children:

A. Oliver Breazeale.

B. Adda Breazeale.

C. Mary Breazeale.

7.   Dickson Bellotte and wife Kate (Rowland) Bellotte had the following children:

A. Ada Bellotte.

B. John Bellotte.

MAJOR DICKSON.

Major Dickson resided on Three and Twenty Creek near Capt. James C. Griffin.   He was highly esteemed and represented Pendleton District in the legislature.   He was no relation to his neighbor, Thos. Dickson.   His daughters never married.   His son, Alex Dickson who resided in the Fork of Anderson County, was the father of young Alex and J. Walter Dickson, a distinguished minister of the Methodist Church.   He left a large family, who I understand are doing well. Maj. Dickson had a sister who married a Mr. Gaston who resided near him on land afterwards owned by Col. T. J. Pickens.   This Mrs. Gaston was an elegant and accomplished woman, and a very determined one also.   A man whipped one of her sons.   Shortly after-wards, while riding on horse-back she met a man, she thought was the one who had whipped her son.   She stopped him in the road and belabored him with her riding whip, very much to his surprise.   She then rode on to the home of her neighbor, Capt. Griffin, and confessed what she had done, and was informed that she had whipped the wrong man.

JOSIAH E. SMITH.

Josiah E. Smith was a son of —— Smith at one time President of the South Carolina College. He married Eliza, daughter of Gov. Seabrook. He came to Pendleton about the year 1850 and purchased the tract of land upon which was located the Pendleton Manual Labor School—afterwards owned by Miss Caroline Taliaferro. His mother and sister, Miss Sallie Smith, and Miss Mary Seabrook, his wife's sister, resided with him. They were elegant, refined and accomplished ladies and gentlemen. Josiah E. Smith and wife Eliza (Seabrook) Smith had several children, but the only two I can now recall are Margaret and Seabrook Smith. Margaret was an exceedingly handsome young woman—tall, slender, black hair and sparkling black eyes. I saw her during the war when her family returned as refugees. She was then engaged to Paul Hamilton, a handsome, brave and gallant young officer. He and Seabrook Smith, Margaret's brother, were both killed during the Confederate War.

JOHN L. NORTH.

John Lawrence North was born in Philadelphia, 1782. His mother with other ladies had been sent from the city of Charleston to that city by the British for some cause now unknown. He married Eliza Elliot Drayton, daughter of General and Elizabeth Drayton. In 1807 he moved to Pendleton and settled at Rusticello farm, purchased from Joseph Whitner and now owned by the Rev. W. W. Mills. They had no children. They were buried in the Episcopal Churchyard at Pendleton.

John Lawrence North had a sister, Mary Eliza North who married Benjamin Savage Smith. They left surviving them one daughter, Sarah North Smith,

who was raised by her uncle, John L. North.   She married her cousin, Wm. Cutino Smith.

BENJAMIN SAVAGE SMITH.

Son of Benjamin and Sarah Smith was great-grandson of Thomas Smith, the first Landgrove.   He married
Mary Eliza North, sister of John   Lawrence   North.
They had one child, Sarah North Smith who married her
cousin, Wm. Cutino Smith and resided at Rivoli,   adjoining Rusticello farm.

Wm. Cuttino Smith and wife, Sarah (North) Smith
had eleven children, seven of whom reached maturity:

I.   Mary E. N. Smith, died unmarried.

II.   Alice Drayton Smith married Dr. J. A.   Tal-
mage.

III.   John L. N. Smith—killed at Seven Pines, Va.
—unmarried.

IV.   Wm. Cutino Smith married Martha Maxcy of
Columbia.

V.   Sarah E. Smith married Rev. W. W. Mills.

VI.   Benjamin Savage Smith—killed   at Malvern
Hill, Va.—unmarried.

VII.   Emily Hayne Smith—unmarried.

IV.   Wm. Cutino Smith and wife Martha (Maxcy)
Smith had five children:

1.   Hart Maxcy Smith—Presbyterian missionary to
China.

2.   Emily North Smith.

3.   Wm. Cutino Smith, Jr.

4.   Ashley M. Smith.

5.   Daniel B. Smith.

V.   Sarah Edith Smith and her husband, Rev. W.
W. Mills had five children:

1.   Wm. Hayne Mills—Presbyterian minister married Louise Pressley.

2.   Lawrence T. Mills married Margaret Johnstone, daughter of Alan Johnstone.

3.   James E. Mills.

4.   Mary North Mills.

5.   Wilson Plumer Mills.

1.   Rev. Wm. Hayne Mills and wife, Louise (Pressley) Mills have two children:

A.   Edith L. Mills.

B.   Wm. Hayne Mills, Jr.

Wm. Cutino Smith, Sr., who married Sarah North Smith married for his first wife, Sarah Elizabeth King and they had one child, Sarah Elizabeth Smith. She married Stephen Mazyck Wilson. About 1850 Mr. Wilson and family moved to Pendleton ,and purchased the plantation near Passmores Bridge on Three and Twenty Creek, now owned by M. B. and A. N. Richardson. Subsequently they all moved to Georgia and later to Alabama. They had nine children:

1.   Sarah Annie Wilson.

II·   Elizabeth Wilson married Lockwood.

III.   Mary Hume Wilson married Audubon Lee.

IV.   Stephen Wilson.

V.   Wm. Cuttino Wilson.

VI.   Eliza North Wilson married John F. O. Bryan.

VII.   Henrietta P. Wilson married Richard Y. Porter.

VIII.   Isaac Hume Wilson.

IX.   Laura B. Wilson married Screven Smith.

Mr. Hume married a Miss Wilson, sister of Stephen M. Wilson. He also resided near Pendleton, but of his descendants I can learn nothing.

The following families settled near Pendleton early in the year 1800: Dr. Hall at the Colin Campbell place, afterwards owned by Mr. W. H. Trescot, and after him by John Owen. Dr. Dart settled close by at the place now owned by John S. Newton's family. Mrs. McGreggor at the Eliot place near Dr. Dart's. Old Ben DuPree settled near Dr. Dart's on the place known as Lorton place, now owned by H. S. Trescot, and Nicholas Bishop settled on land adjoining Dr. Hall. Of these families I can gather but little information. They all came from Charleston, and were refined in their manners, but possessed of moderate means.

Mr. Bishop left two daughters, Jane and Dorcas, who never married, and resided at their father's home on Big Garvin Creek, and lived to a good old age, and were buried at the Old Stone Church.

Gov. Frank Burt married the eldest daughter of Dr. Hall and Samuel Towns of Greenville married another daughter of Dr. Hall.

Mrs. McGregor had three daughters, one of whom, Mary, married Thomas Bowen of Pickens. They all removed from here many years ago, and no further information can be obtained as to their descendants.

BURT FAMILY.

Armistead Burt, Sr., moved from Edgefield to Pendleton and with his wife is buried at Old Lebanon, nearby the former residence of Mr. Thomas Dickson.

He was the father of:

I.   Armistead Burt, Jr.
II. Gov. Frank Burt.
III. Miss Kittie Burt.
IV. Miss Eliza Burt married Campbell Miller.

I.   Armistead Burt, Jr., married Martha Calhoun —no issue. He moved to Abbeville, was at one time a member of United States Congress—and was recognized as a distinguished lawyer.

II. Gov. Frank Burt married Georgiana Hall, daughter of Dr. Hall and had the following children:

1. Georgia Burt married Wm. Dawson of Charleston.
2. Hariet Burt.
3. Joanna Burt.
4. Frank Burt.
5. Armistead Burt.
6. Kate Burt.
7. Mary Burt.

Gov. Frank Burt practiced law at Pendleton, and resided at the residence now owned by Mr. G. E. Taylor. He was appointed by the President, Governor of the Territory of Nebraska during the excitement of the question of slavery. A few months after entering upon his duties in Nebraska he died and his remains were brought home and buried in the Episcopal Churchyard at Pendleton. After this his family removed from Pendleton.

BEE FAMILY.

Col. Barnard Bee came from Charleston and settled on a farm about one and a half miles from the town of Pendleton, on the place still known as the Bee home—now owned by Edward Hall. His remains are buried with other members of his family in the Episcopal churchyard.

Miss Maria Bee, his sister, resided with him. One who knew this lady well says too much cannot be said in praise of her. She was a lovely, refined and Christian woman. Col. Bee was celebrated for his elegant and courtly manners. In fact he was the most elegant gentleman in his manners I ever knew.

Col. Barnard Bee married Miss ——————— and had the following children:

1. Gen. Barnard Bee married Miss Hill.
II. Hamilton Bee.

III.   Ann Bee married Gen. Clement Stevens (See Stevens family.)

IV.   Susan Bee—never married.

V.   Mattie Bee—never married.

VI.   Emma Bee—never married.

I.   Gen. Barnard Bee graduated at West Point, and entered the United States Army as a lieutenant. At the beginning of the Confederate War, he resigned his position in the United States Army ,and was appointed a colonel in the Confederate Army. Shortly thereafter was promoted to be Brigadier General. He was killed at the first battle of Manassas. It was Gen. Barnard Bee who in this battle gave the name of Stonewall to General Jackson. Gen. Barnard Bee married a Miss Hill; there were two children, both of whom died quite young at Pendleton of diphtheria His remains were brought home and buried in the Episcopal churchyard.

II.   Hamilton Bee early in life went to Texas, and figured largely in the war of Texas independence. I can learn nothing further of him.

STEVENS FAMILY.

Mrs. Stevens, a widow and sister of Col. Barnard Bee, came to Pendleton with him and resided at the farm now owned by J. A. Shanklin.

He had the following children:

I.   Gen. Clement Stevens married his cousin, Ann Bee, sister of Gen. Barnard Bee.

II.   Helen Stevens married Dr· Kennedy of Spartanburg, S. C.

III.   Mary Stevens married Dr. Russell of Spartanburg, S. C.

IV.   Henry Stevens.

V.   Ann Stevens.

VI. Rev. Bishop Peter Stevens married, first, Mary Capers, daughter of Bishop William Capers; second, Hattie Palmer.

I. Gen. Clement Stevens became a Brigadier General in the Confederate Army, was killed in battle. His remains were buried in the Episcopal churchyard at Pendleton by the side of his distinguished brother-in-law. He had several children all of whom died at Pendleton of diphtheria.

VI. Bishop Peter Stevens married first Mary Capers and had by this wife two children:

1. Mattie Stevens.

2. Helen Stevens married Prof. Daniel DuPree of Wofford College.

Bishop Stevens by his second wife, Hattie Palmer, had no children.

1. Helen Stevens and her husband, Prof. Daniel DuPree have the following children:

LORTON FAMILY.

Thomas Lorton married Sarah, daughter of Maj. Andrew Hamilton. They had two children.

I. John S. Lorton married Amanda Kilpatrick, widow of J. C. Kilpatrick, daughter of Frank and sister of Judge J. N. Whitner.

II. Mary Lorton married Overton Lewis (See Lewis family.) ·

I. John S. Lorton was a quiet and reserved man. He was a merchant, and was known of all men for his honesty and uprightness of character. I remember well the fact that when any of the gentry of the community sent a child or servant to town to purchase some article, they always told them to go to Mr. Lorton's store, for they well knew that no advantage would be taken of them.

John S. Lorton and his wife, Amanda, had one child:

I.   Ella Lorton married Gideon Lee of Cormel, N. Y., and they had three sons, whose names are unknown.

J. C. Kilpatrick was the son of John Kilpatrick. He married Amanda Whitner, and they had two children:

I.   Clara Kilpatrick married Col. J. W. Livingston.

II.   Whitner Kilpatrick never married.

I.   Clara Kilpatrick was a noted belle when a young lady. She and her husband, Col. J. W. Livingston, had the following children: ————————————

II.   Whitner Kilpatrick was among the noblest young men ever raised in Pendleton. He became a colonel in the Confederate Army, was killed in battle, and his remains were buried at the Old Stone Church.

POTTER.

Rev. Mr. Potter was an Episcopal minister and resided in the house now known as the Railroad house. He married the widow of a Mr. Hamilton, who had a son, Paul Hamilton. Mr. Potter moved away from Pendleton many years ago and died in Charleston.

J. TYLER WHITFIELD.

Mr. Whitfield practiced law in Pendleton and married Martha Griffin, daughter of Capt. James Griffin. They had the following children:

I.   Margaret Whitfield married Rev. Barnard Gaines.

II.   John C. Whitfield married Susan Finley.

I.   Margaret Whitfield and her husband, Rev. Barnard Gaines, had the following children:

1. Ann Gaines married Gassaway and moved to Alabama.
2. Ella Gaines married Dr. Thomas Hudgens.
3. Elizabeth Gaines.
4. Louisa Gaines.
5. Helen Gaines.
6. Jane Gaines.
7. Mary Gaines.
8. Emma Gaines.
9. Capers Gaines.
10. Walker Gaines.
11. Joe Gaines.
12. George Gaines.

2. Ella Gaines and her husband, Dr. Thomas Hudgens, had six children:
A. John Hudgens.
B. Maggie Hudgens.
C. Augustus Hudgens married Lucia Taylor.
D. Elizabeth Hudgens.
E. Kate Hudgens.
F. Arthur Hudgens.

C. Augustus Hudgens and wife, Lucia (Taylor) Hudgens have the following children:
A. Elizabeth Whitner Hudgens.

II. John Whitfield and wife, Susan (Finley) Whitfield had the following children:
1. Ella Whitfield married James Jones.
2. Elbert Whitfield died unmarried.
3. John C. Whitfield, Jr., married Ella Cox of Tennessee.
4. Sue Whitfield, unmarried.

1. Ella Whitfield and husband, James Jones, have one child:
A. Ella C. Jones.

3.   John C. Whitfield, Jr., and wife, Ella Cox, had one child:
A. John C. Whitfield.

WILLIAM HUBBARD.

Had two children:
I.   A daughter who married a Mr. Smith.
II.   William Hubbard, Jr., a well known citizen of Pendleton, married Mahala Waddell.
I.   The daughter of Wm. Hubbard and her husband, a Mr. Smith, had a son:
1.   Munro Smith married Esther Watkins, daughter of Baylis Watkins, and had the following children:
A.   James Smith,—having graduated at Davidson College with first honor, died shortly afterwards, un·· married.
B.   J. P. Smith married Carrie Glenn,   daughter of F. M. Glenn.
C.   Dr. R. Frank Smith married Miss   Hollingsworth.
D.   Dr. Walter Smith married Miss Glenn, daughter of J. M. Glenn.
E.   Elizabeth Smith married J. C. Watkins.   (See Watkins family.)
F.   Amanda Smith married J. P. Glenn, son of F. M. Glenn, no issue.
G.   ——— Smith married Dr. Lawrence Clayton.
H.   Chess Smith married—

B.   J. P. Smith and wife, Corrie (Glenn)   Smith had the following children:
a.   Herbert Smith married—
b.   Lois Smith.
c.   Pearl Smith.
d.   Walter Smith.

D. Dr. Walter Smith and wife, Miss Glenn, had one child:

II. William Hubbard and wife, Mahala Waddell, had the following children:

1. Robt. Hubbard married Jane McFall.
2. Georgia Hubbard married John Brown.
3. Mary Hubbard married Elijah Brown.
4. Hattie Hubbard married Dock Earle.
5. Lillie Hubbard married Barr.
6. Arthur Hubbard married Mary Wilson.
7. Seffie Hubbard.

1. Robert Hubbard and wife, Jane McFall, had five children:

A. Nora Hubbard.
B. John M. Hubbard married Lavinia Cater.
C. Wm. Hubbard married Dessie Keese.
D. Augusta Hubbard.
E. Elizabeth Hubbard married John Broyles. (See Broyles family.)

B. John M. Hubbard and wife, Lavinia (Cater) Hubbard had—

a. ⸺ ⸺ ⸺ ⸺ ⸺ ⸺ ⸺ ⸺ ⸺

C. Wm. Hubbard and wife, Dessie (Keese) Hubbard, had the following children:

a. J. W. Hubbard.
b. Robt. Hubbard.
c. Edward Hubbard.

2. Georgia Hubbard and her husband, John Brown, had three children:

A. Feaster Brown.
B. William Brown.
C. Ernest Brown.

3. Mary Hubbard and her husband, Elijah Brown, had seven children:

A. Hattie Brown married Sam Brownlee.

B. Amelia Brown married Rev. Mr. Edwards, missionary to Mexico.

C. Marie Brown married Joe Magu.

D. Dr. Ralph Brown married.

E. Elijah Brown married Miss Salley of Orangeburg.

F. Eula Brown.

G. Annie Brown.

ANDERSON BURNS.

Anderson Burns married Leah Doyle and had the following children:

I. Mary Burns married Milton Reese.

II. Sarah Burns married William Grogan.

III. Martha Burns, unmarried.

IV. Harriet Burns married Mr. Hunt.

V. Elizabeth Burns, unmarried.

VI. Robt. M. Burns married Miss Blackman.

VII. Thompson Burns, unmarried.

VIII. Maria B. Burns, unmarried.

JOHN PIKE.

John Pike came to this country from England and settled about one mile west of Pendleton near the Old Stone Church. They were people of gentle manners. Mrs. Pike when a widow was employed by Mrs. John C. Calhoun as her companion. They had three children:

I. Ellen Pike, never married.

II. Lucretia Pike married Andrew Stephens.

III. John Pike married Martha Fitzgerald.

ROBINSON FAMILY.

John Robinson was born and raised in Fauquier

County, Virginia, and married there a Miss Benson, and they had the following children:

I.   Dr. John Robinson married Eliza Blassingame, daughter General Blassingame.

II.   Dr. Wm. Robinson married Maria Earle, daughter of Washington Earle.

III.   Eliza Robinson.

John Robinson married the second time Sarah Smith and they had the following children:

IV.   Maj. Willis Robinson.

V.   Margaret Robinson.

VI.   Knox Robinson.

VII.   Mary Robinson.

VIII.   Smith Robinson.

IX.   Catherine Robinson.

I.   Dr. John Robinson practiced medicine for many years in Pendleton and resided in the house subsequently owned by Dr. Joseph Taylor.

Dr. John Robinson and Eliza Blassingame had the following children:

1.   Elizabeth Robinson married Earle Halcomb.

2.   Ann Robinson married Alex Briggs.

3.   Esther Robinson married James E. Hagood.

4.   Mary Robinson, never married.

5.   John Robinson married—

6.   Jane Robinson married Edward Owens of Abbeville.

7.   Sallie Robinson married John Patton.

8.   Julia Robinson married Wm. Lee.

9.   Wm. Robinson married Elvira Hagood.

II.   Dr. Wm. Robinson and wife, Maria Earle, had the following children:

1.   John Robinson married Rebecca Watt of Fairfield County.

2.   Elizabeth E. Robinson married Maj.   John V. Moore.

3.   Sarah Y. Robinson died unmarried.

4.   Dr. George Robinson married Sarah Childs.

5.   Warren D. Robinson died unmarried·

6.   Charles Robinson married Miss Clayton.

7.   Virginia Robinson married E. H. Shanklin, son of Van Shanklin (See Shanklin family.)

2.   Elizabeth E. Robinson and husband, Maj. John V. Moore, had three children ,only one of whom lived to manhood, that was:

A. Wm. R. Moore married Miss—

Major Moore was an officer in the Confederate Army and was killed in battle·

4.   Dr. George Robinson and wife, Sarah (Childs) Robinson had the following children:

A· Charles Robinson married Miss Cox.

B.   Earle Robinson married Miss Cureton of Greenville.

C.   Robert Robinson.

D.   Elizabeth Robinson.

E.   Augusta Robinson.

F.   John Robinson.

IV.   Maj. Willis Robinson was born in Virginia, but spent his early life in Kentucky.   When a young man he came to Pendleton with his two brothers, Dr. John and Dr· Wm. Robinson.   He married twice,—First, Sarah Ann Griffin, daughter of Capt. James Griffin; by this marriage he had one son, Henry C· Robinson, who died unmarried.

He married the second time Rebecca W. Griffin, daughter of Capt. James Griffin and by this marriage he had four children:

I.   Ida Robinson married John T. Hacket.

2.   Anna Robinson, unmarried.

3.   Whitner K. Robinson, unmarried.

4.   Willis S. Robinson, died unmarried.

1.   Ida Robinson and her husband, John T. Hacket, have two children:

A.   Covie Hacket.

B.   John R. Hacket.

DR. GIBBS.

Dr. Gibbs practiced medicine in Pendleton. He came from Beaufort County and resided in the house now owned by Dr. Thos. J. Pickens. He had one daughter, Mary, who attended school under Miss Bates.

DR. STEWART.

Dr. Stewart came to Pendleton from Charleston and practiced medicine here. He resided at the house known as Micassa where H. P. Sitton now resides. He had no children, but an adopted daughter who married Paul Hamilton, the step-son of Rev. Mr. Potter.

DR. THOMAS REESE.

Dr. Thos. Reese, son of David and Susan Polk Reese, married Jane Harris, daughter of Robt. Harris, near Charlotte, N. C., 1773. They had seven children:

I.   Edwin Tasker Reese.

II.   Thomas Sidney Reese.

III.   Elihu Reese.

IV.   Leah Reese.

V.   Lydie Reese.

VI.   Henry Dobson Reese.

VII.   Susan Polk Reese.

I.   Edwin Tasker Reese graduated at Princeton with first honor. His remains were buried at the Old Stone Church, Pendleton, S. C.

II.   Thomas Sidney Reese also graduated at Princeton; was admitted to the bar at Pendleton; shortly thereafter he was killed in a duel by Michie. His second was John Taylor, Esq. He also was buried at the   Stone Church.

III.   Elihu Reese graduated in medicine in Philadelphia; died in Charleston during an epidemic of yellow fever, and was buried there.

IV.   Leah Reese was born 1779. In 1782 she returned with her father to South Carolina and married Maj. Samuel Taylor, son of Maj. Samuel Taylor of Revolutionary fame· Maj. Taylor was an officer in the War of 1812. He moved to Alabama and died there   1833. (See Taylor line.)

V.   Lydie Reese married first Mr. Findley of South Carolina who was killed accidentally by his brother-in-law, Samuel Cherry.   She married the second time John Martin.

VI.   Henry Dobson Reese married Rebecca Harris, grand-daughter of Gen. Andrew   Pickens.   They   had eleven children as follows:

1.   Sidney Harris Reese married late in life an Illinois lady unknown.

2.   Frank Reese unknown.

3.   Maria Reese married Washington Knox.

4·   Edwin Reese married Charlotte McKinstry.

5.   Flora Reese married Mr· Rowland.

6.   Carlos Reese married Mary E. Crenshaw   and moved to Alabama.

7·   Harriet Reese married W. Smith·

8.   Elihu Milton Reese married—

9.   Jane Reese married W. W. Scott.

10.   Thomas Reese.

11.   Mary C. Reese.

VII.   Susan Polk Reese married Samuel Cherry

at the home of Dr. Reese at Pendleton, S. C., 1807. They had twelve children as follows:

1. Robert M. Cherry married Carolina Crenshaw of Alabama·

2. Thomas Reese Cherry married Mary Reese Harris, his cousin·

3. James Alvin Cherry married his cousin, Mary E. Reese.

4. Samuel Sidney Cherry never married, buried at Stone Church.

5. William B. Cherry married Sarah Lewis.

6. Jane Adelaide Cherry married Dr. A. H. Reese and moved to West Point, Ga.

7. Edwin Augustus Cherry died unmarried.

8. Sarah Ann Cherry married John Smith.

9. David E. Cherry married Edmonia Schull of Virginia·

10. John C. Cherry died unmarried—buried at Stone Church.

11. Mary E. Cherry married Elijah McKinley.

12. Charles Henry Cherry—unmarried.

2. Thomas Reese Cherry and wife, Mary Reese Harris, had eight children as follows:

A. Edward B. Cherry.

B. Mary Story Cherry.

C. Annie Reese Cherry.

D. Laura Cherry.

E. Thomas R· Cherry.

F. Nathaniel H. Cherry.

G. Lillie B. Cherry.

H. Kate Cherry.

5. Dr. William B. Cherry and Sarah Lewis, his wife, had three children as follows:

A. Lorty Cherry died young.

B.   Samuel D. Cherry married Minnie Johnson of Atlanta.

C.   Fanny Lewis Cherry married Warren R. Davis.

GEORGE REESE, BROTHER OF DR. THOS. REESE.

George Reese, son of David and Susan Polk Reese, married Anna Story of Sumter, S. C. Their eldest daughter, Mary Story Reese, married David Cherry of Pendleton, S. C. They had one child, George Reese Cherry, who married Sarah Creswell, and they had one child, Mary George Cherry.

CATHERINE REESE.

Catherine Reese, eldest daughter of David and Susan Polk Reese, sister to Dr. Thomas and George Reese, married William Sharpe of Maryland. William Sharpe was a son of Thomas Sharpe—he was a distinguished patriot of the Revolution. He was a lawyer by profession. He was a member of the State Congress, and Aid-de-Camp to Gen. Rutherford and afterwards a member of the Continental Congress at Philadelphia. The said William Sharpe and Catherine Reese, his wife, left a number of children, among them Elizabeth and Elam settled in Pendleton. Elizabeth married Capt. R. Starke, died without issue. Elam Sharpe married Elizabeth Miller, daughter of John Miller (See Miller line.) They had the following children:

I.   Oscar Sharpe.

II.   Elam Sharpe.

III.   Edwin Sharpe.

IV.   Marcus Sharpe.

V.   Elizabeth Sharpe.

I. Oscar Sharpe married Susan Harrell. They had the following children:

1. Edwin Reese Sharpe.
2. Susan Elizabeth Sharpe.
3. Frances H. Sharpe.
4. Mary C. Sharpe.
5. Annie E. Sharpe.
6. Rose Harrell Sharpe.
7. Pinkie Sharpe.
8. Wm. Oscar Sharpe.
9. Gertrude E. Sharpe.

II. Elam Sharpe married Fanny Hayne, daughter of Gov. Robert Y. Hayne of South Carolina. They had the following children:

1. Martha Sharpe married James Overton Lewis.
2. Elam Sharpe.

III. Edwin Sharpe never married.

IV. Dr. Marcus Sharpe never married.

V. Elizabeth Sharpe married Rev. John M. Carlisle. They had the following children:

1. Rev. John E. Carlisle.
2. Wm. Mayson Carlisle, died young.
4. James B. Carlisle.
5. Charles H. Carlisle.
6. Susan Elizabeth Carlisle.
7. Rev. Marcus L. Carlisle.

1. Rev. John E. Carlisle married first, Emma Jones,—no issue; married second, Kate Roland,—no issue.

3. Edwin Sharpe Carlisle married Annie Bowden. They had seven children, namely:

Elizabeth, Annie, William, Sarah, John, Mary R., and Gladys Carlisle.

4. James B. Carlisle married Eliza Allen. They

have three children, Eliza Allen, James A. and Lilly
Carlisle.

5. Charles H. Carlisle married Alice Pyles. They
have boys, namely: Charles E., Francis M., and John
S. Carlisle.

6. Susan Elizabeth Carlisle married John K. Jennings. They have five children, namely:

John Carlisle Jennings, Wm. Coke, Lucius K., Emma C· Jennings.

7. Rev. Marcus L. Carlisle married Annie Rast.
They have two chillren, namely, Charles E. and Wm.
A. Carlisle.

DUPREE FAMILY.

Benjamin DuPree came to Pendleton early in the
18th century and settled on a farm on Little Garvin
Creek, now owned by H. S. Trescot. As far as could
be ascertained he had eight children:

I. Benjamin DuPree, Jr., married Eliza Frances
Carne 1819.

II. Cornelius Portervine DuPree married Esther
Mary Carne 1827.

III. Mary DuPree married Dr. Dart·

I· Benjamin DuPree, Jr., and wife, Eliza F. (Carne)
DuPree, had the following children:

1. Sarah C. DuPree.

2. Augustus N. DuPree.

3. Eliza Caroline DuPree.

4. Samuel A. DuPree.

II. Cornelius Portervine DuPree and wife, Esther
M. (Carne) DuPree had the following children:

1. Amanda C· DuPree.

2. Julius Franklin C. DuPree married Mary P.
Huckabee·

3. Cornelius H. DuPree.

4. M. Rosa Eugenia DuPree married M. L. Kennedy.

5. M. Emma V. DuPree.

6. B. C. DuPree.

2. Julius Franklin C. DuPree was elected the first Professor of Horticulture of Clemson College and died at Clemson College. He and his wife, Mary P. (Huckabee) DuPree, have the following children:

A. Julius H. DuPree married Josephine Hill.

B. Jannette DuPree, died unmarried.

C. Eugene M. DuPree married Anna K. McKellar.

D. Wm. C. DuPree married Sarah W. Shillito.

E. Frank C. DuPree married Sarah N. Marshall.

F. A. Mason DuPree married—

G. Mary C. DuPree, unmarried.

H. Anna R. DuPree, died unmarried.

4. M. Rosa Eugenia DuPree and her husband, M. L. Kennedy, have the following children:

A. Eala Kennedy married Mr. Haddon.

B. Alice Gertrude Kennedy married John N. Bleckley.

The two brothers, Benjamin DuPree, Jr., and Cornelius Partervine DuPree built two houses on the eastern part of Pendleton exactly alike and resided there for many years. One of these houses was purchased by the Episcopal Church for a parsonage. The other was recently torn down by F. E. Boggs.

SAMUEL CRAIG.

Samuel Craig came to Pendleton with the Lewis family from North Carolina. His people were originally from Virginia. He married Ruth Briggs and had one son, David Craig, who married Catherine Smith, daughter of Capt. Aaron Smith.

David Craig and wife Catherine (Smith) Craig had the following children:

I.   Sam T. Craig married Mary Partlow.
II.   D. M. Craig married Leah Rochester.
III. Luther Craig never married.
IV. Ruth Craig married Joseph N. Smith.
V.   Kate Craig unmarried.

I.   Sam T. Craig and wife Mary (Partlow) Craig have the following children:

1. Sam Craig, Jr.
2. James Craig.
3. Mamie Craig.
4. Marshall Craig.

II.   D. M. Craig and wife Leah (Rochester) Craig have the following children:

1. Marcus Craig.
2. Augustus Craig.
3. Ray Craig.
4. Ruth Craig.

DAVID SLOAN.

David Sloan born 1753 married Susanah Majors. They resided on Seneca River at the place now known as Sloan Ferry and were buried at the family graveyard on his homestead.

David and Susanah (Majors) Sloan had twelve children as follows:

I.   William Sloan died 1804.
II.   Elizabeth Sloan married Jesse Stribling (See Stribling Family.)
III. David Sloan married Nancy Trimmier.
IV. Susan Sloan married Robert Bruce.

V. Nancy Sloan married Col. Jos. Taylor (See Taylor Family.)

VI. Mary Sloan died 1810.

VII. Rebecca Sloan married Dr. Joe Berry Earle (See Earle Family.)

VIII. Benjamin F. Sloan married Eliza C. Earle.

IX. Thomas Majors Sloan married Nancy Blasingham.

X. Catherine E. Sloan married Jno. P. Benson. (See Benson Family.)

XI. William Sloan married Eliza Hackett.

XII. J. Madison Sloan married Rebecca Linton.

III. David Sloan and his wife, Nancy (Trimmier) Sloan had eight children as follows:

1. William David Sloan married Martha Jones.

2. Sallie Sloan married first, John Blasingham, second, John Bomar.

3. John T. Sloan married Eliza Benson.

4. Emily Sloan married G. W. Bomar.

5. Susan Sloan married Andrew F. Lewis.

6. Lucy Sloan married Dr. Robert Maxwell.

7. Thomas Sloan married Sallie Seaborne.

8. Ben Parker Sloan married Mary Reeder.

3. John T. Sloan and wife, Eliza (Benson) Sloan had children as follows:

A. Enoch Berry Sloan married Mary Benson.

B. Alice Sloan—unmarried.

C. Essie M. Sloan married Wm. H. Whitner, no issue.

D. Eliza Sloan—unmarried.

E. David B. Sloan married Nancy Poe.

F. Wm. Henry Sloan—died.

G. John T. Sloan twice married; first, Janie Beverly; second, Mrs. Gilliam.

H. Dr. Henry N. Sloan married Ella Townsend.

I.   Gourdin Sloan married first, Sallie Carpenter; second, Ella Justice.

J.   Emma Sloan—died.

K.   McBurnie Sloan married Cynthia Gibbes.

L.   Barny Cleveland Sloan married Luve Vrooman.

A.   Enoch Berry and Mary (Benson) Sloan had three children as follows:

a.   Edward Sloan.

b.   D. Prue Sloan.

c.   Essie Sloan.

a.   Edward Sloan married Alice White and has two children, Mortimer Sloan and New Sloan.

E.   David B. and Nancy (Poe) Sloan, his wife, have six children as follows:

a.   Joseph Henry Sloan married Carrie Marshall.

b.   Winslow Sloan married Daisy Russell.

c.   Ellen Sloan—unmarried.

d.   Alice Sloan—unmarried.

e.   Janie Sloan—unmarried.

f.   Neila Sloan—unmarried.

a.   Jos. Henry and Carrie (Marshall) Sloan, his wife have two children,—David Sloan and Mamie Sloan.

b.   Winslow and Daisy (Russell) Sloan, his wife have children as follows: Gus Hoke, Joseph Henry Sloan.

G.   John T. and Janie (Beverley) Sloan, his wife had three children: Beverley, Annie and John.

H.   Dr. Henry N. and Ella (Townsend) Sloan, his wife had the following children:

Henry Townsend Sloan married Maggie Rice .

John Benson Sloan married Reuby Anderson.

Joldsby Sloan—unmarried.

Eliza Trimmier Sloan—unmarried.

I.   Gourdin and Sallie (Carpenter) Sloan and Ella

(Justice) Sloan had two children, Annie and Louise Cleveland.

K. McBurnie and Cynthia (Gibbs) Sloan, his wife have one child, James Trimmier Sloan.

L. B. Cleveland and Luve (Vrooman) Sloan, his wife, have one child, John Cleveland Sloan.

4. Emily Sloan married G. W. Bomar and had children as follows:

A. David S. Bomar—killed in Civil War.

B. Edward D. Bomar—married Eugenia Earle.

C. Annie Bomar,—died.

D. Mary Bomar married Albert Twitchell.

E. Robert Bomar married Julia Sims.

F. George Bomar married Sallie Elford.

G. William Bomar—died.

H. Landrum Bomar—died.

I. Emma Bomar married James Gilfillin.

J. Berry Bomar—died.

K. Eli Geddings Bomar married, first, Miss Keit; second, Fanny Johnson.

L. Henry Bomar married—

5. Susan Sloan and Andrew F. Lewis. (See Lewis line.)

6. Lucy Sloan and Dr. Robt. D. Maxwell. (See Maxwell line.)

7. Tomas Sloan and Sallie (Seaborne) his wife, had children as follows:

A. Douglas Sloan married, first, Fannie Dye; second Mamie Tresevant.

B. George Sloan—died.

C. Eva Sloan married E. B. Murray.

D. Julius Sloan—drowned.

E. Duff Sloan married Lilian Trowbridge.

F. Meta Sloan married Dr. J. O. Wilhite.

A. Douglas and Fanny (Dye) Sloan had two children as follows:

James Marshall Sloan.

Francis Dye Sloan.

A. Douglas and Mamie Trezevant Sloan have children as follows:

Douglas Sloan.

Mary Sloan.

George Sloan.

Seaborne Sloan.

Bessie Orr Sloan.

C. Eva Sloan married E. B. Murray and had the following children:

    a. Felicia Hall Murray.

    b. J. Scott Murray—died unmarried.

    c. Eva Sloan Murray married Mr. Cumnock.

    d. Edward B. Murray.

    e. Duff S. Murray.

    f. Douglas Murray.

E. Duff and Lilian (Trowbridge) Sloan, his wife have two children:

George Seaborne Sloan.

Annie Lilian Sloan.

F. Meta Sloan married Dr. J. O. Wilhite and they have children as follows:

    a. J. O. Wilhite, Jr.

    b. Lydie G. Wilhite.

    c. Sarah Earle Wilhite.

    d. Cora Wilhite.

    e. Philip A. Wilhite.

    f. Frank T. Wilhite.

8. Ben Parker and Mary (Reeder) Sloan had eight children:

    A. Nancy Sloan—died.

    B. Manning Sloan.

    C. Lewis Sloan.

    D. Hattie Sloan.

    E. Lucy Sloan married C. Perley.

    F. Susan Sloan.

G.   David Sloan.

VIII.   Benjamin F. Sloan, son of David and Susan (Majors) Sloan, married Eliza C. Earle and had   the following children:

1.   Sallie T. Sloan married W. H. D. Gaillard.

2.   David Sloan married Sallie Taylor.

3.   Col. John B. E. Sloan married Mollie Seaborne.

4.   Joe Berry Sloan married Mary E. Earle—killed in Civil War.

5.   Susan Sloan married Wm. P. Hall.

6.   Benjamin Franklin Sloan, Jr., married, first, Rebecca Benson; second, Ellen Lewis.

7.   Dr. P. H. E. Sloan married Ella Maxwell.

1.   Sallie Sloan married W. H. D. Gaillard and had the following children:

A.   Rebecca Gaillard married B. C. Crawford.

B.   Benj. Gaillard—unmarried.

C.   Eliza Gaillard married James T. Hunter.

D.   Wm. H. D. Gaillard, Jr., married Lena Greene.

E.   Susan Gaillard married Joseph J. Sitton.

F.   Henrietta Gaillard married Wm. Seabrook.

G.   Pauline Gaillard married Miles M. Hunter.

H.   P. Cordes Gaillard married Eoline Merchant.

A.   Rebecca Gaillard married B. C. Crawford and they have the following children:

a.   Mary Bell Crawford.

b.   B. C. Crawford, Jr.

c.   Eliza Crawford.

d.   Frank Crawford.

e.   Sue Crawford.

f.   Henry Crawford.

g.   James Crawford.

h.   Paul Crawford.

C.   Eliza Gaillard married James T. Hunter and they have the following children:

a.   Thomas E. Hunter.

  b. James William Hunter.

  c. Miles N. Hunter.

  d. Sallie Gaillard Hunter.

  e. Louise Hunter.

  b. James William Hunter married Miss Skinner of Raleigh, N. C.

  D. Wm. H. D., Jr., and his wife, Lena (Green) Gaillard had the following children:

  a. Margaret.

  b. Irene.

  c. Henrietta.

  d. W. H. D.

  e. Perkins Green Gaillard.

  E. Susan Gaillard married Joseph J. Sitton and had the following children:

  a. Emma Sitton.

  b. Henrietta Sitton married Benjamin Aull.

  c. Arthur Sitton.

  d. Louis Sitton.

  e. John Sitton.

  f. Henry Sitton.

  g. Joseph Sitton.

  h. Ben Gaillard Sitton.

  F. Henrietta Gaillard married William Seabrook and had the following children:

  a. Wm. Seabrook, Jr.

  b. Henrietta Seabrook.

  c. P. C. Seabrook.

  d. Edward Seabrook.

  G. Pauline Gaillard married Miles M. Hunter and had the following children:

  a. Bessie Hunter.

  b. Galliard Hunter.

  c. Ralph Hunter.

  d. Sallie Hunter.

  e. James Hunter.

f. Pauline Hunter.

g. Miles Hunter.

H. P. Cordes and Eoline   (Merchant)   Gaillard have two children:

P. C. Gaillard, Jr.

James Culbraith Gaillard.

3. Col. John Baylis E. Sloan and   Mollie   (Seaborne) Sloan have the following children:

A. Earle Sloan married Alice Witte.

B. Louis F. Sloan—unmarried.

C. Annie Lee Sloan—unmarried.

D. Leila Sloan married L. Johnson.

E. Joe Berry Sloan—unmarried.

F. Vivian S. Sloan—unmarried.

G. Helen Gaines Sloan married Dr. Torrence.

H. Margarite E. Sloan—unmarried.

A. Earle Sloan and Alice Witte Sloan, his wife, have the following children:

a. Carla W. Sloan.

b. Eliza Earle Sloan.

4. Joe Berry Sloan and Mary E. (Earle) Sloan, his wife have two children as follows:

A. Harriet Sloan—unmarried.

B. Mary Mayes Sloan.

B. Mary Mayes Sloan married William H. Lyles and had children as follows:

a. Mary Mayes Lyles.

b. Saray Lyles.

c. Joe Berry Lyles.

d. William Lyles.

e. Preston Lyles.

f. Mayes Lyles.

5. Susan Sloan married Wm. P. Hall and they have the following children:

A. Felicia Hall married Wm. B. Chisholm.

B. Eliza Hall married Andrew Crawford.

    C.   Tudor Hall married.
    D.   Henry G. Hall—unmarried.
    E.   Wm. P. Hall married Floride Orr.

    A.   Felicia Hall married Wm. B. Chisholm and they have the following children:
    a.   Sue Chisholm married Lieut. Dwight.
    b.   Wm. B. Chisholm.
    c.   Tudor Hall Chisholm.
    d.   Caspar Chisholm.
    e.   Felix Chisholm.
    f.   Alexander Chisholm.
    g.   Felicia Chisholm.
    h.   Esteria Chisholm.
    i.   Harry Chisholm.
    B.   Eliza Hall married Andrew Crawford and they have the following children:
    a.   Kate Lorraine Crawford.
    b.   Wm. Hall Crawford.
    c.   Andrew Crawford, Jr.
    d.   Stateria Crawford.
    e.   John Crawford.
    f.   Daniel Crawford.
    g.   J. B. E. Crawford.
    h.   Susan Crawford.
    i.   Eliza Earle Crawford.
    E.   William P. Hall, Jr., married Floride Orr and they have the following children:
    a.   Wm. P. Hall, Jr.
    b.   Lawrence Orr Hall.
    6.   Benjamin Franklin Sloan married first, Rebecca Benson, and had two children—married second, Ellen Lewis—no issue.
    A.   Dora Sloan married H. T. Poe.
    B.   Baylis Sloan married Hess Porcher.

    A.   Dora Sloan married H. T. Poe and they have the following children:

a. Harry T. Poe., Jr.
b. Ellen Poe.
c. Baylis Poe.
d. Frank Poe.
e. Thomas Poe.
f. Dora Poe.
  B. Baylis Sloan married Hess Porcher and they had one son, Frank Sloan.
  7. Dr. P. H. E. Sloan married Ella V. Maxwell, daughter of Dr. Robt. D. Maxwell, and they have the following children:
  A. Paul H. E. Sloan, Jr., married Susan James Simpson.
  B. Harry A. Sloan married Hattie Smith.
  C. Susan Hall Sloan—unmarried.
  D. Baylis Franklin Sloan married Emma Merrick.
  E. Sloan Maxwell Sloan married Walden.
  F. Elise Sloan—died young.

  A. Paul H. E. Sloan, Jr., married Susan James Simpson, daughter of R. W. and Maria L. Simpson and they have the following children:
  a. Maria Louise Garlington Sloan.
  b. Ella Maxwell Sloan.
  c. Paul H. E. Sloan, Jr.
  d. Susie Simpson Sloan.
  e. Jean Conway Sloan.
  f. Eliza Earle Sloan.
  g. Margaret Taliaferro Sloan.
  h. Lucy Maxwell Sloan.

  B. Harry A. Sloan married Hattie Smith and they have the following children:
  a. Suny May Sloan.
  b. Elise Sloan.
  c. Harry A. Sloan, Jr.
  d. Paul E. Sloan.
  V. Nancy Sloan, daughter of David and Susan

(Majors) Sloan married Col. Joseph Taylor. (See Taylor line.)

VII.   Rebecca, daughter of David and Susan (Majors) Sloan married Dr. Joe Berry Earle. (See Earle line.)

THOMAS MAJORS SLOAN.

IX.   Thomas Majors Sloan, son of David and Susan Majors Sloan, married Nancy Blasingham and had the following children:

1.   John B. Sloan married Lucilla Houston.
2.   Susan M. Sloan married J. W. Crawford.
3.   David M. Sloan married Mary Easley.
4.   Elizabeth Sloan married Samuel Easley.
5.   Carrie Sloan married W. K. Easley.
6.   Wm. Sloan married Timoxina Houston.
7.   Thomas M. Sloan married Cornelia Houston.
8.   Nancy Sloan married T. S. Crayton.
9.   Benjamin Sloan married Annie Maxwell.
10.   James M. Sloan married Sallie Lynch.
11.   Robt. E. Sloan married Sallie Maxwell.
12.   Mary Sloan married Thomas O. Jenkins.
13.   Catherine Sloan married Frank Maxwell.
14.   Lucilla Septima Sloan married J. T. Gresham.
15.   Julia Octavia Sloan—unmarried.

1.   John B. Sloan married Lucilla Houston and had the following children:
A.   Loula Sloan married John Easley.
B.   Curran Sloan married Kate Hyde.
C.   Thomas M. Sloan married Anna Johnson.
D.   Lucilla Sloan married Karr Tupper.

2.   Susan M. Sloan married James W. Crawford and had the following children:
A.   B. C. Crawford married Rebecca Gaillard. (See Gaillard line.)

B.   Fanny Crawford married Charles Bradford.

C.   Nannie S. Crawford married Nelson Poe.   (See Poe line.)

D.   Sloan Crawford married Lucia Earle.

D.   Sloan Crawford married Lucia Earle, daughter of Judge and U. S. Senator Joseph H. Earle and had the following children: ———————

3.   David M. Sloan married Mary Easley and removed to Texas many years ago.   They have the following children:

A.   Martha Sloan married John Kretzer.

B.   David Sloan.

C.   William Sloan married Alice Farmer.

D.   Nancy Sloan married ——— Frame.

E.   John B. Sloan.

4.   Elizabeth Sloan married Samuel Easley and had the following children:

A.   Mary Easley married Daniel Wilcox.

B.   Samuel Easley married Roberta Crow.

C.   Nancy Easley married ——— Brunell.

D.   South Carolina Easley married James Root.

E.   Elizabeth Easley married Frederick Turner.

F.   Florence Easley married Harry Derit.

G.   T. M. Sloan Easley.

5.   Carrie Sloan married W. K. Easley and had the following children:

A.   John Easley married, first, Loula Sloan; second, Nannie Hyde.

B.   Elizabeth Easley.

C. Carrie Easley.

D.   Robert Easley married Mary Farmer.

E.   Ogier Easley.

F.   Thrace Easley married Thomas Mauldin.

G.   Carlus Easley.

H.   Mamie Easley married Louis Wilbanks.

6.   William Sloan married Timoxina Syler and had the following children:

A. Jesse Sloan married Georgiana McDowel.

B. Hattie Sloan married George L. Jones.

C. Carrie Sloan.

D. Nancy Sloan married Dr. Ed Kennebrew.

E. William Sloan.

F. Leon Sloan.

7. Thomas M. Sloan married Cornelia Houston and had the following children:

A. Houston Sloan.

B. John Sloan.

8. Nancy Sloan married T. S. Crayton and they have the following children:

A. Nanny Crayton.

B. Julian Crayton.

C. Lizeve Crayton.

D. Maxwell Crayton.

9. Benjamin Sloan married Annie Maxwell, daughter of John Maxwell and they had one daughter:

A. Annie Sloan who married Bradshaw Beverley of Virginia and had one son.

10. Dr. James M. Sloan married Sallie Lynch and had one child, Susan Sloan.

11. Robert E. Sloan married Sallie Maxwell, daughter of Dr. Robt. D. Maxwell and they have the following children:

A. Robt. E. Sloan, Jr.

B. Felix J. Sloan—died.

C. Lucy Maxwell Sloan.

D. Eloise Verner Sloan.

E. Nancy Blasingham Sloan.

F. Mary Easley Sloan.

G. Fannie Wallace Sloan.

H. Hattie Poe Sloan.

I. Benjamin F. Sloan.

J. David M. Sloan.

12. Mary Sloan married Thos. O. Jenkins (No issue.)

13. Catherine Sloan married Frank Maxwell. (See Maxwell line.)

14. Lucilla Septima Sloan married Rev. G. T. Gresham and had one child, Julia Gresham.

15. Julia Octavia Sloan—unmarried.

X. Catherine Sloan, daughter of David and Susan (Majors) Sloan married John P. Benson and had the following children. (See Benson line.)

XI. William Sloan, son of David and Susan (Majors) Sloan married Eliza Hackett and had the following children:

Samuel Maverick, the father of Samuel Augustus Maverick, Mary Elizabeth (Maverick)—Weyman and Thompson and Lydia Ann (Maverick) Van Wyck came to Pendleton from Charleston when Pendleton was first settled. He became very wealthy and was the largest land owner in the United States in his day. He was no ordinary man. Gen. Robert Anderson married his widowed mother. Samuel Augustus Maverick went to Texas when a young man, and joined the Texans under Houston in their war with Mexico; was taken prisoner and was condemned to be shot, but was saved by Gen. Waddy Thompson of Greenville, S. C., who was at the time Minister to Mexico. He, like his father, Samuel Maverick, invested largely in land and in his day was the largest land owner in the United States—owning more land than his father.

SAMUEL MAVERICK.

Was born at Charleston, S. C., December 30th, 1772. He was a son of Samuel Maverick, who was the son of John or Samuel Maverick, two brothers who came from London, England to Carolina among the first settlers before Charleston was built. Samuel Maverick, the father of the Samuel who was born December 30th, 1772, was a soldier of the Revolution; was taken prisoner by the British and was kept on board a ship of war off New York in handcuffs for twelve months. When released he walked and begged his bread until he reached home in Charleston, S. C. He married Lydia Turpin, and had six children all of whom except Samuel, at the head of this article, died without issue. Lydia Turpin was the daughter of Capt. Joseph and Mary Turpin of Providence, R. I. Capt. Joseph Turpin and Mary Turpin had three children, Joseph, Lydia and William Turpin. Joseph was the father of Capt. William Turpin of Greenville, S. C., and of Catherine Weyman and Mary Footman. Catherine Weyman had Mary, Robert and Edward. Edward was the father of Joseph T. Weyman who married Mary Elizabeth Maverick. Samuel Maverick married Elizabeth Anderson, daughter of Gen. Robert Anderson of Pendleton, S. C. They had three children:

    1.   Samuel Augustus Maverick.
    II.   Mary Elizabeth Maverick.
    III.   Lydia Ann Maverick.

    I.   Samuel Augustus Maverick married Mary Adams of Alabama and had Samuel, Lewis, Agatha, Augustus and Mary E. Maverick.

    II.   Mary Elizabeth Maverick married Joseph T. Weyman, her first husband. They had:

    1.   Eliza Houston Weyman.
    2.   Augustus Maverick Weyman.
    3.   Joseph B. Weyman.
    3.   Joseph B. Weyman married Emmala Maxwell, daughter of Capt. John Maxwell and had two children:

    A.   Samuel T. Weyman married Miss Le Fontaine.
    B.   Josephine Weyman married Bryan Houston.

    II.   Mary Elizabeth Maverick married second time Joseph Thompson of Kentucky and had two children:

    1.   Josephine Thompson married first, —————; second, Mr. Hardin.

2. Samuel Maverick Thompson.

III. Lydia Ann Maverick, daughter of Samuel and Elizabeth (Anderson) Maverick, married William Van Wyck of New York and had:

1. Dr. Samuel Maverick Van Wyck.
2. William Van Wyck.
3. Zeruah Van Wyck.
4. Augustus Van Wyck.
5. Robert Anderson Van Wyck.
6. Lydia Maverick Van Wyck.
7. Benjamin Stephens Van Wyck—died unmarried.

1. Dr. Samuel M. Van Wyck married Margaret C. Broyles and they have two children:
A. Samuel Maverick Van Wyck.
B. Oze Van Wyck.

A. Samuel M. Van Wyck married Nina Harrison, daughter of Gen. J. W. Harrison, and they have seven children:
a. Maverick Van Wyck.
b. Maggie May Van Wyck.
c. Sallie Ann Van Wyck.
d. Nina Harrison Van Wyck married Julian Johnson.
e. Robert Anderson Van Wyck.
f. Lillie Van Wyck.
g. Grace Van Wyck.

B. Oze B. Van Wyck, son of Dr. Samuel M. and Margaret (Broyles) Van Wyck, married Mary Elizabeth Keith and they have four children:
a. Wm. Overman Van Wyck.
b. Lydia Maverick Van Wyck married T. S. Shuford.
c. Oze Keith Van Wyck.
d. Elizabeth Hale Van Wyck.

2. William Van Wyck, son of Wm. and Lydia Ann (Maverick) Van Wyck, married 1st, Mary Battle, Chap-

el Hill, N. C., and had one child, Mary Battle Van Wyck.   Married 2nd time Hallie Early of Baltimore and had two children:

A.   Ann Early Van Wyck.

B.   William Van Wyck.

3.   Zeruah Van Wyck, daughter of William and Lydia Ann (Maverick) Van Wyck, married Charles Banks of New York and they have two children:

A.   Zeruah Banks.

B.   Annie Banks married—

4.   Augustus, son of William and Lydia Ann (Maverick) Van Wyck married Leila Wilkins of Richmond, Va.. and they have two children:

A.   William Van Wyck.

B.   Leila Gray Van Wyck married Walker Osborne.

Augustus Van Wyck was a Justice of the Supreme Court of the City of New York and the democratic candidate for Governor of the State of New York.

5.   Robert Anderson Van Wyck, son of William and Lydia An n (Maverick) Van Wyck is unmarried.   He was Judge of the City Court of New York and the first Mayor of Greater New York City.

6.   Lydia Maverick Van Wyck, daughter of William and Lydia Ann (Maverick) Van Wyck married Gen. R. F. Hoke of North Carolina and they have four children:

A.   Van Wyck Hoke.

B.   Michael Hoke married Laurie Hardee Harrison.

C.   Lydia M. Hoke married Alexander Webb.

D.   Frances Burton Hoke.

TAYLOR FAMILY.

James Taylor of Virginia, son of James Taylor, came from England, 1654, married Hannah Williams

of Pennsylania and settled on a farm which is now a
part of Philadelphia, Pa. Upon his deatn his widow
and one son, Samuel Taylor, survived him. His widow married Mr. Van Swearenger. His son, Samuel
before the Revolution was an officer in the British army
but joined the American army and served as captain,
when he was transferred to the South, and served faithfully to the end of the war, having been promoted to the
position of colonel. He married Mrs. Eleanor Hudgens,
nee Cannon. Large tracts of land on Seneca River near
Pendleton were deeded to him by the Government. He
died in 1798, and he and his wife were buried on his
farm now owned by the children of A. F. Lewis. They
left the following children:

I.   John Taylor.
II. Samuel Taylor.
III. William Taylor.
IV. Joseph Taylor.
V.   Dilly Taylor.
VI. Elizabeth Taylor.

The eldest daughter married Gen John Baylis Earle.
(See Earle family.)

I.   John Taylor, a lawyer and member of Congress
from Pendleton, married first, Mary Smith, daughter of
Judge Smith, and had one child, a daughter, Mary, who
married a Mr. Calhoun. He moved to Alabama and
was a member of Congress from that State. His second wife was Miss Fanny Owens of Baltimore, Md.

II. Samuel married Miss Reese and moved to Alabama.

VI. Elizabeth married Bales and moved to Alabama.

IV. Joseph, Col. Joseph Taylor, married Nancy
Sloan, daughter of David and Susanah Sloan. Their
children were:

1.   Col. David S. Taylor.

2. Susan Taylor married Jesse P. Lewis. (See Lewis family.)

3. John Baylis married —— ——— of Augusta, Ga., and moved to Texas.

4. Dr. Joseph Taylor married—moved to Marshall, Texas.

5. Samuel Taylor married—moved to Texas.

6. Ellen C. Taylor married Mr. Wm. Poe. (See Poe family.)

7. Dr. William S. Taylor married Virginia Holcombe of Mobile, Alabama and moved to Alabama.

2. Col. David S. Taylor married Lucy Hannah Taliaferro and had the following children:

A. Zachariah T. Taylor.

B. Rosa A. Taylor.

C. Joseph D. Taylor.

D. Lucy C. Taylor.

E. Susan Ann Taylor.

F. Samuel J. Taylor—died in army unmarried.

G. David S. Taylor.

H. John Carter Taylor—died unmarried.

I. Wm. B. Taylor—died unmarried.

J. Ernest M. Taylor.

K. Edward W. Taylor.

A. Zachariah T. Taylor, son of David S. and Lucy H. Taylor, married Mary Merriwether and had the following children:

a. Mary Rosa Taylor married Lou De Yampert.

b. Zack T. Taylor married Alma Rogers.

c. Joseph P. Taylor—married.

d. David S. Taylor, married Rebecca De Yampert.

e. James M. Taylor married Sallie Tupper.

f. Wm. S. Taylor unmarried.

g. Samuel J. Taylor married Sallie Tucker.

h. Gertrude Taylor married Prue Benson of Abbeville, S. C.

B. Rosa A. Taylor, daughter of Col. David S. and Hannah Taylor married Dr. Daniel D. Bacot and had the following children:
  a. David Taylor Bacot.
  b. Laura D. Bacot.

  a. David Taylor Bacot married Florence Norton of Virginia and had the following children:
  1a. D. Norborne Bacot married Daisy Marshall.
  2a. Florence Bacot.
  3a. George Bacot.
  4a. Rosalie Bacot.

  b. Laura D. Bacot married Paul T. Jenkins and had the following children:
  1a. Paul Jenkins.
  2a. Daniel Jenkins.
  3a. Ada Jenkins.
  4a. Rosamond Jenkins.

C. Joseph D. Taylor, son of David S. and Lucy H. Taylor married Ellen King and had the following children:
  a. Ellineta Taylor married Wm. Henry Heyward.
  b. Lucia Taylor married Moultrie Clement.
  c. Pauline Taylor—died unmarried.
  d. Taliaferro Taylor married Anna Cuthbert.
  e. Gordon H. Taylor married Alma Melchers.

  a. Ellenita Taylor, daughter of Joseph D. and Ellen Taylor married Wm. Henry Heyward and had the following children:
  1a. Taliaferro Taylor Heyward.
  2a. Helen Taylor Heyward.

D. Lucy C. Taylor, daughter of Col. David S. and Lucy H. Taylor married R. Edmund Belcher and had one son, Robert E. Belcher who married Miss Ligon.

E. Susan Ann Taylor, daughter of Col. David S. and Lucy H. Taylor, married Capt. Edward L. Parker, and had one child, Sue Parker, who married Cuthbert Fripp.

F.   David S. Taylor, son of Col. David S. and Lucy H. Taylor, married Bessie Rucker, and had the following children:
   a.   Marion Taylor married John Ligon.
   b.   Lucia Taylor married W. A. Hudgens.
   c.   Eubank Taylor.
   d.   Rucker Taylor.
   e.   Frank Taylor.

J.   Ernest M. Taylor, son of Col. David S. and Lucy H. Taylor married Mary Bacot and had the following children:
   a.   Ernest Taylor.
   b.   Louise Taylor.
   c.   Leila Taylor married Stephen Prevost.
   d.   Richard Taylor.

K.   Edward W. Taylor, son of Col. David S. and Lucy H. Taylor, married Annie Bacot, and had one son, David Samuel Taylor.

DICKINSON FAMILY.

I.   Francis W. Dickinson, a lawyer of Charleston, S. C., married Rachel Miles (old Mrs.) Dickinson, as lovely a woman as ever lived in Pendleton.)   They had the following children:
   1.   Jeremiah Dickinson married Adaline E. Legare.
   2.   Susan Dickinson.
   3.   Rachel K. Dickinson married James F. Green.
   4.   Sarah Dickinson married Dr. Lawrence Lee.

1.   Jeremiah and Adaline E. Dickinson had the following children:
   A.   Francis W. Dickinson.
   B.   Adaline E. Dickinson—unmarried.
   C.   Susan L. Dickinson—unmarried.

D. Caroline C. Dickinson.

E. J. Hamilton Dickinson married.

F. Rachel M. Dickinson married.

D. Caroline C. Dickinson, daughter of Jeremiah and Adaline E. Dickinson, married Maj. J. J. Lewis and had two children:

    a. Sue Ellen Lewis married J. Lee Carpenter.

    b. Nina D. Lewis married Wm. S. Hunter.

    a. Sue Ellen (Lewis) Carpenter and J. Lee Carpenter have the following children:

    1a. Ellen S. Carpenter.

    2a. Lewis Carpenter.

    3a. Nina Carpenter.

    b. Nina D. (Lewis) and Wm. S. Hunter have the following children:

    1a. Carry L. Hunter.

    2a. Ellen Hunter.

    3a. Annie Hunter.

3. Rachel K. Dickinson, daughter of Francis W. and Rachel W. Dickinson, married Capt. Jas. F. Green and had one child, Lawrence Lee Green, who married Mary Clement and they have two children:

    a. Charles Green.

    b. May Green married Mr. Grant.

4. Sarah Dickinson, daughter of Francis W. and Rachel W. Dickinson, married Dr. Lawrence Lee and had four children:

    A. Francis W. Lee married Miss Thompson.

    B. Susan D. Lee.

    C. Elizabeth Lee married Wm. D. Gaillard.

    D. J. Moultrie Lee married Harriet Bruce.

A. Francis W. Lee married Sarah Thompson and had the following children:

    a. Lawrence Lee.

    b. Margaret Lee.

c. Francis W. Lee.
d. Lillian Lee.
C. Elizabeth Lee married Wm. D. Gaillard   and they have the following children:
a. Elizabeth Gaillard.
b. Wm. Gaillard.
c. Lawrence Gaillard.
d. Theodore Gaillard.
e. Prioleau Gaillard.
f. Susan Gourdin Gaillard.
D. J. Moultrie Lee married Harriet Bruce and they had the following children:
a. Cornelia Lee.
b. Lawrence Lee.
c. J. Moultrie Lee.

COL. DAVID K. HAMILTON.

Thomas Hamilton was a soldier of the Revolution under Sumter, and was the first Elder of Carmel Presbyterian Church where he was buried. He married Annie Kennedy, herself a Revolutionary heroine. During the war a band of Tories came to her house and found her spinning flax. One of the Tories attempted to set fire to the flax, whereupon a struggle began, she seized him and he placed the chunk of fire against her wrist to force her to let him go, but she then caught him by the coat collar and the seat of his pants and pitched him into the yard. He then started to shoot her, but the others were so much amused they interfered to prevent him. She carried the scar on her wrist to her grave. This good woman lies buried in the family graveyard, on the land now owned by T. S. Glenn.

Thomas Hamilton and his wife Annie K. Hamilton were the father and mother of Col. David K. Hamilton. Colonel Hamilton was a soldier under Jackson in 1812. After his return home he married Jane E. Walker. By this marriage Colonel Hamilton had four daughters and one son:

    A.   Louisa A. Hamilton married Rev. G. W. Boggs and died childless.

    B.   Martha Jane Hamilton married Thos. H. Russell.

    C.   Mary E. Hamilton married W. N. Martin.

    D.   Matilda Hamilton married Benjamin Pooser.

    E.   Thomas W. Hamilton died unmarried.

    B.   Martha Jane Hamilton married Thomas H. Russell and raised twelve children, namely:

    a.   David H. Russell was school commissioner and member of the Constitutional Convention from Anderson County.

    b.   Thomas W. Russell.

    c.   William W. Russell.

    d.   Edw. A. Russell.

    e.   Geo. W. Russell.

    f.   Benjamin F. Russell.

    g.   Emma Russell.

    h.   Mary Russell and Marion Augustus (twins.)

    i.   John A. Russell.

    j.   Louisa A. Russell and Matilda A. Russell (twins).

Col. David K. Hamilton was a prominent man in his day, and was Colonel of the Regiment of Cavalry that had camp musters at Old Pickensville and was among the first members of the Pendleton Farmers' Society.

At one time he with others was summoned as a posse by E. B. Benson, then sheriff, to arrest a noted desperado one, Corbin. Corbin was killed and Sheriff Benson and the members of his posse were tried for murder. They were defended by Armisted Burt and Joseph N. Whitner (Judge) and were acquitted.

(Furnished by D. H. Russell.)

JAMES DAWSON SMITH.

Came to Pendleton from Greenville when a young
man and was for many years a successful merchant. He
early volunteered in the Confederate service and served
through the whole war. Died in 1896 and was buried
in the Baptist cemetery at Pendleton. In 1858 he married Mary Jane Bates, and had nine children, two of
whom died in infancy. The living are namely:

    I.   Ella Smith.
    II.   Mamie Smith.
    III.   William Hovey Smith.
    IV.   J. Dawson Smith, Jr.
    VI.   Hattie Smith.
    VII.   Gordon L. Smith, unmarried.

    I.   Ella Smith married Wm. S. Brown, of Anderson,
and had two children, Joel E. Brown and Irene V. Brown.

    II.   Mamie married first, C. V. Bostic, of North
Carolina, and had one child, J. V. Bostic. Married sec-
ond time, J. E. Sitton, and, dying, left two children,
Macie Sitton and Glennella Sitton.

    III.   Wm. Hovey Smith married Lollie J. Gilmore,
and died leaving one child, Mary Lollie Smith.

    IV.   J. Dawson Smith, Jr., married Lena J. Russell
and they have four children, Marion R. Smith, Robert
Smith, Alice Smith and Lena Smith.

    VI.   Hattie Smith married Harry A. Sloan and they
have the following children: Sunie M. Sloan, Elise M.,
Harry A., Jr., and Paul Earle Sloan.

JAMES T. LATTA.

A son of James Latta, of Yorkville, was born in
1872, graduated at Yale College, and married Angela
Lott, of New Jersey, 1850, and shortly thereafter moved
to Pendleton and purchased from Dr. O. R. Broyles the

Plantation now owned by Francis J. Pelzer. James T. Latta died near the end of the Confederate war. During his comparatively short life he was in feeble health, and as he was not able to volunteer for service, he contributed largely from his private means to the Confederate government and to the hospitals. Mrs. Latta was a beautiful and lovely woman, and in her elegant home entertained her friends with whole souled hospitality, coupled with such simplicity, dignity and refinement that won the love and respect of all who had the pleasure of associating with her.

James T. Latta and his wife Angela (Lott) Latta had four children, one daughter Angela, who died in Europe and three sons:

I. Edward Dilworth Latta.

II. Wm. Latta died unmarried.

III. Walter Latta died unmarried.

I. Edward Dilworth Latta, the only survivor of the family, married Hattie Nisbet, of Macon, Ga., and now resides in Charlotte, N. C., and they have three children, namely:

1. Marion Nisbet Latta.

2. Edward D. Latta, Jr.

3. Janet Acton Latta.

Mr. and Mrs. Latta and their two sons are buried in the Episcopal cemetery at Pendleton.

REV. W. H. HANCKEL.

Son of Rev. Christian and Ann Stuart Hanckel, moved to Pendleton and purchased the Flat Rock farm, formerly the home of Colonel Hayne. Married Elizabeth Clark and they have the following children:

I. William Hanckel died in infancy.

II. Henry Hanckel died in infancy.

III. Alfred Hanckel died unmarried.

IV.   Christian Hanckel married Arna E. White
V.   Lilly Hanckel, unmarried.

IV.   Christian Hanckel married Anna E. White
and has the following children:
1.   Richard W. Hanckel.
2.   Elizabeth C. Hanckel.
3.   Mary G. Hanckel married Marvin Franks.
4.   Christine E. Hanckel.
5.   William H. Hanckel.
6.   Annie E. Hanckel.
7.   Emily G. Hanckel.
8.   Alfred S. Hanckel.
3.   Mary G. Hanckel married Marvin Franks of
Laurens, S. C.   The others are unmarried.

SAMUEL HALL.

Came from Ireland and settled in Pendleton early
in its history.   He had four children, namely:
I.   Yancy Hall.
II.   Rebecca Hall.
III.   Julia Hall.

IV.   John Calvin Hall married, first, Nancy Mulligan and had one child, Edward McD. Hall, a soldier
in the Confederate war, and died from wounds in Vir-
gina.   Married second, Lucinda Mulligan and had eleven
children:
1.   Lucy Hall married Till Powers.
2.   Amanda Hall married————— Crenshaw.
3.   Josephine Hall married C. D. Madden.
4.   Mary Hall married Thos. Traynham.
5.   J. C. Hall married Elizabeth Moore.
6.   J. S. Hall married Florence Mulligan.
7.   Samuel P. Hall married Lou Crenshaw.
8.   Andrew C. Hall died.
9.   W. Y. Hall married Ophelia Summers.

10.   Hadden Hall, unmarried.

11.   Pink Hall, unmarried.

5.   J. C. Hall and his wife, Elizabeth (Moore) Hall
had six children.

A.   W. E. Hall married Miss Evatt.

B.   J. C. Hall, Jr., Married.

C.   James S. Hall.

D.   Henry L. Hall.

E.   Florence Hall married Brooks Cooper.

F.   Emma Hall.

6.   J. S. Hall married Florence Mulligan and they
have the following children:

A.   Prue Hall.

B.   Doyle Hall.

7.   S. P. Hall married Lou Crenshaw and had eight
children:

A.   Hattie Hall married Oscar Kay.

B.   Bernice Hall.

C.   Marvin M. Hall.

D.   Clarence Hall.

E.   Grover Hall.

F.   Wilton Hall.

G.   Arthur Hall.

H.   Alice Hall.

REV. THOS. L. McBRYDE.

Son of John and Lucy Livingston McBryde, graduated at the University of Georgia and at the Theological
Seminary at Columbia, S. C.   Married Mary Williamson
McClerky.   Soon after his marriage he and his wife
went as missionaries to China in 1840.   After three
years they had to return on account of Mr. McBryde's
health.   Mr. McBryde and his devoted wife spent their
lives doing good and were loved and respected as are but
few in this world.   He and his wife are buried at the

Old Stone Church.   He left surviving him nine children:

    I.   Sarah Boon McBryde.
    II.   Lucy Newton McBryde—unmarried.
    III.   Rev. John T. McBryde.
    IV.   Jeanie McBryde.
    V.   Agnes Law McBryde.
    VI.   Fannie L. McBryde.
    VII.   Lizzie M. McBryde.
    VIII.   Elizabeth Adger McBryde.
    IX.   Randell W. McBryde.

    I.   Sarah Boon McBryde married William Gaillard Jenkins and died leaving nine children, all of whom are married except Nannie.   They are as follows:

    1.   Thomas McB. Jenkins.
    2.   Jane G. Jenkins.
    3.   Mary W. Jenkins.
    4.   Lucy McB. Jenkins.
    5.   Margaret H. Jenkins.
    6.   Joseph Wardlaw Jenkins.
    7.   Laurens S. Jenkins.
    8.   Nannie M. Jenkins.

    III.   Rev. John T. McBryde married, first, Frances Hutson—no issue; married second, Ada Dickinson and had one child who died in infancy; third, Sarah Chappel —no issue.

    IV.   Jeanie McBryde married Rev. James A. McLees—no issue.

    V.   Agnes Law McBryde married Rev. Hugh W. McLees and had three children, namely:
    1.   Mary B. McLees married A. L. Blake.
    2.   Sophronia H. McLees marred C. L. Link.
    3.   Hugh L. McLees—unmarried.

ADGER FAMILY .

James Adger, native of Moneynick, Antrim County, Ireland, married Sarah E. Ellison, of South Carolina, resided in Charleston and amassed a large fortune. He had the following children:

I. Margaret M. Adger married Rev. Thos. M. Smyth, D. D.

II. Susan D. Adger—unmarried.

III. John B. Adger. D. D., married Elzabeth K. Shrewsbury.

IV. James Adger—never married.

V. Robert Adger married Jane E. Fleming.

VI. William Adger married Margaret H. Moffett.

VII. Sarah Adger—never married.

VIII. Jane Adger—never married.

IX. Joseph Ellison Adger married Susan C. Johnson.

I. Margaret M. (Adger) Smythe was the mother of Maj. A. T. Smythe who owns a large stock farm near Pendleton and resides there a part of each year, and of Ellison A. Smythe, the president of the Pelzer Mills.

III. John B. Adger, D. D., resided for many years in Pendleton and was a distinguished divine of the Presbyterian Church. Both he and his wife are now dead, and only three children survive them. Mrs. D. Mullally, Mrs. Anna Neal and Miss Susan D. Adger, who owns and resides at her father's homestead in Pendleton.

V. Robert Adger resided for years at Rivoli near Pendleton; some time after the war he returned to Charleston. While residing at Pendleton one daughter, Sarah E. Adger, married William Dalton Warren, who owned and resided at the place now owned by F. J. Pelzer. William Dalton Warren and Sarah E. (Adger) Warren had two children:

1. Jane Warren married John B. Adger, son of J. Ellison Adger.

2. Anna M. Warren—unmarried.

After the death of his wife he married the second time Jane Pendleton Dandridge, daughter of Alexander Spotswood Dandridge, M. D. By this marriage he has no children.

VI. William Adger married Miss Margaret Moffett and had nine children. William Adger died and his widow and children moved to Pendleton and resided at Duncan, which place she sold to Mrs. John C. Calhoun. The family now resides in Spartanburg.

IX. Joseph E. Adger and wife, Susan C. (Johnson) Adger resided at Woodburn, now owned by Maj. A. T. Smythe, his nephew. They had twelve children. Mr. Adger and his boys donned the red shirt in 1876 and took an active part in the redemption of the State from negro rule. Some time after this he and family returned to Charleston. His son John married Jane Warren, daughter of William Dalton Warren, and is now president of a large enterprise near Belton, S. C.

Robert Adger subscribed largely to the Confederate government, and at the beginning of the war gave many thousand dollars for beef which was pickled at Pendleton for the soldiers.

BOWEN FAMILY.

O. A. Bowen, son of Capt. George Bowen, of Laurens County, S. C., married Clarissa W. Adger, a daughter of Robert Adger, and owned and resided at Ashtabula near Pendleton, which is now owned by F. J. Pelzer. He afterward bought Rivoli, the former home of his father-in-law, Robert Adger. After Mr. Bowen's death, Mrs. Bowen and family removed to Georgia. O. A. Bowen and wife, Clarissa W. (Adger) Bowen have four living children:

I. O. A. Bowen, Jr., married Mary Taylor, daughter of Geo. E. Taylor.

II. Robt. Adger Bowen—unmarried.

III. Jane E. Bowen married Frank E. Taylor, son of George Taylor.

IV. George Bowen married Florida Bethel.

II. O. A. Bowen, Jr., and his wife Mary (Taylor) Bowen have five children.
1. O. A. Bowen, Jr.
2. Edwin T. Bowen.
3. Robt. Adger Bowen.
4. M. Evelyn Bowen—dead.
5. Catherine S. Bowen.

III. Jane E. Bowen and her husband, Frank E. Taylor have three children:
1. Frank E. Taylor, Jr.
2. Clarissa W. Taylor.
3. Jane Adger Taylor.

JENKINS.

Dr. William Seabrook Jenkins married Susan M. Ogier. She died and left one daughter—Susan M. Jenkins.

1. Susan M. Jenkins married George Thomas Anderson, a grandson of Gen. Robert Anderson. She had several children, one of whom was Robert Anderson at one time reading clerk in the South Carolina legislature. Robt. Anderson died and left several children, names unknown to me.

Dr. William Seabrook Jenkins married the second time, Keith Ogier, sister of his first wife, and by this marriage had one son, Dr. W. L. Jenkins for many years a practicing physician at Pendleton.

1. Dr. W. Y. Jenkins married Jane H. Gaillard and had six children:
1. Wm. G. Jenkins married Sallie McBryde.

2.   Thomas O. Jenkins married Mary Sloan—no issue.

3.   Robert M. Jenkins married Ann Gaillard.

4.   Henry H. Jenkins—unmarried.

5.   Florence A. Jenkins married J. E. Wofford.

6.   Mary J. Jenkins—unmarried.

1.   W. G. Jenkins and wife, Sallie McBryde Jenkins had nine children:

A.   Thomas McBryde Jenkins.

B.   Jane G. Jenkins.

C.   Mary Jenkins.

D.   Wm. L. Jenkins, Jr.

E.   Lucy McB. Jenkins.

F.   J. W. Jenkins.

G.   Margaret H. Jenkins.

H.   Laurens S. Jenkins.

I.   Nanny M. Jenkins.

J.

3.   Robt. M. Jenkins and wife, Ann (Gaillard) Jenkins have seven children:

A.   Robt. G. Jenkins.

B.   L. C. Jenkins.

C.   Eliza P. Jenkins.

D.   A. Louise Jenkins.

E.   Mary C. Jenkins.

F.   C. B. Jenkins.

G.   Turner G. Jenkins.

5.   Florence A. Jenkins and her husband, J. E. Wofford have two children:

A.   John E. Wofford, Jr.

B.   Wm. Jenkins Wofford.

I.   Dr. Wm. L. Jenkins married second time Anna R. Gaillard and by this marriage had three children:

1.   Anna M. Jenkins—unmarried.

2.   John G. Jenkins married.

3. Susan M. Jenkins married Jas. H. Gaillard—no issue.

Dr. Wm. Seabrook Jenkins married the second time Jane Keith Ogier. He died and his widow married John B. Ferrell and had five children, namely:

I. Martha Ogier Ferrell married Chauncy Stevens.
II. Louis O. Ferrell.
III. John B. Ferrell.
IV. Jane K. Ferrell married George G. Matthews.
V. Charlotte M. Ferrell.

I. Martha Ogier Ferrell married Chauncy Stevens and had the following children:

1. William Stevens.
2. Elizabeth Stevens.
3. Janie Stevens.
4. Sarah Stevens.
5. Carrie Stevens.
6. Ella Stevens.
7. Thomas Stevens.
8. Lucius Stevens.
9. Mattie Stevens.
10. Kate Stevens.

DAVANT FAMILY.

Richard James Davant married Evylin Judith Cherry. Among others born of this marriage was Dr. Charles Davant.

1. Dr. Charles Davant was twice married, first to Mary H. Bostick, daughter of Wm. Mann Bostick. They had the following children:

1. Evylin Cherry Davant married C. J. Porter.
2. Mary Bostick Davant—unmarried.
3. Laura Elmore Davant—unmarried.
4. William Bostick Davant married Miss Clarke.

1.   Evylin Cherry Davant and her husband, C. J. Porter, have the following children:

A.   May Porter.

B.   Clarence Porter.

C.   Charles Porter.

D.   James Porter.

Dr. Charles Davant married second time, Mary But-ler Pickens, daughter of Col. Thomas J. Pickens. By this marriage he had no issue.

POE FAMILY.

Ellen C. Taylor, a daughter of Col. Joseph and Nancy (Sloan) Taylor, (See Sloan family) married Mr. William Poe, and removed from Pendleton. After Mr. Poe's death Mrs. Poe returned to Pendleton. Mrs. Poe was an uncommon woman. Left a widow with a family of small children, she portrayed her excellent motherly qualities by raising and educating a family of children honored and esteemed for many admirable qual-ities. The writer knew Mrs. Poe well, and if space would permit would take pleasure in putting on record his high regard for this good, true and lovable woman. Wm. Poe and Ellen C. (Taylor) Poe had the following children:

1. Wm. Poe—never married. Died from wounds secured in battle.

II.   Ellen M. Poe married Dr. G. H. Symmes.   (See Symmes Family.)

III.   Azalia J. Poe married Dr. James Mayes. (See Mayes Family.)

IV.   Nanny T. Poe married D. B. Sloan. (See Sloan Family.)

V.   J. Taylor Poe married Nela Taylor of Mobile, Ala.

VI.   Nelson C. Poe married Nanny Crawford.

VII.   Frank W. Poe married Hattie Maxwell.

VIII.   Hal T. Poe married Dora Sloan.

VI.   Nelson C. Poe married Nanny Crawford, daughter of James W. Crawford and they have three children:

1.   Nelson C. Poe, Jr.

2.   Ellen Poe.

3.   Wilkins Poe.

VII.   Frank W. Poe and Hattie (Maxwell) Poe had five children:

1.   Eugenia M. Poe—unmarried.

2.   Harriet A. Poe—unmarried.

3.   Zadie Poe—unmarried.

4.   Lucy Poe—unmarried.

5.   Frank W. Poe, Jr.—unmarried.

VIII.   Hal T. Poe married Dora Sloan, daughter of B. Frank Sloan and had five children:

1.   Harris T. Poe—unmarried.

2.   Nell Poe—unmarried.

3.   Baylis S. Poe—unmarried.

4.   Thomas Poe—unmarried.

5.   Dora Poe—unmarried.

THE EARLE FAMILY.

This family has been distinguished from its first advent into South Carolina and its descendants have intermarried extensively with other prominent families. So numerous are the members of this family it is impossible to give a complete genealogy of them, but as many of them are identified with Pendleton by marriage and otherwise I am compelled to set out only those branches of the family as are connected with the history of Pendleton.

The Earles came from England in the early history of this country and settled in Virginia.   John Earle of

Westmoreland, Va., and wife, Mary, had three children: Samuel, John, and Mary Earle. Sam Earle, the first, had a son, Sam Earle, second. Sam Earle, second, had a son Sam, third, and Hannah and Elizabeth. Sam Earle, third, married first time Ann Sorrell; married second time, E. Holbrook and by the second marriage had two sons, (John and Baylis). John Earle, son of Sam, third, and his wife E. Holbrook, married Miss Prince and had three sons, Gen. John Baylis, Washington and Joe Berry Earle. Gen. John Baylis married Ellen Taylor, daughter of Maj. Samuel Taylor and sister of Col. Joseph Taylor and had the following children:

Mary Earle married Purvis.

Eliza Earle married B. F. Sloan.

Sarah Earle married Maj. George Seaborne.

Jack Earle—unmarried—killed in Texas war.

Paul Earle—unmarried—surgeon in Navy—lost at sea.

Dr. Sam Earle married Harriet Wright.

Dr. Baylis Earle moved to Texas.

Joe Earle moved to Alabama.

Washington Earle, son of Sam, third, brother of Gen. John Baylis Earle, married Elizabeth Earle, daughter of Col. Elias Earle and had children, one of whom married Dr. Wm. Robinson and another married Amanda, daughter of E. B. Benson, and he had a son, Dr. G. W. Earle—one daughter married W. L. Yancy.

Baylis, son of Sam, third, and E. Holbrook his wife, and brother of John, married Miss Prince and had one son.

Samuel fourth (Blinky Sam) Earle.

Samuel (Blink) Earle married Harriet Harrison and had the following children:

Mary Earle married R. A. Maxwell. (See Maxwell family.)

Elizabeth Earle married Capt. John Maxwell. (See Maxwell Family.)

Harriet Earle married Elias Earle.

Miriam Earle married ———— Mayes. (See Mayes Family.)

Judge Baylis Earle—never married.

One daughter married Dr. J. W. Lewis.

One daughter married Thos. Harrison.

Sam Earle moved to Marietta, Ga.

Edward Earle moved to Marietta, Ga.

Col. Elias Earle, son of Samuel Earle, third, and his first wife, Ann Sorrell, married Frances Melton Robinson and subsequently moved to Centerville, S. C. His children were:

Frances Melton Earle married Tillinghast.

Elizabeth A. married George Washington. They had a son, Elias D. Earle, who married a Miss Haynsworth and had three sons, Judge and U. S. Senator J. H. Earle, Dr. T. T. Earle and George W. Earle.

Nancy Earle married McClanahan.

Sarah Earle married James Harrison of Andersonville.

Robinson Earle married Eliza Thompson, sister of Waddy Thompson.

B.   John Baylis Earle married.

Elias Earle married Harriet Earle, daughter of Samuel (Blinky) Earle.

Elias Earle and Harriet Earle, his wife, had the following children:

Miriam Earle married Thos. B. Lee.

Mary Earle married Joe Berry Sloan son of B. F. Sloan and wife, (Eliza Earle) Sloan.

Florence Earle married Dr. James H. Thornwell.

E. P. Earle married Nettie Harrison, daughter of Col. F. E. Harrison of Andersonville.

Fannie Earle—never married.

Wilton Earle—never married and was killed in battle.

Mary Earle married Joe Berry Sloan and had two children. (See Sloan Family, B. F. Sloan.)

John Baylis Earle, son of Elias D. Earle of Centerville, married ——— ——— and had daughters:

One married Maj. Joseph Adams, son of Dr. Jasper Adams of Pendleton. He had one son, Quincy Adams.

One married Dr. Cooley, and after his death J. S. Fowler.

One married Judge and U. S. Senator Joseph H. Earle.

Dr. Robinson Earle, son of Elias D. Earle of Centerville and wife, Eliza Thompson, had the following children: Elias, killed in the Mexican War; Harrison; Dr. James W. Earle; Thompson Earle; Henrietta Earle married Col. James Irby, father of J. L. M. Irby, U. S. Senator; Corry; Carry; and Emily Earle. Dr. Robinson Earle was killed by Wm. L. Yancy.

ZACHARIAH TALIAFERRO.

Zachariah Taliaferro was born in Amherst County, Virginia, in 1759. At the early age of eighteen he became a private soldier in the War of the Revolution, and was a faithful soldier to the end of the war, so says a number of well known Virginia gentlemen who signed the required recommendation to obtain permission to practice law in South Carolina. After the war he studied law, and was admitted to practice in the courts of Virginia, but soon thereafter removed to South Carolina, and settled on the head waters of Three and Twenty Mile Creek near Pickensville, where he practiced law until the courts at that place were abolished in 1800. In 1802 he returned to Virginia and married Miss Margaret Chew Carter, a daughter of John Carter and Hannah Chew, his wife of Caroline County, Virginia. After the removal of the Court House from Pickensville he removed and settled on the homestead, three miles east of Pendleton, and continued to practice law at Pendleton until 1826 when the District of Pendleton was divided. He died in 1831 and was buried in the family grave-yard on his homestead which he devised to his daughter, Margaret M. Taliaferro, who married Maj. R. F. Simpson and they continued to reside thereon until their death, and both were buried in the family grave-yard. Other members of his family, including Col. Benjamin Taliaferro, settled on Broad River in Georgia. Zachariah Taliaferro and Margaret Chew (Carter) Taliaferro, his wife, left surviving them four daughters:

I. Sarah A. Taliaferro married Dr. O. R. Broyles.

II. Lucy Hannah Taliaferro married Col. David S. Taylor, son of Joseph and Nancy Taylor.

III. Mary Margaret Taliaferro married Maj. Richard F. Simpson.

IV. Caroline Virginia Taliaferro married Dr. H. C. Miller.

BROYLES FAMILY.

I. Sarah A. Taliaferro married Dr. O. R. Broyles. They resided for a time on Beaver Dam, Anderson County, then removed to Pendleton and purchased and resided for years at the home now owned by F. J. Pelzer. This place they sold to James T. Latta and then moved to the Town of Anderson, and died there and are both buried in Silver Brook Cemetery. They had the following children:

1. Augusta Taliaferro Broyles, never married, was a distinguished lawyer and is buried in Silver Brook Cemetery.

2. Charles Edward Broyles married Lucy Johnson, second. He too was a lawyer of distinction. Was colonel in Confederate War, and now resides in Colorado with his second wife.

3. Zachariah Broyles—died unmarried.

4. Wm. Henry Broyles married Rebecca Taliaferro.

5. Margaret Caroline Broyles married Dr. Sam M. VanWyck.

6. Dr. Robt. Broyles married Ella Keith of Charleston.

7. Sarah Ann Broyles married Wm. D. Williams of Greenville, Tenn.

8. Dr. Thomas T. Broyles married first Mary Rainey; second, Bettie Harrison.

9. John P. Broyles married Bettie Hubbard.

2. Charles Edward and wife, Lucy Johnson Broyles had the following children:

A. Charles Broyles.

B. Laura Broyles married Dr. Boyd.

C. Sarah Broyles married Dr. Boyd.

D. Frank Broyles.

E. Robt. Broyles.

F. Price Broyles.,

4. Wm. Henry and wife, Rebecca (Taliaferro) Broyles had the following children:

A. Minnie Broyles married John Lockhart.

B. Jeffie Broyles married Tom Lockhart.

C. Gussie Broyles married Tom Middlebrook.

D. Rebecca Broyles married John Clark.

E. Charles Broyles married Hallie Schille.

F. Bruer Broyles married Annie Walker.

G. Oze Broyles married Mamie Little.

H. John Broyles—unmarried.

5. Margaret Caroline Broyles married Dr. Sam VanWyck, son of Wm. and Lydia Ann Maverick Van Wyck. Dr. VanWyck was surgeon to Forrest's regiment and was killed in Confederate War. They had the following children:

A. Sam Maverick VanWyck.

B. Oze B. VanWyck. (See VanWyck Family).

6. Dr. Robt. Broyles married Ella Keith and they had the following children:

A. Mattie Broyles.

B. Taliaferro Broyles—died.

C. Robt. Broyles—killed on railroad.

D. Keith Broyles.

E. Mary Broyles.

7. Sarah Ann Broyles married Wm. D. Williams of Tennessee and had the following children:

A. Wm. D. Williams, Jr.—unmarried.

B. Lucian Williams—died unmarried.

C. Margaret Williams—died unmarried.

D. John Q. Williams—unmarried.

E. Minnie Williams—unmarried.

F. Zae Williams—unmarried.

8. Dr. Thos. T. Broyles married first, Mary Rainy; second, Bettie Harrison and had the following children:

(No data.)

9. John P. and wife, Bettie (Hubbard) Broyles have the following children:

A. Augustus T. Broyles, Jr.—unmarried.

B. John P. Broyles, Jr.—unmarried.

C. Douglass Broyles—unmarried.

D. Zae Broyles—unmarried.

I. Lucy Hannah Taliaferro, daughter of Zachariah and Margaret Chew (Carter) Taliaferro, married Col. David S. Taylor, son of Col. Joseph Taylor and Nancy Taylor, his wife, and had the following children. (See Taylor Family.)

SIMPSON FAMILY.

III. Mary Margaret Taliaferro, third daughter of Zachariah and Margaret Chew (Carter) Taliaferro married Maj. Richard F. Simpson of Laurens, S. C.

Maj. Simpson was Major of a battalion of cavalry in the Seminole War in Florida, was State Senator from Laurens County—was member of U. S. Congress for three terms, beginning 1842 or 1849—was a member of the South Carolina Secession Convention from Anderson County. He was a son of Col. John and Mary (Wells) Simpson of Laurens County. After his marriage to Miss Taliaferro in 1836 he resided on the home place of Zachariah Taliaferro and he and his wife are buried in the family burial ground on the plantation on which he resided, the same having been devised to his wife, Margaret, by her father, Zachariah Taliaferro. They had the following children:

1. Taliaferro Simpson—unmarried. Killed at Battle of Chickamauga, Ga. His remains were buried at the old family cemetery by the side of his father and mother.

2. Richard W. Simpson married Maria Louise Garlington, daughter of John and Susan Washington (James) Garlington of Laurens, S. C.

3. Mary Simpson married Capt. Thos. Lanier Williams of Greenville, East Tenn. Capt. Williams was a gallant soldier of the Confederate Army.

4. Anna Tallulah Simpson—died unmarried.

5. John Garlington Simpson—died unmarried.

2. Richard Wright Simpson was a private in the Confederate War, Company A, Third S. C. V. and Calhoun's Co. Adams Battalion of Cavalry. He owns the old Zachariah Taliaferro homestead but resides in the town of Pendleton and is an attorney-at-law. He married Maria Louise Garlington, daughter of John and Susan Washington (James) Garlington and they have nine children as follows:

A. Margaret Garlington Simpson married Dr. W. W. Watkins—no issue.

B. Susan James Simpson married P. H. E. Sloan, Jr.

C. Maria Louise Simpson—unmarried.

D. Annie Ball Simpson married Alister G. Holmes.

E. Elizabeth Conway Simpson married   Samuel
Maner Martin.

F. Richard W. Simpson, Jr.—unmarried.

G. John Garlington Simpson married Lucy W.
Jones.

H. Taliaferro Strother Simpson married   Mary
Caldwell Bradfield.

I. Jean Stobo Simpson married   Williston W.
Klugh.

B. Susan James Simpson married P. H. E. Sloan,
Jr., and they have eight children.

   a. Maria Louise Garlington Sloan.

   b. Ella Maxwell Sloan.

   c. Paul H. E. Sloan, Jr.

   d. Susan Simpson Sloan.

   e. Jean Conway Sloan.

   f. Eliza Earle Sloan.

   g. Margaret Taliaferro Sloan.

   h. Lucy Maxwell Sloan.

   i. Mary Richard Sloan.

   j. B. Frank Sloan.

D. Annie Ball Simpson married Alester G. Holmes
and they have the following children:

   a. Alester G. Holmes, Jr.

   b. Louise Garlington Holmes.

E. Elizabeth Conway Simpson married   Samuel
Maner Martin and they have three children:

   a. Samuel Maner Martin, Jr.

   b. Richard W. Simpson Martin.

   c. Ben Vincent Martin.

   g. Maria Garlington Martin.

G. John Garlington Simpson married Lucy   W.
Jones and they have one child:

   a. John Garlington Simpson, Jr.

H.　Taliaferro Strother Simpson married Mary Caldwell Bradfield and they have two sons:

　　a.　Taliaferro S. Simpson, Jr.
　　b.　Richard Wright Simpson.

I.　Jean Stobo Simpson married Wiliston W. Klugh and they have three children:

　　a.　Williston W. Klugh, Jr.
　　b.　Louise Klugh.
　　c.　Jean Simpson Klugh.

3.　Mary Simpson, daughter of Richard F. and Margaret Taliaferro Simpson, married Capt. Thos. Lanier Williams of Tennessee and had the following children:

　　A.　Eliza Snead Williams married Robt. O. Hunter of Abbeville, S. C.
　　B.　Richard Franklin Williams—unmarried.
　　C.　Wm. D. Williams, Jr.—unmarried.
　　D.　Thos. Lanier Williams—killed on railroad.
　　E.　Maria Louise Williams—died unmarried.
　　F.　Anna Simpson Williams—unmarried.

MILLER FAMILY.

IV.　Caroline Virginia Taliaferro married Dr. Henry C. Miller and had the following children:

1.　Henry C. Miller, Jr.—killed in battle of Cedar Mountain, Va., C. S. A.
2.　Ressie E. Miller married J. N. Hook—no issue.
3.　Caroline Virginia Miller married W. W. Simons—no issue.
4.　George W. Miller married Edith E. Walker.

4.　George W. Miller and Edith E. (Walker) Miller had the following children:

A.　Harry Pinckney Miller married Lillian Hallwood of Ohio.

B.   Percy Walker Miller married Marion Marston, New York.

C.   Dorothea Modd Miller—unmarried.

D.   Mattie Porter Miller—unmarried.

E.   Caroline Taliaferro Miller married Edgar H. Morton, Georgia.

F.   Edith Miller—unmarried.

G.   Beatrice Miller—unmarried.

H. Henry Campbell Miller—unmarried.

CAPT. WILLIAM SIMPSON.

Capt. Wm. Simpson's parents came from the North of Ireland and settled in Union County. His father was a soldier under Gen. Green in the Revolutionary War. Capt. William Simpson married Miss Elizabeth Snoddy of Spartanburg, S. C., and moved to Pendleton in 1852. They had three children:

I.   John W. Simpson married Augusta Foster, daughter of Col. Garland Foster.

II.   Mary J. Simpson married William Graham of Mississippi.

III.   Richard Augustus Simpson married Margaret Agnew of Union, S. C.

I.   John W. and Augusta (Foster) Simpson had five children:

1.   Robert Raymond Simpson married Mattie Hudgens.

2.   Augustus Norman Simpson—never married.

3.   Wm. Graham Simpson married Mamy Long.

4.   Annie Hampton Simpson married —— Wright.

5.   John Orland Simpson—not married.

1.   Robert Raymond and Mattie (Hudgens) Simpson had three children:

A.   Foster Simpson.

B.   Raymond Simpson.

C. Lura Lee Simpson.

II. Mary J. Simpson and her husband Wm. Graham had four children:
1. Bessie Graham.
2. Bertie Graham.
3. Genella Graham.
4. David Graham.

III. Richard Augustus and Margaret (Agnew) Simpson had six children, all dead except one, Gussy Simpson—unmarried.

CALHOUN FAMILY.

In 1733 Patrick Calhoun came from Donegal, Ireland with his wife, Katherine, they had five sons, and one daughter, namely: William Calhoun, Ezekiel Calhoun, John Calhoun, Patrick Calhoun, James Calhoun, Katherine Calhoun. They first settled in Pennsylvania and then removed to Albemarle County, Virginia. Patrick Calhoun, Sr., died there. In 1755 Katherine, Patrick's widow, and children removed to Abbeville County, S. C. The mother, Katherine, and I. James, her son, were killed by the Indians in 1760. A rude stone marks the spot.

II. William Calhoun married Agnes Long.
III. Ezekiel Calhoun married Jane Ewing.
IV. John Calhoun.
V. Katherine married Alexander Noble.
VI. Patrick Calhoun married Martha Caldwell.

III. Ezekiel Calhoun and his wife, Jane (Ewing) Calhoun, had among others, one son, James Ewing Calhoun, who was a Senator in Congress. They had the following children:
1. John E. Calhoun married Martha Davis.
2. Floride Calhoun married John Caldwell Calhoun.

3.   James Edward Calhoun married—no issue.

1.   John E. Calhoun married Martha Davis, a sister of Warren R. Davis, a distinguished lawyer, statesman and wit.   They resided at Keowee, near Fort Hill. They had the following children:

A.   Capt. Randsom Calhoun—killed in a duel by R. B. Rhett.

B.   Martha C. Calhoun—died unmarried.

C.   Henry Davis Calhoun—died during Confederate War.   No issue.

D.   Edward B. Calhoun married Sarah Norwood.

D.   Edward B. Calhoun and his wife, Sarah (Norwood) Calhoun had four children:.

a.   Martha M. Calhoun and Sarah L. Calhoun (twins).   Martha died unmarried.

b.   Floride B. Calhoun and Willie N. Calhoun (twins)—unmarried.

Sarah L. Calhoun married Allen M. Schoen and has two children, Edward and Sarah Schoen.

V.   Patrick Calhoun and his wife, Martha Caldwell Calhoun, had four sons and one daughter:

1.   William Caldwell Calhoun.

2.   James Calhoun.

3.   John Caldwell Calhoun.

4.   Patrick Calhoun.

5.   Katherine Calhoun.

3.   John Caldwell Calhoun, the great statesman, married Floride Calhoun, the granddaughter of his uncle, Ezekiel Calhoun, his father's brother, being his first cousin once removed.   They settled early in life at Clergy Hall, known afterwards as Fort Hill from a fort built upon the place by that name.   Mrs. Calhoun's mother, the widow of Senator James Ewing Calhoun, settled at Cold Spring, a plantation adjoining Fort Hill, and afterwards was the home of J. W. Craw-

ford.   Cold Spring, the home place of Mrs. Floride Calhoun's mother, the widow of Senator James Ewing Calhoun, also adjoined the home place of Col. John E. Calhoun, the brother of Mrs. John C. Calhoun (Floride).

3.   John Caldwell Calhoun and his wife, Floride
(Calhoun) Calhoun had seven children:

A.   Andrew P. Calhoun married first, Miss Eugenia Chappell, daughter of Congressman Chappell—
no issue.   Married second time Margaret Green,
daughter of Duff Green.

B.   James Edward Calhoun—never married.

C.   John Caldwell Calhoun, Jr., married first, Angie Adams, no issue.   Married second time Miss Putnam.

D.   Patrick Calhoun—dead, never married.

E.   William L. Calhoun married widow of his
brother John.

F.   Anna M. Calhoun married Thos. G. Clemson.

G.   Cornelia Calhoun—dead—never married.

A.   Andrew P. Calhoun and Margaret (Green)
Calhoun had the following children:

a.   Duff Green Calhoun married and had one son,
Andrew Pickens Calhoun.

b.   Andrew P. Calhoun, Jr.—died unmarried.

c.   John C. Calhoun married Linnie Adams of
Kentucky.

d.   James E. Calhoun—died unmarried.

e.   Margaret Calhoun—unmarried.

f.   Patrick Calhoun married Sallie Williams,
daughter of George W. Williams.

a.   Duff Green Calhoun and his wife had one
son, Andrew P. Calhoun, who married Floride Lee,
granddaughter of Anna M. Clemson.

c.   John C. Calhoun and his wife, Linny (Adams)
Calhoun, have the following children:

James Edward Calhoun—unmarried.

David Adams Calhoun—unmarried.

Julia Johnson Calhoun—unmarried.

John Caldwell Calhoun—unmarried.

f. Patrick Calhoun and Sallie (Williams) Calhoun have the following children, names unknown:

C. John Caldwell Calhoun, Jr., married first Miss Angie Adams, no issue; married second time Miss Putnam and by this marriage had one child, Ben Calhoun.

E. William Lowndes Calhoun married Miss Putnam, the then widow of his brother, John Caldwell Calhoun, Jr., and had two sons, John and William.

F. Anna M. Calhoun married Thos. G. Clemson, a graduate from the School of Mines in Paris, France. Mr. Clemson offered his services to President Davis, and served during the war. After the war he and his family permanently resided at Pendleton with Mrs. John C. Calhoun, and after her death removed to Fort Hill, which had been willed to his wife, Anna M. Clemson. He survived his wife and two children for quite a time and dying devised the Fort Hill plantation and a large fortune to the State for the purpose of establishing thereon an agricultural and mechanical college, a noble institution, Clemson Agricultural College only a short distance from the home of his father-in-law, the great statesman, John C. Calhoun. The writer hereof was for several years previous to his death Mr. Clemson's attorney, wrote his will and was appointed therein his Executor. Mr. and Mrs. Clemson made mutual wills, giving their property to each other, with a promise that the survivor should will the whole estate, except certain provisions to their granddaughter, Floride Lee. Mr. Clemson's will was attempted to be broken by his son-in-law, Gideon Lee of New York in behalf of his daughter, Floride Lee, but the will was sustained by the Supreme Court of the United

States. No man in South Carolina has ever erected a nobler monument to himself than Mr. Clemson in establishing Clemson College.

Thos. G. Clemson and Anna M. (Calhoun) Clemson had two children:

Capt. Calhoun Clemson—killed in a railroad Collision near Seneca, S. C.,—unmarried.

Floride Clemson who married Giedon Lee of New York.

Floride Clemson Lee died seventeen days after her brother was killed and left one daughter, Floride Lee, who married Andrew P. Calhoun as stated above.

Mr. and Mrs. Clemson after the death of their only two children resided at Fort Hill. Shortly after her children's death, Mrs. Clemson died suddenly while her husband was absent from home. Thereafter, Mr. Clemson lived the life of a hermit until his death. He and his wife and son are buried in the Episcopal Churchyard at Pendleton and their daughter in New York.

DAVIS FAMILY.

Warren R. Davis and his sister, Martha Davis, came to Pendleton in its early history. I think they came from Sumter County. Warren R. Davis practiced law at Pendleton and was Solicitor for several years, and was elected to the U. S. Congress in which he served several terms. He died and was buried in Washington City, D. C. He was perhaps the most noted wit, and the most popular man in Pendleton. He never married. His sister, Miss Martha Davis, married John E. Calhoun, brother of Mrs. John C. Calhoun. (See Calhoun family.) W. R. Davis and his sister, Mrs. Martha Calhoun, were first cousins to Gen. Wade Hampton.

COL. HAYNE'S FAMILY.

Col. Alston Hayne was a son of Robt. Y. Hayne,
U. S. Senator, and his wife, Miss Alston. He married Miss Stiles and had several children. He resided at Flat Rock, a plantation now owned by C. Hanckel.
After the Confederate War Col. Hayne and his family
moved to California and there he was a member of the
legislature. His sons became prominent, one of them
was Judge of the Circuit Court. I regret I can obtain no more than this meagre information about this
polished and distinuished citizen of Old Pendleton.

COL. THOMAS PINCKNEY.

Was one of the first members of the Pendleton
Farmer's Society and was active in all things looking
to the upbuilding of the country. He built and resided at the home now owned by the McCrarys, and Cotes-
worth Pinckney, his brother, built and resided at the
home now owned by Maj. A. T. Smythe.

RANDELL FAMILY.

Carver Randell of Newberry married Miss Mary
C. Johnstone, daughter of Judge Job Johnstone, and
sister of Silas Johnstone. They came to Pendleton and
purchased the farm now owned by R. E. Sloan, about
1845-6. They had no children, but for many years
were distinguished citizens of Pendleton and were noted
for their generous hospitality, having large means.

REV. JASPER ADAMS.

Rev. Jasper Adams was the first President of Hobart
College, New Jersey. He came to Pendleton early in

the eighteenth century and settled at the place known as the Adams place, adjoining Fort Hill, the home of John C. Calhoun.

He married Placidia Mayrant of —————— and had the following children:

I.   Angie Adams married John C. Calhoun, Jr.—no issue.

II.   Elizabeth Adams married A. C. Campbell and had one son, Jasper Campbell, who resides in New York.

III.   Caroline Adams—never married.

IV.   Maj. Joseph Adams married Miss Earle, daughter of J. Baylis Earle. He had one son, Quincy Adams.

V.   Fannie Adams married.

After the Confederate War the survivors of the family, Mrs. Campbell and her son, Jasper, her sisters, Caroline and Fannie went to New York and have been lost sight of. Jasper is married and is successful in business.

CORNISH FAMILY.

Rev. A. H. Cornish, an Episcopal minister, resided for many years in Pendleton and was known of all men for his Christian piety and his unblemished deportment. He was the personal friend of John C. Calhoun, Andrew P. Calhoun and Mr. and Mrs. Thos. G. Clemson. He married Miss ————— —————, a lady universally beloved, and well remembered as the most artless of women. They had two children, Miss Kate Cornish and Miss Elizabeth Cornish. Neither of them married.

MAYS FAMILY.

Mr. James Butler Mays married Miriam Earle, daughter of Maj. Sam Earle, and had two children:
I. Samuel Earle Mays.
II. James Butler Mays.

I. Samuel Earle Mays married Catherine Mosely and they had the following children:
1. James F. Mays.
2. Samuel E. Mays.
3. Miriam C. Mays.
4. Earle W. Mays.

1. James F. Mays married E. Walton and they have the following children:
A. Annie Mosely Mays.
B. Catherine Mays.
C. Tombs Mays.
D. James F. Mays.
E. Miriam Mays.
F. Maud Mays.

2. Samuel E. Mays married Rowena Lee Evers. Their children are:
A. Rowena Mays.
B. Frances C. Mays.

II. Dr. James Butler Mays married Azalia Josepha Poe, daughter of William and Ellen (Taylor) Poe Their children are:
1. James B. Mays.
2. William Poe Mays.
3. Wilton Earle Mays.
4. Sam B. Mays.
5. Ellen Poe Mays.
6. Josepha Mays.
7. Hallie Poe Mays.
8. F. W. Poe Mays.

6.   Josepha Mays married John D. Hobbs and they
have one child, Ellen Mildred Hobbs.

Mrs. Miriam Mays resided at the residence now owned by Mrs. Holmes.

Samuel E. Mays graduated at South Carolina College
with first honor.   Both sons served through the Confederate War, and both after the war removed to Florida,
and both are alive at this time.

LIGON FAMILY.

William Jackson Ligon was born at Prince Edward
Court House, Virginia, and came to South Carolina and
graduated at the South Carolina College.   Adopting the
profession of teaching he became a noted educator.   He
married Louise Caroline Seibels of Lexington County,
South Carolina.   He came to Pendleton about 1859 and
taught the Pendleton Male Academy for many years.
He and his wife, Louise C. (Seibels) Ligon, had the following children:

I.   William Baker Seibels Ligon married Cora S,
Reed—died—no issue.

II.   Lucy Lavinia Ligon—died unmarried.

III.   Henry Arthur Ligon married Lucy Reed.

IV.   Thos. C. Ligon married Mary Towers.

V.   Richard Simpson Ligon married Helen Reed,
daughter of Clifton Reed.

VI.   Lavinia B. Ligon died in infancy.

VII.   Lucian Louis Ligon died in infancy.

VIII.   Eliza Manda Ligon died in infancy.

IX.   Robert Emmet Ligon married Mamie Benson.

X.   Marshall Orr Ligon died unmarried.

XI.   Lucia Louise Ligon died unmarried.

XII.   John Temple Ligon married Mary Brice.

III.   Henry Arthur Ligon and wife, Lucy (Reed)
Ligon, have the following children:

1.   Eoline Ligon.

2. Lucy Ligon.

3. Henry Arthur Ligon, Jr.

4. William Pinckney Ligon.

IV. Thos. C. Ligon and wife, Mary (Towers) Ligon, have the following children:

1. Mary C. Ligon.

2. William Jackson Ligon.

3. Alex Towers Ligon.

4. Louis L. Ligon.

5. Daniel R. Ligon.

6. Law Ellen Ligon.

V. Richard Simpson Ligon and wife, Helen (Reed) Ligon, have the following children:

1. Frances K. Ligon married Thomas Allen.

2. Annie Louise Ligon.

3. Clifton R. Ligon.

IX. Robert Emmet Ligon and wife, Mamie (Benson) Ligon, have the following children:

1. Prue B. Ligon.

2. Mack Ligon.

3. Eugenia Ligon.

4. May Ligon.

5. Charlton Ligon.

6. Robert C. Ligon.

XII. John Temple Ligon and wife, Mary (Brice) Ligon, have the following children:

1. John Temple Ligon, Jr.

JOHN HASTIE.

Uncle John, as we called him, was an old bachelor, but a kind hearted man. He was for years one of the foremost merchants not only in Pendleton but in the up-country. He had a brother, William Hastie, in Charleston and a half brother, Abe Isaacs, who clerked for him and during the war was a noted soldier of the

Confederate Army and after the war married in Greenville and died there. Mr. Hastie never married.

SEABORN FAMILY.

George Seaborn emigrated from Virginia and settled on the Grove near Piedmont. He left one son, James Seaborn, and died in 1818.

James Seaborn, son of the above George Seaborn, died on the Grove in Greenville County in 1804. He left a son, George Seaborn (Major Seaborn) who married Sarah Ann, daughter of Gen. John B. Earle, and resided at Cherry Hill, a mile or so from Pendleton. Maj. George Seaborn and wife, Sarah Ann Earle Seaborn, had the following children:

1. Sallie Taylor Seaborn married Thos. J. Sloan (See Sloan family).

II. James Seaborn married Laura Annie Mason.

III. B. Earle Seaborn married Marie Dunham.

IV. Mollie S. Seaborn married Col. J. B. E. Sloan (See Sloan family).

V. Grace Greenwood Seaborn—died unmarried.

VI. Hannah Earle Seaborn—died unmarried.

VII. William Robinson Seaborn—killed in battle of Seven Pines.

VIII. Eliza Seaborn—died unmarried.

IX. Mattie Seaborn married Gregg G. Richards—no issue.

X. Sue Vivian Seaborn—unmarried.

II. James Seaborn and wife, Laura Annie (Mason) Seaborn, had the following children:

1. Deanie S. Seaborn married Boon R. Moss.

2. George Seaborn married Gussie Holleman.

3. W. E. Seaborn.

4. Mason C. Seaborn.

5.   James Seaborn.
6.   Douglass S. Seaborn.

PIKE FAMILY.

Daniel Pike married in England a Miss Phelps and there had two children, John and Letitia, and then came to Pendleton in 1831. . One more child was born to him in Pendleton, Ellen Pike—died unmarried.

John Pike and Martha Fitzgerald had the following children:

I.   Alice Pike married Baylis Whitten.
II.   Warren Pike married Flora Reese.
III.   George Pike married Mattie Perry.
IV.   William Pike married Florrie Jefferson.
V.   Albert Pike married Rosa Philpot.
VI.   Mary Pike married A. L. Whitten.

I.   Alice Pike and her husband, Baylis Whitten, have the following children:

1.   Eugene Whitten.
2.   Norman Whitten.
3.   George Whitten.
4.   Edith Whitten.
5.   Colin Whitten.
6.   Floyd Whitten.
7.   Clyde Whitten.

II.   Warren Pike and wife, Flora (Reese) Whitten have the following children:

1.   Sam Pike.
2.   George Pike.
3.   Henry Pike.
4.   Oscar Pike.
5.   Ellen Pike.
6.   Maggie Pike.
7.   Richard Pike.
8.   John Pike.

VI. Mary Pike and her husband, A. L. Whitten, have the following children:

1. Walter Whitten.
2. Furman Whitten.
3. Ernest Whitten.
4. Mamie Whitten.
5. Lewis Whitten.
6. John Whitten.
7. Green Whitten.
8. Ressie Whitten.
9. Alice Whitten.

Letitia Pike married Andrew Stephens and they had following children:

I. J. Stewart Stephens.
II. Hayne Stephens.
III. Zeruah Stephens.
IV. Angie Stephens.
V. Dora Stephens.
VI. Daniel Stephens.
VII. Hampton Stephens.
VIII. Samuel Stephens.

SHAW FAMILY.

William Shaw came to Pendleton from England. He was a lawyer and practiced at Pendleton. He married Jane Anderson, daughter of Gen. Robert Anderson —no issue. His sister, Ann Shaw, who married a Mr. Smith, in England, had four children:

Thomas Smith.
William Smith.
Matilda Smith.
Maria Smith.

William Shaw, when he came from England brought with him his sister's two sons, Thomas and William Smith. Mrs. Smith, then a widow, followed her brother to this country bringing her two daughters, Matilda and Maria Smith. She settled in Laurens County and there married a Mr. Barlow—no issue.

Mr. Shaw educated his two nephews, Thomas and William Smith. Thomas became a practicing physician and married and settled at Society Hill in Darlington County. He had no children, but adopted two, Caroline and Francis McIver.

Caroline married Jonathan Lucas.

Frances married a Mr. Williams. To these two adopted daughters he gave all of his large estate, except a tract of land in Anderson County and an annuity of $250.00 to his sister, Maria Smith. William Smith settled in Augusta, Ga., and nothing is known of his family. Matilda Smith never married. Maria Smith married William Watson and had the following children:

I. Matilda Watson married Elijah Owen.

II. Drucilla Watson married Joshua Owen.

III. Louisa Watson married Ferdinand Watson killed in Confederate War.

IV. Elizabeth Watson married Jasper Owen.

V. Thomas Watson—unmarried—killed in Confederate War.

VI. Allen Watson married Sarah Erskine.

VII. Emma Watson married Henry Crenshaw.

VIII. Maria Watson married Joseph Erskine— died in prison.

IX. Jane Watson married John Mitchell.

X. Joseph N. Watson—unmarried—killed in Confederate War.

VIII. Maria Watson and her husband, Joseph Erskine, had the following children:

1. Jefferson Erskine.

2. Joseph Erskine married Ida Watson.

3. Martha Erskine married T. E. McConnell.

4. Mary Erskine married G. F. McConnell.

The last two named were twin sisters and married twin brothers.

IX.   Jane Watson and her husband, John Mitchell, have the following children:

1.   William Mitchell.
2.   John Mitchell.
3.   Cary Mitchell.
4.   Augustus Mitchell married Theo. Owen, daughter of John Owen.
5.   Leonidas Mitchell.
6.   Oswald Mitchell.

Augustus and Oswald reside near Penlleton.   All the others now reside in Texas and California.

Maria (Smith) Watson lived until she was ninety-two years of age.   When she was ninety she came to the office of the writer hereof to have him write her will. on account of her extreme age three lawyers were called in to witness the will.   Before doing so they were requested to talk with Mrs. Watson, and they agreed that she was the most remarkable woman of her age they had ever met.

SYMMES FAMILY.

Dr. Frederick W. Symmes was for many years one of the most prominent and influential citizens of Pendleton in its best days.   He was a noted physician, a man of sterling character, and a fluent writer.   He was for years editor of the Pendleton Messenger, a newspaper and political organ that did more to shape public opinion in South Carolina than any other paper in the State. Dr. Symmes was a close relative of President Benjamin Harrison, and was possessed of many of the characteristics peculiar to that celebrated family.   He resided at the time I knew the family in the house near the Blue Ridge Railroad bridge, now owned by Mr. S. L. Eskew and was buried at the Old Stone Church.

Dr. F. W. Symmes married Sarah Whitner, daughter of Joseph Whitner, and sister of Judge Joseph N. Whitner. Their children were:

I.   Cornelia Symmes.
II. William Symmes—died unmarried.
III. Edward Symmes.
IV. Dr. G. H. Symmes.
V.   Mary Symmes.
VI. James Whitner Symmes.

I. Cornelia Symmes married William R. Jones, a graduate of the South Carolina College. Their children are:

1. William R. Jones, Jr.
2. Mamie Jones.
3. G. Thomisena Jones.
4. Eugene Jones.

1. William R. Jones, Jr., married Miss Bobo and they have two children, names not given.

3. G. Thomisena Jones married Jacob T. Grey and their children are:

A. Clelia Grey.
B. Dora Grey.
C. Thomas Eugene Grey—married.

III. Edward Symmes married Mary Jones—no issue.

IV. Dr. Gustavus H. Symmes married Ellen Matilda Poe, daughter of William and Ellen (Taylor) Poe. Their children are:

1. Frederick W. Symmes.
2. Lewis Symmes.
3. Gustavus H. Symmes, Jr.
4. Edgar Poe Symmes.
5. Nelson Poe Symmes. (See Poe Family.)

2. Lewis Symmes married Hallie Moody. Their children are:

A. William Henry Symmes.

B.   Lewis Frederick Symmes.

3.   Gustavus H. Symmes, Jr., married Martha Myers and they have one child:

A.   Rita Close Symmes.

4.   Edgar Poe Symmes married Mrs Martha Sanders nee Christian, and they have one child:

A.   Ellen Miriam Symmes.

V.   Mary Symmes married Dr. J. H. Dean.   Their
children are:

1.   Hamilton Symmes Dean.

2.   J. Harry Dean.

VI. James   Whitner   Symmes   married   Anneta
Alexander.   Their children are:

1.   Julia Symmes.

2.   Mary Symmes.

3.   Daisy Symmes.

4.   Nettie Symmes.

5.   Frederick Wm. Symmes.

6.   Lucena Symmes.

7.   Alexander Symmes.

3.   Daisy Symmes married Charles E. Gambrell.
Their child is:

A.   Jane Anne Gambrell.

JOHN MILLER.

John Miller, commonly called Printer John Miller,
was born in London and was one of the printers of the
celebrated Junius Letters. He was tried among others
in London, but feeling was so strong in favor of the
Junius Letters he was acquitted. Disgusted with the
proceedings connected with these celebrated trials, he
left London and came to America in 1782 and settled
first in Philadelphia, Penn. The delegation of South
Carolina at that time was Edward Rutledge, Thomas
Heyward, and Arthur Middleton, by them John Miller

was induced to move to Charleston, S. C., to become printer for the State.   There he commenced the publication of the South Carolina Gazette and General Advertiser.   He removed to Pendleton in 1785, and obtained a grant of a tract of land containing 640 acres on Eighteen Mile Creek.   (The Stone Church is located on a part of this land.)

Some time after removing to Pendleton he began the publication of a newspaper, called Miller's Weekly Messenger. About what time he commenced the publication of this paper is unknown, but it was probably in 1795. This paper he continued to publish until 1806, when its name was changed and it was then edited by Dr. F. W. Symmes and Gov. Francis Burt.   John Miller was elected the first Clerk of the Court of Pendleton in 1790.   He died at Pendleton in 1809 and was buried at the Old Stone Church.   He left two sons, Crosby and John.

Crosby Miller married Miss Hammond.

John Miller married and left five sons and five daughters, one of his sons was named John, who was the father of S. F. W. Miller and Dr. Thaddeus Miller.   The other sons removed west. The daughters, Miss Jane Miller Mrs. Charlotte Kay, Mrs. James Duké, Mrs. Richard Wilson, and Mrs. Elizabeth Sharpe, who was the mother of Elam Sharpe, who married a daughter of Governor Hayne, Dr. Marcus Sharpe and Elizabeth who married Rev. John M. Carlisle.   (See Sharpe Family.)

A SKETCH OF JOHN MILLLER, FOUNDER
OF THE PENDLETON MESSENGER.

BY A. T. BROYLES.

Mr. Editor:—In compliance with your request I herewith send you a biographical sketch of John Miller, who about the beginning of the present century published at Pendleton Miller's Weekly Messenger, the first newspaper ever published in this county. This paper he con-- tinued to publish until the year 1806 when its name was changed to the Pendleton Messenger, which was afterwards so ably edited by Dr. F. W. Symmes and Gov. Frances Burt.

John Miller was an Englishman and resided in the City of London. He was one of the fifteen partners who owned the London Evening Post, as the account book of that paper shows, and was connected with it from 1769 to 1780. This account book, which was most neatly kept, together with many other interesting manuscripts, have been kindly furnished me for the purpose of this sketch, by Mr. S. F. W. Miller, his great-grandson, by whom they have been carefully preserved. From this account book it appears to have been the practice of the partners to appoint a committee of their number from time to time to examine these accounts, and in 1775 Henry Sampson Woodfall, the publisher of the celebrated letters of Junius, was one of the committee appointed at that time, showing that he was also a partner. The letters of Junius, however, were published by Woodfall in the Daily Advertiser.

The object of these letters was to denounce official corruption wherever it existed, whether in the ministry, the Parliament of the Judiciary, and to hold it up to the odium and execration of the English people. The author whoever he was, was undoubtedly a man of splendid genius, and the intrepidity with which he used his polished weapons, sparing neither rank nor station, cannot fail to command the admiration of mankind. For simplicity force and elegance of diction these letters are unsurpassed by any other compositions in our language. Who the author really was is even today a matter of speculation, but he undoubtedly despised the honors of authorship, for in assigning all his right, title and interest in these letters to Woodfall, as fully and effectually as it was possible for any author to do, no doubt as a reward for what he had suffered by their publication, he declared that he alone was the repository of his own secret, and that it should die with him. At last he addressed one of these letters to George III—the king himself. It was first published by Woodfall in the Daily Advertiser and immediately thereafter it was reprinted by John Miller in the London Evening Post and by Almon, a bookseller.

Without going into details further than may be necessary to show the importance of the issues involved and the interest which these cases excited, Lord Campbell's account of the matter is simply this: That the Attorney General at once filed criminal information against all three of these parties. In the case against Almon, who was defended by Sergeant Glyn, it was not denied that the letter was a libel, but it was insisted that the purchase of the letter at the shop of Almon, who was a bookseller and publisher of pamphlets, from a person in the shop acting as his servant, with his name on the title page as publisher, was not sufficient evidence to convict Almon of the publication. But Lord Mansfield instructed the jury that in the absence of any proof that Almon was not privy or assenting to it, a sale of the letter by Almon's servant was *prima facie* evidence of a publication of the matter and the jury found a verdict of guilty. In the case of Woodfall a different course was pursued.

There was no doubt of his liability as publisher, but it was denied that the letter was libellous, and the grand dispute which then arose was whether the libellous character of the paper was a question for the jury, or one of law exclusively for the court. Lord Mansfield held that the simple inquiry for the jury was whether the defendant printed and published the letter charged in the information as libellous. Having done their duty in this respect the question whether the paper was a libel or not, was a question of law for the court. The jury were out many hours, but having at length agreed they were taken in coaches from Guildhall to Lord Mansfield's house in Bloomsbury Square, where the foreman rendered in a verdict of "Guilty of the printing and publishing only." The legal result of this finding being doubtful, Lord Mansfield, granted a new trial, but Woodfall was from that time safe as there was not a jury in London that would have found a verdict of "guilty" against the publisher of Junius. On the trial of John Miller Lord Campbell says: "Half the population of London were assembled in the streets surrounding Guildhall and remained several hours impatiently expecting the result. Lord Mansfield had retired to his home, and many thousands proceeded thither in a grand procession when it was announced that the jury had agreed. At last a shout proceeding from Bloomsbury Square and reverberated from the remotest quarters of the metropolis proclaimed a verdict of not guilty.

These three famous cases were tried in the latter part of the year 1770, a short time before our Declaration of Independence. A summary of the law as laid down by Lord Mansfield was that the jury were not only limited to the simple inquiry whether the defendant printed and pulished the paper charged to be libellous, but that in making up their verdict upon this issue they had no right to inquire into the intention of the defendant as in other criminal prosecutions or into the innocence or criminality of the paper charged to be malicious and seditious, because these were questions of law for the court to be determined by the court upon the mere reading of the record. This he maintained had been the law of Eng-- land from the revolution of 1688, and that no complaint had ever been made of it, until the reign of George III. There was no doubt of the sincerity and honesty of his convictions, and that he was sustained by precedent. But it is evident that the law was founded upon the no- tion of imposing some limitations and restraints upon the freedom of the press, because if the jury were per- mitted to inquire into those matters which were held to be questions of law for the court, they would have been at once invested with the power of deciding the questions of law, as well as the facts, in a libel case, and this it was apprehended would lead to a freedom of dis- cussion that would be subversive of law and order. The law thus laid down was denounced as an invasion of the province of the jury, an attack upon the liberty of the press, and dangerous to the liberties of the people. In fact it would seem that very little of the public attention had been attracted to this condition of the law of libel un- til the time of Junius when these three prosecutions were commenced. His letters had been read with universal, applause, and no doubt the great name of Junius aroused much of the public interest which was manifested in these causes. But they also involved an important con- stitutional principle, and their trial was therefore at- tended by an intense public excitement. The question was an important one and brought into requisition the talent and learning of some of the most distinguished men in England.

It may not be an uninteresting digression to say that no man ever won a more splendid forensic victory than that which was achieved by Lord Camden over the great Lord Mansfield, when he challenged him to a discussion of his law of libel. Lord Camden had said that if he

could obtain a copy of the opinion and it should appear
to him contrary to the known and established principles
of the constitution he would not scruple to tell the author
of his mistake boldly and openly in the House of Lords.
Lord Mansfield thereupon caused a copy of the opinion
in the case of Woodfall to be filed with the assistant
clerk of the House. Lord Camden, after inspecting it,
said that he considered this action as a challenge directed
to him, personally, and that he accepted it. He (Lord
Mansfield) has thrown down the gauntlet and I take it
up. His doctrine is not the law of England, and I am
ready to enter into the debate whenever the noble lord
will fix the day for it. I desire and insist that it shall be
an early one. Lord Mansfield was much confused by
the questions propounded by Lord Camden as the
basis of the debate. Aware of the strong alliance which
existed between Lord Camden and Lord Chatham, who
would be aided by the Duke of Richmond and other allies,
and that he himself had no one to give him the slightest
assistance in the debate his courage forsook him and he
seemed so much distressed that the matter was allowed
to drop.

Lord Mansfield himself lived to see the day when his
doctrine on this subject was subverted by Mr. Fox's Libel
Bill, and that bill and Lord Campbell's Libel Bill, which
was subsequently passed have settled the law of libel sub-
stantially upon its present basis. The important constitutional principles thus established is contained in
Section 8 of the Declaration of Rights, Article I of our
present State Constitution, which, among other things,
declares that in all indictments for libel the jury shall
be judges of the law and the facts, a doctrine which
is now universally recognized in this country.

These three cases which led to this result have
passed into history, and although John Miller, the subject
of this sketch, was only a defendant in one of these prosecutions, in which he was sought to be victimized by an

administration which regarded freedom of speech as
dangerous to the safety of the State, yet even in this
capacity he is entitled to his share of the celebrity these
cases have acquired. His name has thus been associated
with the settlement of a very important constitutional
question, and with the freedom of the press. Disgusted
no doubt with a country where it was deemed criminal
to publish an appeal to the king to mediate between
his Ministry and the people, and to afford his subjects
that redress they were entitled to demand, he left his
native shores and arrived in Philadelphia in January,
1782, shortly after the news of the evacuation of Charleston in December 1782, had been received in England.
Our delegation in Congress at that time consisted of
Edward Rutledge, Thomas Heyward, and Arthur Middleton, and by them he was sent to Charleston to be
printer to the State. There he commenced the publication of the South Carolina Gazette and General Advertiser, and in his prefatory address he said that his ambi-
tion could not have been more truly gratified than by
finding himself the printer of the commonwealth of
South Carolina. His family followed him to Charleston
and reached there in November, 1783. Mr. William L.
King, in his little work entitled, "The Newspaper Press
of Charleston," gives an account of him, and make many
extracts from his editorials, which are very creditable to
him. He sold the Gazette and Advertiser to Tymothy &
Mason, and went to Pendleton about the year 1785, for
during that year he obtained from his Excellency Benjamin Guerard a grant for a tract of land, containing
640 acres, on Eighteen Mile Creek, which, as the writer
is informed, was on both sides of said creek on the road
from Pendleton to Fort Hill.

There has been placed in my possession a copy of
the City Gazette, of Charleston, containing a communication dated, "Pendleton County, Washington District,
September 25, 1785," made by John Miller, corresponding

secretary of the "Franklin or Republican Society of Pendleton County," asking the publication of the pre· amble and resolutions prepared by him for the Society, and adopted by the several Brigades at the Governor's Reviews, denouncing the treaty concluded in 1794 by Mr. Jay with England and expressive of strong sympathy with France.   At the request of General Washington Mr. Jay resigned the Chief Justiceship of the Supreme Court of the United States to effect this treaty, but it was bitterly denounced in the United States Senate and in many parts of the country.

There is a memorandum in Miller's own handwriting stating that in 1795 he had made proposals for the publication of a newspaper, but that the project had been postponed until now that the rapid increase of population in the back country had rendered it practicable. There is no doubt that it was then he commenced the publication of Miller's Weekly Messenger, but as the memorandum is without date it is impossible to fix the precise time.

John Miller died at Pendleton in 1809, and was buried at the Old Stone Church.   He left behind him many highly respected descendants, most of whom reside in Anderson County.   His   son   John,   who assisted him in the publication of the Pendleton Messenger, had five sons and as many daughters.   One of these sons was also named John, who remained in this county, and was the father of Mr. S. F. W. Miller and Dr. Thaddeus Miller.   The other two sons removed west.   The daughters were Miss Jane Miller, who died at Pendleton, Mrs. Charlotte Kay, Mrs. Duke, Mrs. Sharpe and Mrs Wilson. Mrs. Elizabeth Sharpe was the mother of Elam Sharpe who married Governor Hayne's daughter; Dr. Marcus L. Sharpe, our fellow townsman, Edwin Sharpe and Miss Elizabeth Sharpe, who married Rev. John M. Carlisle, and these are his descendants so far as I have been able to ascertain.

LEWIS FAMILY

The Lewis family is of Welch decent. Four brotners of this family emigrated from Wales. Two of them, General Robert and John Lewis, settled in Virginia.

General Robert had a son John, Sr. John Sr.,had a son John, Jr., who married Frances Fielding. Their son married Bettie Washington, a sister of Gen. George Washington. John, the emigrant from Wales, born 1640, had a number of children, one of whom, David Lewis, is the ancestor of the Lewis descendants in South Carolina and particularly in Pendleton. David Lewis married Miss Terrell and raised eight children, among them John Lewis who married Sarah Taliaferro of Virginia. Just before the Revolution he, John, and his family removed from Virginia and settled in Rutherford County, North Carolina.

John and Sarah Taliaferro Lewis raised nine children.

John, their son, married Ann Berry Earle, a sister of Gen. John Baylis Earle and Washington Earle (as to this family see the Earle Family). Their children were:

I. John Taliaferro Lewis married Eleanor Earle, daughter of Gen. John B. Earle.

II. Madison Earle Lewis married Mary Griffin.

III. Jesse Payne Lewis married Susan M. Taylor.

IV. Baylis Washington Lewis married Frances Gaines.

I. John Talliaferro Lewis at the age of twenty-one was appointed Clerk of the Superior Court of Pendleton for life. He married as above stated, Eleanor Earle, and had a number of children, one Rev. Henry T. Lewis practiced law at Pendleton for a while, then became a preacher and removed to Mississippi. He was the author of that celebrated sermon, The Harp of a Thousand Strings. Also Samuel W. Lewis who married Annie

166   HISTORY OF PENDLETON

McCurry and Hannah Elizabeth Lewis. These two last
named I remember very well.

II.   Madison Earle Lewis and wife, Mary Griffin.

III. Jesse Payne and Susan M. Taylor Lewis, his
wife (daughter of Joseph Taylor, a son of Maj. Samuel
Taylor. As to Susan M. Lewis, see Taylor Family) had
the following children:

1.   Nancy Lewis—died unmarried.

2.   Robert O. Lewis—died in Confederate Army.

3.   John Joseph Lewis married Carrie C. Dickinson.

4.   Jesse A. Lewis—died unmarried.

5.   Ellen M. Lewis married B. Frank Sloan (See
B. F. Sloan Family).

6.   Earle S. Lewis—killed in Confederate War—
unmarried.

3.   John Joseph Lewis and wife, Carrie C. (Dickinson) Lewis had two children:

A.   Sue Ellen Lewis married J. Lee Carpenter.

B.   Nina D. Lewis married William S. Hunter.

A.   Sue Ellen Lewis married J. Lee Carpenter and
they have three children:

a.   Ellen S. Carpenter.

b.   John Lewis Carpenter.

c.   Nina Hunter Carpenter.

B.   Nina D. Lewis married William S. Hunter and
they have two children:

a.   Carrie Hunter.

b.   ———

3.   John Joseph Lewis married second time Maggie
Wilkinson and they have the following children:

A.   Robert Earle Lewis.

B.   Jennie Hall Lewis.

C.   John Joseph Lewis.

Col. Richard Lewis, another son of John and Sarah
Taliaferro Lewis, was Clerk of the Court of Rutherford
County North Carolina and a member of the Convention

for revising the North Carolina Convention. He married Sarah Miller, daughter of Gen. James Miller of North Carolina, who was an officer in the Revolution and commanded at Augusta, Ga. He and his wife emigrated to South Carolina and settled on Seneca River near Pendleton, and he and his wife are both buried at the Old Stone Church. They had nine children:

I.   Mary M. Lewis married Hon. John McDowell of North Carolina.

II. James Overton Lewis married Mary Lorton.

III. Ann Elvira Lewis married Joseph Van Shanklin (See Shanklin Family).

IV. Sarah Ann Lewis married Edwin Reese (See Reese Family).

V.   Andrew F .Lewis married Susan Sloan.

II. James Overton and wife, Mary (Lorton) Lewis, had the following children:

1.   Sarah Lewis married Dr. William B. Cherry of Pendleton.

2.   Mary Lewis married Dr. Beverly A. Henry of Georgia.

3.   Dr. Thomas L. Lewis married Eliza Maxwell, daughter of Capt. John Maxwell.

4.   Capt. Richard L. Lewis married Sue Gaines.

5.   Frances Lewis married E. A. Tate of Georgia.

6.   John E. Lewis married Florence Boatwright of Columbia.

7.   R. Fielding Lewis married ————

8.   Lucy Lewis married John Lebby of Charleston.

9.   James Clarkson Lewis.

10. James Overton Lewis married Martha R. Sharpe, grand-daughter of R. Y. Hayne.

1.   Dr. William B. Cherry and Sarah Lewis Cherry, his wife, had the following children:

A.   Mary Lorton Cherry—died unmarried.

B.   Samuel Cherry married ————

    C.   Fannie Lewis Cherry married Warren R. Davis.

    3.   Dr. Thomas L. and Eliza (Maxwell) Lewis, his wife, have the following children:

    A.   Elizabeth Earle Lewis—unmarried.

    B.   Mary T. Lewis—unmarried.

    C.   Mattie D. Lewis—unmarried.

    D.   Julia K. Lewis married Overton Henry.

    E.   Emily W. Lewis—unmarried.

    F.   James Lewis married Miss Birnie.

    G.   Thomas Lewis.

    H.   Edward Lewis married Miss Pope.

    I.   Ben Lewis.

    4.   Capt. Richard and Sue (Gaines) Lewis have no issue.

Capt. Richard Lewis volunteered in the Confederate War and rose to captain.

    V.   Andrew F. Lewis (son of Col. Richard Lewis and Susan (Sloan) Lewis had ten children

    1.   Richard Lewis married ———————— Lawrence.

    2.   David Lewis died in Confederate War.

    3.   John E. Lewis married Anna Smith.

    4.   Sue A. Lewis—unmarried.

    5.   William Lewis—killed himself accidentally.

    6.   Sallie M. Lewis—unmarried.

    7.   James P. Lewis married Anna Porcher.

    8.   Andrew F. Lewis, Jr., died unmarried.

    9.   Emma E. Lewis—died unmarried.

    10.   Barnard Bee Lewis—unmarried.

    11.   Thomas Lewis—married.

SHANKLIN FAMILY.

Joseph Van Shanklin, a lawyer by profession, practiced at Pendleton. He married Nancy Elvira Lewis, daughter of Col. Richard Lewis, and raised three children:

    I.   Joseph Augustus Shanklin.

II.   Capt. Julius L. Shanklin.

III.   E. Henry Shanklin.

I.   Rev. Joseph Augustus Shanklin, an Episcopal minister, married Catherine Ann Sadler of Florida, and had five children:

1.   Catherine Ann Shanklin.

2.   Edwin Alvesti Shanklin.

3.   Mary Lewis Shanklin.

4.   Lila Shanklin.

5.   Joseph Augustus Shanklin, Jr.

After the death of Rev. Joseph A. Snanklin his widow married Rev. J. H. Elliott, of Georgia.

II.   Julius L. Shanklin married Julia Doyle and raised four sons. He graduated at University of Virginia. was captain in Confederate War and State Senator for several terms.

1.   Augustus Shanklin married Miss Neville.

2.   J. Barbour Shanklin—married.

3.   S. Morris Shanklin.

4.   Edgar R. Shanklin.

III.   E. Henry Shanklin graduated at Virginia University and served faithfully during the whole Confederate War.   He married Virginia Robinson, daughter of Dr. William Robinson and Maria Earle, his wife. They have three sons and two daughters:

1.   Julius A. Shanklin married Conyers Pickens. daughter of Dr. T. J. Pickens.

2.   Edward H. Shanklin married Miss Hagood.

3.   George Shanklin—unmarried.

4.   Bessie Shanklin—unmarried.

5.   Annie Shanklin—unmarried.

1.   Julius A. Shanklin and his wife, Conyers (Pickens) Shanklin have three children:

A.   Virginia Shanklin.

B.   Julius A. Shanklin, Jr.

C.   Sue Conyers Shanklin.

WHITNER FAMILY

Joseph Whitner came from Germany when a lad of twelve or thirteen years of age. He had no relatives in this country, and it is stated that he was an orphan in Germany and was entitled to a large property there and that he was shipped to this new country by some of his relatives in order to get possession of his property. He landed in Charleston and when about grown he came to Pendleton. He was a surveyor and acquired considerable property and much influence. He resided at the North place, subsequently at Flat Rock, now owned by C . Hanckel. He married Elizabeth Shackelford and had the following children:

I. Benjamin F. Whitner married Miss Spann.

II. John Whitner died—unmarried.

III. Rebecca Whitner died—unmarried.

IV. Joseph N. Whitner and Elizabeth Whitner (twins.)

Joseph N. Whitner married Elizabeth Hampton Harrison.

Elizabeth Whitner married Anthony W. Ross. (See Ross Family.)

VI. Sarah Whitner married Dr. Frederick W. Symmes. (See Symmes Family.)

I. Benjamin F. and wife, Miss Spann, had the following children:

1. Amanda Whitner married J. C. Kilpatrick. (See Kilpatrick Family.)

2. B. F. Whitner, Jr., married Sarah Church.

3. Joseph N. Whitner married ———

4. John C. Whitner married Martha Cobb, sister to Howell and T. R. R. Cobb.

2. B. F. Whitner, Jr., and wife, Sarah (Church) Whitner had the following children:

A. Alonzo Church Whitner married ———

B. B. F. Whitner married Elizabeth Randolph of Florida.

3. Joseph N. Whitner married ——— resided in Florida.

4. John C. Whitner and wife, Martha (Cobb) Whitner had a number of children, one of whom, (A) John A. Whitner married Lidie Farrow, daughter of Col. H. P. Farrow and Cornelia (Simpson) Farrow.

A. John A. Whitner and wife, Lidie (Farrow) Whitner had the following children:
(The data could not be obtained for this.)

IV. Judge Joseph N. Whitner and wife, Elizabeth Hampton (Harrison) Whitner had the following children:

1. Joseph N. Whitner, Jr., married Amelia M. Howard, of Marion, S. C.

2. Sarah F. Whitner married Elbert M. Rucker.

3. James H. Whitner married Ellen Stovall of Augusta, Ga.

4. Benjamin F. Whitner married Annie P. Church of Athens, Ga.

5. Wm. W. Whitner married, first, Esther Sloan, no issue; second, Jane Randolph, of Florida—no issue.

6. Elizabeth Toccoa Whitner married Col. Thos. J. Glover.

7. Elias E. Whitner married, first, Miss Williams; second, Miss Duval of Virginia.

8. Tallulah Whitner married Col. John L. Eubanks of Virginia.

2. Sarah Whitner and husband, Elbert Rucker, had the following children:

A. Joseph N. Rucker.

B. Elizabeth Rucker married David S. Taylor, Jr.

C. James H. Rucker—married.

D. E. Marion Rucker married Miss Kinard of Columbia, S. C.

E.   Guy G. Rucker—unmarried.

B.   Elizabeth Rucker married David S. Taylor, Jr. (See Taylor family.)

4.   Benjamin F. Whitner and wife, Annie P. (Church) Whitner, have the following children:

A.   Frank C. Whitner—unmarried.

B.   Annie Lee Whitner—died unmarried.

C.   James Harrison Whitner married Annie Barna of Atlanta, Ga., no issue.

D.   Wm. C. Whitner married Catherine Roddy of Rock Hill, S. C.

E.   Elizabeth H. Whitner married Wm. Latta Law.

F.   Hugh Earle Whitner—died unmarried.

D.   Wm. C. Whitner and wife, Catherine (Roddy) Whitner, have the following children:

a.   Wm. C. Whitner, Jr.

b.   Lyle R. Whitner..

c.   Catherine Whitner.

d.   Anna B. Whitner.

e.   James Harrison Whitner.

E.   Elizabeth H. Whitner and husband, Wm. Latta Law, have the following children:

a.   Wm. Latta Law, Jr.

b.   Elizabeth McIver Law..

c.   Margaret Law.

d.   Frank Whitner Law.

e.   Jane Law.

HARRISON FAMILY.

James Harrison, of Andersonville, S. C., a son of James Harrison and Elizabeth (Hampton) Harrison, married Sarah Earle, daughter of Col. Elias Eearle and wife, Frances Wilton (Robinson) Earle, and had the following children:

I.   Elizabeth Hampton Harrison married Judge Jos. N. Whitner.   (See Whitner Family.)

II.   Wm. Henry Harrison—died unmarried.

III.   Elias Earle Harrison—died unmarried.

IV.   Gen. James W. Harrison married Mary, daughter of E. B. and Esther Benson, of Pendleton.

V.   Samuel Earle Harrison—died unmarried.

VI.   Francis Eugene Harrison married Anna, daughter of Rev. A. W. and Elizabeth Ross.

IV.   Gen. James W. and his wife, Mary (Benson) Harrison, had the following children:

1.   Elizabeth Harrison married Dr. Thomas T. Broyles—no issue.

2.   Lucia Harrison married Vincent F. Martin—no issue.

3.   Isham Harrison married Meta Darby—no issue.

4.   John B. Harrison married Imogene Baughn, of Baltimore—had children.

5.   Ida Harrison married Dr. B. D. Darby—had children.

6.   Nina Harrison married Samuel M. Van Wyck —had children.

7.   Frank E. Harrison married Miss Connor of Charleston—had children.

8.   George A. Harrison married Hannah Earle, or Spartanburg—had children.

9.   Josephine Harrison married Mr. Norman, of Walhalla—had children.

VI.   Francis Eugene Harrison married first Anna Ross and had the following children:

1.   Elizabeth Harrison—died unmarried.

2.   James Harrison married Martha Cunningham— had one child, Elizabeth.

3.   Sarah Harrison married Joseph G. Cunningham.

4.   Antoinette Harrison married E. Preston Earle (See Earle Family.)

3.   Sarah Harrison and husband, Joseph G. Cunningham, had the following children:

A.   Frank Harrison Cunningham.

B.   Joseph G. Cunningham, Jr.
C.   Anna Ross Cunningham.
D.   Thomas Harrison Cunningham.
E.   Jennie E. Cunningham.
F.   Sallie A. Cunningham.
VI.   Col. Francis E. Harrison married the second
time and had the following children:
1.   Thomas P. Harrison.
2.   Dr. Frank Harrison.
3.   ——— Harrison.
——— Harrison, brother of ——— Harrison, married ————— and had one child, a daughter, who
married Gen. Stephen D. Lee.

ANDERSON FAMILY.

John Anderson and his wife, Jean, came from Ireland to Philadelphia and thence about 1735 they removed
to Staunton, Va.   They had among other children
1.   Robert Anderson.
2.   James Anderson.

1.   Robert   Anderson   married   Ann   Thompson, November 6th, 1765, and shortly thereafter removed
to South Carolina and settled in that part of the State
which afterwards was known as   Pendleton   District.
Robert Anderson was an officer in the Revolutionary
War and rose to rank of Colonel.   After the war he was
prominent in the organization of Pendleton District and
was one among the Judges who held the first court in
Pendleton District in 1790.   He was subsequently appointed Brigadier General of the militia and is now
known as Gen. Robert Anderson.
2.   James Anderson married December 10th, 1771,
Agnes Craig, of Augusta County, Virginia, and in1786
or 1789 he removed to Pendleton District.   He was a
captain in the Revolutionary War.

Gen. Robert Anderson and his wife, Ann Thompson, had five children:

I.   Elizabeth Anderson married Samuel Maverick. (See Maverick Family.)

II.   Mary Anderson married, first, Capt. Robert Maxwell; second, Mr. Corruth.

III.   Jane Anderson married Mr. Shaw, an Englishman.

IV.   Annie Anderson married Dr. William Hunter. (See Hunter Family.)

V.   Robert Anderson married Maria Thomas from Nassau.

II.   Capt. Robert Maxwell who married Mary Anderson was a prominent citizen and officer in the Revolutionary War.   He came from Ireland.   At the close of the war he married and settled on Saluda River in Old Pendleton District.   In 1797 he was shot from ambush and killed near his home and was buried in the family graveyard, and over his grave his son has erected a monument which is still standing.   Capt Robert Maxwell and wife, Mary (Anderson) Maxwell, had two sons:

1.   Capt. John Maxwell married Elizabeth Earle, daughter of Samuel Earle.

2.   Robert Anderson Maxwell married Mary Prince Earle, daughter of Samuel Earle.

1.   Capt. John Maxwell was a member of the Legislature and a member of the Secession Convention in 1860 and 1861.   He and his wife, Elizabeth (Earle) Maxwell, had the following children:

A.   Dr. Robert Maxwell married Lucy Sloan, daughter of David Sloan.

B.   Samuel Maxwell married Julia Keels.

C.   Harriet Maxwell married Dr. Baylis Earle.

D.   Mary Maxwell—died unmarried.

E.   Baylis Maxwell—died unmarried.

F.   Eliza Maxwell married Dr. Thos. Lewis, son of Overton Lewis.   (See Lewis Family.)

G.   Dr. John H. Maxwell married Mary Alexander —no issue.

H.   Emily Maxwell married Joe Waymon.

I.   Martha Maxwell married John Keels.

J.   Annie Maxwell married Maj. Benjamin Sloan.

K.   Miriam Maxwell—unmarried.

B.   Samuel Maxwell and wife, Julia (Keels) Maxwell, had the following children:

a.   Frank Maxwell married Kate Sloan, daughter of Thos. Sloan.

b.   Keels Maxwell married Maud Shelton.

c.   Sue Maxwell married Dr. Thos. J. Pickens, son of Col. T. J. Pickens.   (See Pickens Family.)

a.   Frank Maxwell and wife, Kate (Sloan) Maxwell had the following children:

Kate Maxwell married Edmund Cudworth.

Nanny Maxwell married Ramie Hughes.

George K. Maxwell married Miss Hutchinson.

Traynham Maxwell—unmarried.

Julia Maxwell married James Ansel.

Annie Maxwell married Frank Crawford.

Frank L. Maxwell—unmarried.

Samuel E. Maxwell—unmarried.

Sue Conyers Maxwell—unmarried.

b.   Keels Maxwell and wife, Maud (Sheldon) Maxwell, had the following children:

Sue Maxwell married Charles Neild.

Mary Maxwell married Wm. Nix.

Samuel E. Maxwell—unmarried.

John H. Maxwell—unmarried.

Fannie Maxwell married ———— Ferguson.

Thomas P. Maxwell—unmarried.

Jesse Maxwell married Miss Murphy.

Julia Maxwell—unmarried.

Lucian Maxwell—Unmarried.

Olive Maxwell—unmarried.

C.   Harriet Maxwell and husband, Dr. Baylis Earle, had one child:

a.   Theron Earle married Miss Price.

H.   Emily Maxwell and husband, Joseph Waymon, had two children:

a.   Samuel Waymon, married.

b.   Josephine Waymon married Mr. Houston.

I.   Martha Maxwell and husband, John Keels, had the following children:

a.   Fannie Keels married Dr. Swandale.

b.   John Keels—unmarried.

c.   Sue Keels married John G. Capers.

d.   Emily Keels married Frank Capers.

J.   Annie Maxwell and her husband, Maj. Benjamin Sloan, had one child, Annie Sloan who married Bradshaw Beverly, of Virginia. She died and left one son, Benjamin Sloan Beverly.

2.   Robert A. Maxwell and wife, Mary Prince Earle, had the following children:

A.   Robert A. Maxwell, Jr.,—unmarried.

B.   Anna M. Maxwell married Maj. John D. Wright, died in Confederate War.

C.   Harriet Earle Maxwell—unmarried.

D.   Maria Louisa Maxwell married Col. Thos. J. Warren—killed in Confederate war.

E.   Mary E. Maxwell married Prof. J. R. Blake— no issue.

F.   Priestly Maxwell—died unmarried.

G.   T. Edward Maxwell—killed in Confederate War.

B.   Anna M. Maxwell and her husband, Maj. John D. Wright, had two children, Richard M. Wright and Maria Louisa Wright, both of whom died unmarried.

D.   Maria Louisa Maxwell and her husband, Col. Thomas J. Warren, had three children:

a.   Robert   Maxwell   Warren—unmarried—killed on railroad train.

b.   Elizabeth Taylor Warren—unmarried.

c.   Mary Earle Warren married William P. Pickens, son of Col. T. J. Pickens.

c.   Mary Earle Warren and her husband, William P. Pickens, have one child, Robert Warren Pickens.

II.   Mary (Anderson) Maxwell, after the death of her husband, Capt. Robert Maxwell, married a Mr. Corrouth and they had one child, Louisa Corrouth, who married General Gilliam, of Greenwood, S. C.—no issue.

V.   Robert Anderson, Jr., and his wife, Maria Thomas, had the following children:

1.   Martha Anderson married   Samuel   Bonneau Pickens, grandson of Gen. A. Pickens—no issue.

2.   Robert Anderson married Mary Barksdae Pickens, grand-daughter of Gen. A. Pickens.

3.   Thomas Anderson married Susan Jenkins, sister of Dr. William L. Jenkins.

4.   Ann Anderson married Jos. Pickens Harris, grandson of Gen. A. Pickens.   (See Harris Family.)

5.   Edmund Anderson married Miss McIver.

6.   Edward Anderson—unmarried.

7.   John Anderson married Kate Bissell.

8.   Caroline Anderson married Leroy Halsey, D. D.

9.   Julius Anderson—unmarried.

10.   William H. Anderson married Miss Burchmyer.

2.   Robert Anderson and his wife, Mary Barksdale Pickens, grand-daughter of General Pickens, had the following children:

A.   Eliza Anderson.

B.   Mary Anderson.

C.   Maria Anderson

D.   Annie Anderson.

E.   Kizzie Anderson.

F.   Susan Anderson.

G.   Pickens Anderson.

H.   Septima Anderson.

I.   Robert Anderson.

J.   Kate Anderson.

K.   Barksdale Anderson.

L.   Rosalie Anderson.

3.   Thomas Anderson and wife, Susan (Jenkins) Anderson, had the following children:

A.   Martha J. Anderson.

B.   Robert Anderson.

C.   Thomas Anderson.

D.   William Anderson.

E.   Julius Anderson.

F.   Annie Anderson.

5.   Edmund Anderson and wife, Miss McIver, had one daughter who married Rev. W. A. Rogers.

7.   John Anderson and wife, Kate (Bissell) Anderson, had the following children:

A.   Robert Maxwell Anderson.

B.   Bissell Anderson.

C.   Edward Anderson.

D.   Claudia Anderson.

E.   Samuel Pickens Anderson.

8.   Caroline Anderson and husband, Rev. Leroy Halsey, had the following children:

A.   John Halsey.

B.   Martha Halsey.

C.   Leroy Halsey (2)

D.   Lucy Halsey.

E.   Samuel Pickens Halsey.

10.   William H. Anderson and wife, Miss Burchmyer, had one son, Samuel Pickens Anderson.

Capt. James Anderson, brother of Gen. Robert Anderson, and wife, Agnes Craig, had eleven children, seven daughters and four sons, all of whom are dead and their children have removed to other states, except

Dr. William Anderson. Dr.William Anderson married Mary McE. Hunter (Mary Hunter was a daughter of Thomas and Sarah Gilkie Hunter. This was a brother of John Hunter and came from Ireland) 'and resided at the place called Orrville, ten miles east of Pendleton. He was a noted man, of large means. His children were:

A.   R. Harrison Anderson married ——— Miss Mc-Conn, daughter of H. McConn.

B.   W. Anderson.

C.   Mrs. S. C. McLees, of South Carolina.

D.   Mrs. R. H. Reid, of South Carolina.

E.   Mrs. Ann E. Tarrant, of South Carolina.

F.   Mrs. Eliza C. Orr,of Atlanta, Ga.

G.   Mrs. A. L. Burkhead, of Virginia.

H.   Mrs. Augusta V. Anderson, of Alabama.

I.   Miss Belle Anderson, of Alabama—unmarried.

The other two brothers of Gen. Robert Anderson and Capt. James Anderson were william Anderson who moved to Kentucky and Andrew remained at the old homestead in Virginia. All four brothers were officers in the Revolutionary War.

A.   R. Harrison Anderson and wife, Josephine (McConn) Anderson, had the following children:

a.   Ida N. Anderson married J. D. Smith.

b.   Hampton G. Anderson married Olive Brown.

c.   Julius H. Anderson married Mary Norris.

d.   Minnie M. Anderson Married Dr. M. A. Thompson.

e.   Wm. DeWitte Anderson—unmarried.

HUNTER FAMILY.

——— Hunter married Mary McEldownie. They lived and died in Ireland. They had a number of children, one John Hunter, who came to Carlisle, Pennsylvania, and died there.   John Hunter married, first, Margaret ———, 1774, and had three children:

I.   Dr. William Hunter married Ann Anderson, daughter of Gen. Robert Anderson.

II.   Jennie Hunter.

III.   James Hunter married Sarah Folk.

John Hunter married Mary Crawford in 1781 and had the following children:

IV.   Joseph Hunter.

V.   D. John Hunter married Catherine Pickens, daughter of Gen. Andrew Pickens.

VI.   Margaret Hunter.

VII.   Mary Hunter—never married—was a noted school mistress in Pendleton.

VIII.   Thomas Hunter.

IX.   Robert Hunter.

X.   Cyrus and Crawford Hunter—twins (died).

XI.   Joseph Crawford Hunter.

XII.   Mandana Hunter—never married.

XIII.   Etherlinda Hunter—never married.

XIV.   Cyrus Hunter.

I.   Dr. William Hunter and wife, Ann (Anderson) Hunter, had the following children.

1.   Wm. Hunter married first ———; second, Miss McFall—no issue.

2.   John Hunter—unmarried.

3.   Ann Hunter married ——— Smith.

4.   Mary Hunter married Rev. David Humphreys —no issue.

5.   Andrew Hunter married Mary Simpson.

5.   Andrew Hunter and wife, Mary (Simpson) Hunter, had the following children:

A.   William Simpson Hunter married Nina D. Lewis, daughter of J. J. Lewis.

B.   Mary Alice Hunter married E. B. Farmer.

C.   Agnes L. Hunter married J. L. Farmer.

D.   Annie M. Hunter—unmarried.

A.   William Simpson Hunter and wife, Nina D. (Lewis) Hunter had the following children:
a.   Carrie Lewis Hunter.
b.   May Reamer Hunter—dead.
c.   Sue Ellen Hunter.
d.   Annie Hunter.

B.   Mary Alice Hunter and her husband, E. B. Farmer, had the following children:
a.   Mary Hunter Farmer.
b.   Cathline B. Farmer.
c.   Louise Farmer.
d.   Andrew E. Farmer.
e.   Nina Lewis Farmer.
f.   Alice Farmer.
g.   Nathaniel Farmer.
h.   Edwin Farmer.

C.   Agnes L. Hunter and husband, J. L. Farmer, had the following children:
a.   W. Frank Farmer.
b.   Mary Reamer Farmer.
c.   Annie Hunter Farmer.
d.   James L. Farmer.
e.   Robert Farmer.
f.   Joseph Simpson Farmer.
g.   Lewis Hunter Farmer.
h.   Wm. Anderson Farmer.

III.   James Hunter and wife, Sarah (Folk) Hunter had the following children:
1.   Sarah Ann Hunter married Carter Clayton.
2.   John Folk Hunter—never married. Command-ed a regiment from Pennsylvania in Mexican War, was presented with a sword by the Legislature of Pennsylvania, which sword is now owned by his nephew, M. M. Hunter. He removed to Pendleton after the Mexican War.

3. Mary Crawford Hunter—never married.
4. William Hunter married Sallie Ellenburg.
5. Thomas Hunter—unmarried.
6. James Hunter married Eliza Norton.
7. Etherlinda Hunter married Madison Barton—
no issue.
8. Susan Hunter married John McDaniel.
9. ——— Hunter married Emily Haiium.

6. James Hunter and wife, Eliza (Norton) Hunter,
had the following children:
A. Virginia Eliza Hunter married J. C. Stribling.
B. J. Norton Hunter married Nettie Pinkhind.
C. James T. Hunter married Eliza Earle Gaiiiard.
D. Miles M. Hunter married Pauline Gaillard.
E. Elizabeth S. Hunter married E. L. C. Terrie

A. Virginia Eliza Hunter and her husband, J. C.
Stribling, had the following children:
a. Harry Lee Stribling married Ella M. Osborne,
of Atlanta.
b. Jesse C. Stribling married Meta Henshall.
c. James Hunter Stribling—unmarried.
d. Mary Eliza Stribling—unmarried.
e. Thomas E. Stribling—died unmarried.
f. Elizabeth Stribling—unmarried.
g. Roxie Alice Stribling—unmarried.

a. Harry Lee Stribling and wife, Ella M. Osborne
Stribling, have the following children:
Augustus Lee Stribling.
Raymond W. Stribling.
Robert Stribling.

B. J. Norton Hunter and wife, Nettie (Pinkhind)
Hunter, have one child, Aneska Hunter.

C. James T. Hunter and wife, Eliza E. (Gaillard)
Hunter, have the following children:
a. Thomas Earle Hunter—died unmarried.

b.   James William Hunter married Kate Skinner, of Raleigh, N. C.

c.   Miles Norton Hunter—unmarried.

d.   Sallie Gaillard Hunter—died unmarried.

e.   Louise Hunter—unmarried.

D.   Miles M. Hunter and wife, Pauline (Gaillard) Hunter, have the following children:

a.   Bessie Hunter.

b.   Ben Gaillard Hunter.

c.   Ralph Hunter.

d.   Sallie Sloan Hunter.

e.   James Hunter.

f.   Pauline Hunter.

g.   Miles Hunter.

E.   Elizabeth S. Hunter and husband, E. L. C. Terrie, have the following children:

a.   Edwin L. Terrie.

b.   James Hunter Terrie.

c.   Nettie Pinkhind Terrie.

ROSS FAMILY.

Rev. Anthony Ross, a Presbyterian minister, came from North Carolina to Pendleton early in the eighteenth century. He married Elizabeth Whitner, daughter of Joseph Whitner, the boy emigrant, and twin sister of Judge Joseph N. Whitner. They had the following children:

I.   Anna E. Ross married Col. Frank E. Harrison. (See Harrison Family.)

II.   Joseph Whitner Ross—died unmarried.

III.   Henry Ross—died unmarried.

IV.   Anthony W. Ross married Miss McCown of Marion, S. C.

V.   Julius N. Ross—killed in the Confederate War —unmarried.

VI.   Sarah Ross married W. Y. Miller.

IV.   Anthony W. Ross and wife, Miss (McCown) Ross, had one child:

1.   Henry Ross.

VI.   Sarah Ross and husband, W. Y. Miller, had the following children:

1.   Willie Miller married J. T. Price—no issue.

2.   Nettie Miller married Dr. F. L. Narramore —no issue.

3.   Julius Ross Miller married Mary Mattison.

4.   Joseph W. Miller—unmarried.

3.   Julius Ross Miller and wife, Mary Mattison, had the following children:

A.   Lydia M. Miller.

B.   Edith Miller.

C.   William Y. Miller, Jr.

NEWTON FAMILY.

Isaac Newton and wife, Sarah Spicu, were residents of Caroline County, Virginia. When their eldest son, Willis, was fourteen years of age (that is 1815) they removed to South Carolina and settled a few miles east of Pendleton. They had the following children:

I.   Willis Newton married first, Ruth Swords; second, Widow Dickson.

II.   Patsy Newton.

III.   Catherine Newton.

IV.   Frances Newton.

V.   Isaac Newton.

I.   Willis Newton and Ruth (Swords) Newton had the following children:

1.   Mary Newton married, first, Warren Forsyth; second, John Hinton.

2.   Larkin Newton married Ruth Welborn.

3.   John S. Newton married Eveline Neighbors.

4.   Sarah Newton married ———— Johnson.

2.   Larkin Newton and wife, Ruth (Welborn) New-
ton, had the following children:
A.   J. C. C. Newton married Letty Lay.
B.   Marion Newton married Ellen Martin.
C.   Josephus Newton married Alice Boggs.
D.   Olivia Newton married J. W. Evatt.
E.   Julius Newton married, first, Florrie Carson;
second, Miss Ellis.
F.   Lula Newton married W. H. Martin.
G.   Henry Newton.

A.   Rev. J. C. C. Newton, of the Methodist Church,
has been for years a missionary in Japan.   He and his
wife, Letty (Lay) Newton, have the following children:
(Could not get data)

C.   Josephus Newton and wife,   Alice   (Boggs)
Newton, have the following children:
(Could not get data.)

B.   Marion Newton and wife, Ellen (Martin) Newton, had the following children:
(Could not get data.)

F.   Lula F. Newton and her husband, W. H. Mar-
Newton, had the following children:
(Could not get data.)

3.   John S. Newton and wife, Eveline (Neighbors)
Newton, had the following children:
A.   Matilda Newton married J. W. Evatt.
B.   Sarah R. Newton married M. B. Richardson.
C.   Leard Newton married Mary Boggs.
D.   Annie Newton married C. J. Boggs.
E.   Emmie J. Newton—unmarried.
F.   J.   Willis Newton   married Lillie Reeves—no
issue.
G.   J. Calhoun Newton married Alice Day.

B. Sarah R. Newton and husband, M. B. Richard-son, had the following children:
a. Henry Richardson.
b. Effie Richarson married Andrea—had one child.
c. Sallie Richardson.

C. Leard Newton and wife, Mary (Boggs) Newton, had the following children:
a. Eva Newton.
b. Bessie Newton.
c. Wilmer Newton.
d. Nellie Newton.
e. Alice Beth Newton.
f. Blanche Newton.

D. Annie Newton and husband, C. J. Boggs, have the following children:
a. DeWitt Boggs.
b. Annie Lee Boggs.
c. Ruth Boggs.

G. I. Calhoun Newton and wife, Alice Lay Newton, have one child:
a. Ellen Newton.

4. Sarah Newton and husband ——— Johnson, had the following children:
A. Sedgwick Johnson married Ellen Brewer.
B. John Thomas Johnson.

A. Sedgwick Johnson and wife, Ellen (Brewer) Johnson, had the following children:
a. Lizzie Johnson married Joseph Bates.
b. James Johnson—died unmarried.
c. Edward Johnson.
d. Hampton Johnson married Della Harris.
e. May Johnson married S. E. Whitten.
f. Bessie Johnson.
g. Gertrude Johnson.
h. Grayton Johnson.

e.   May Johnson and husband, S. E. Whitten, have three children:
Thelma Whitten.
Allie Whitten.
May Whitten.

GENERAL ANDREW PICKENS.

(This sketch was taken from the obituary of General Pickens published in the Pendleton Messenger on the 27th day of August, 1817.)

Was born in Buck County, Pennsylvania, September 13, 1739, and died August 11th, 1817. His ancestors left France after the Edict of Nantes. They went first to Scotland, then to Ireland and then to America. The family then removed to Augusta County, Virginia, and soon after to the Waxhaws in South Carolina before he had attained the age of manhood. In 1761 he served as a volunteer with Moultrie and Marion, in a bloody but successful expedition under Colonel Grant against the Cherokees. After the termination of that war he removed to Long Cane settlement in Abbeville. At an early period he took a positive stand against Great Britain, and at the commencement of the war was appointed captain of militia; rose to Major, Colonel and Brigadier General. In the most despondent period of the war with such leaders as Sumter and Marion he kept up the spirit of resistance against the British, Tories and Indians. In 1781 he commanded in chief the expedition against the Cherokees in the northwest corner of the State and such was his success in a short time he so subdued the spirit of that then powerful nation that a peace so permanent was effected that it since has not been disturbed. He fought at Cowpens, Eutaw, King's Mountain, and in many minor engagements both with British and Indians. In fact he stood as a power of strength, and was the great protector of all the Whig settlers in upper South Carolina. Peace being restored he served his country continuously in some public office until 1801. He made a treaty with the Cherokees by which that territory embraced in the counties of Greenville, Anderson, Pickens, and Oconee was ceded to the State. This treaty was made at Hopewell on the banks of the Seneca River nearby Cherry's Crossing on the Blue Ridge Railroad. Soon after this treaty General Pickens removed to Hopewell and erected a dwelling on the hill a short distance from the tree under which the treaty was made. He owned a large body of land on Seneca River, the lower part of which he subsequently gave to his son, Ezekiel Pickens. He served in the State Convention, in the Legislature and in Congress. He was appointed Major General of militia. While residing at Hopewell, he with Gen. Robert Anderson, built the first Presbyterian Church near where the old Stone Church now stands. When Pendleton District was formed he was one of the county judges, and held the first court ever held therein. About what time he removed to his beautiful and valuable farm, Tomassee, now in Oconee County, is not known, but he was evidently residing there when the war of 1812 broke out. In this emergency he was again pressed into public service. He accepted a seat in the Legislature and was pressed to accept the office of Governor at this eventful crisis, which he declined because he thought the office should be left to more youthful hands. He died August 11th, 1817, and was buried at the Old Stone Church. Early in life General Pickens married Rebecca Calhoun, March 19th, 1765, a sister of John Ewing Calhoun who was a senator in Congress, and the daughter of Ezekiel Calhoun, the brother of Patrick Calhoun. They had a numerous family:

I.   Mary Pickens married John Harris.

II.   Ezekiel Pickens married, first, Elizabeth Bonneau; second, Eliza Barksdale.

III.   Ann Pickens married John Simpson—moved away.

IV. Jane Pickens married Dr. John Miller—moved to Mississippi.

V. Margaret Pickens married Dr. George Bowie —moved to Alabama.

VI. Andrew Pickens married, first, Susan Wilkinson; second, Mary Nelson, of Virginia—no issue.

VII. Rebecca Pickens married William Noble, son of Maj. Alexander Noble.

VIII. Catherine Pickens married Dr. John Hunter —moved to Alabama.

IX. Joseph Pickens married Caroline Henderson —moved to Alabama.

I. Mary Pickens and her husband, John Harris, had the following children:
1. Andrew Harris.
2. John Harris.
3. Rebecca Harris.
4. Mary Harris.
5. Ezekiel Harris.
6. Nathaniel Harris.
7. Thomas Harris.
8. Joseph Harris.
9. Eliza Harris.
10. Benjamin Harris.

II. Ezekiel Pickens and wife, Elizabeth (Bonneau) Pickens, had the following children: (Elizabeth Bonneau was a sister to Floride Bonneau who married Col. John Ewing Calhoun and whose daughter married John C. Calhoun.)

1. Ezekiel Pickens (Second)—unmarried.
2. Samuel Pickens married Martha Anderson—no issue—moved to Alabama.
3. Andrew Pickens—accidentally shot.
4. Elizabeth Pickens married Gov. Patrick Noble.

4.   Elizabeth Pickens and husband, Gov. Patrick Noble, had the following children:

A.   Ezekiel Noble.

B.   Floride Noble.

C.   Patrick Noble.

D.   Edward Noble.

E.   Alexander Noble.

F.   Elizabeth Noble.

G.   Samuel Noble.

II.   Ezekiel Pickens and his second wife, Eliza (Barksdale) Pickens, had the following children:

1.   Thomas J. Pickens married Kizziah A. Miles.

2.   Andrew Pickens married, first, Agnes Bell; second, Mary Boone.

3.   Mary Pickens married Robert Anderson, grandson of Gen. Robert Anderson.

1.   Col. Thomas J. Pickens married K. A. (Miles) Pickens and had the following children:

A.   Dr. Thomas J. Pickens married Sue Maxwell.

B.   Eliza D. Pickens—unmarried.

C.   J. Miles Pickens—unmarried.

D.   Ezekiel Pickens—died unmarried.

E.   Col. Samuel B. Pickens married Anna Ingraham.

F.   Anna Pickens married Jerry Miles.

G.   Mary Pickens married Dr. Chas. Davant—no issue.

H.   Andrew Pickens—died unmarried.

I.   Kizzie Pickens married Frank Waring.

J.   Francis Pickens married Lou Pickens, of Alabama.

• NOTE—Maj. Alexander Noble married Catherine Calhoun, daughter of Ezekiel Calhoun and sister of Rebecca, wife of Gen. Andrew Pickens. Their children were William, John, Ezekiel, Patrick, Catherine, Alexander and Joseph. William Noble married Rebecca, daughter of Gen. Andrew Pickens. Patrick, his brother, married Elizabeth, daughter of Ezekiel Pickens, son of Gen. Andrew Pickens.

K.   Patrick Pickens married, first, Miss Pettigrew;
second, Annie Waring.

L.   Wm. P. Pickens married Mary Warren.

A.   Dr. Thos. J. Pickens and wife, Sue (Maxwell)
Pickens, had the following children:

a.   Samuel Pickens married Nellie Trowbridge.

b.   Julia Pickens married William Gaillard—no
issue.

c.   Sue Conyers Pickens married Julius A. Shanklin.   (See Shanklin Family.)

a.   Samuel Pickens married Nellie Trowbridge and
they have the following children:

Joel C. Pickens.

Thomas T. Pickens.

Samuel M. Pickens, Jr.

Jessie C. Pickens.

Phillip A. Pickens.

Nellie Sue Pickens.

Julia Eliza Pickens.

E.   Col. Samuel B. Pickens and wife, Anna (Ingraham) Pickens, had the following children:

a.   Mary Pickens married James Simons.

b.   Eliza Pickens—unmarried.

c.   Emily Pickens—unmarried.

d.   Anna Belle Pickens.

e.   Floride Pickens.

f.   Hallie Pickens.

F.   Anna Pickens and husband, Jerry Miles, have
the following children:

a.   Allen Miles.

b.   Jerry Miles.

c.   Samuel Miles.

I.   Kizzie Pickens and husband, Frank Waring,
have one child:

a.   Kizzie Waring.

J.   Francis Pickens and wife, Lou (Pickens) Pick·
ens, have the following children:
(Could not get data.)

K.   Patrick Pickens and second wife, Annie Waring Pickens, have the following children:
(No data.)

L.   William P. Pickens and wife, Mary (Warren)
Pickens, have the following children:
a.   Robert Warren Pickens.

2.   Andrew Pickens and first wife, Agnes (Bell)
Pickens, had three children:
A.   Ezekiel Pickens—died unmarried.
B.   Rebecca Pickens married Captain Sally, of
Orangeburg.
C.   Eliza Pickens—unmarried.

2.   Andrew Pickens and second wife, Mary (Boon)
Pickens, had two children:
A.   Andrew Pickens.
B.   Mary Pickens.

3.   Mary Pickens and husband, Robert Anderson,
had fourteen children.   (See Anderson Family.)

III.   Ann Pickens, born 1770, and husband, John
Simpson, had the following children:
1.   Leah Simpson.
2.   Rebecca Simpson.
3.   Andrew Simpson.
4.   John Simpson.
5.   Ezekiel Simpson.
6.   Jane Simpson.

IV.   Jane Pickens and husband, Dr. John Miller,
had the following children:
1.   Robert Miller.
2.   John Miller.
3.   Eliza Miller.

V. Margaret Pickens and husband, Dr. George Bowie, had children:

1. Louisa Bowie.

VI. Gov. Andrew Pickens and first wife, Susan (Wilkinson) Pickens, had the following children.

1. Gov. Francis W. Pickens, married first, Miss Simpkins; second, Miss Marion Dearing; third, Miss Lucy Holcombe.

2. Susan Pickens married James M. Calhoun— moved to Alabama.

1. Gov. Francis W. Pickens married, first; Eliza Simpkins; second, Marion Dearing; and third, Lucy Holcombe.

Children by first marriage are:

A. Susan Pickens.

B. Eliza Pickens.

C. Maria Pickens.

D. Eldred Pickens.

Children by second marriage are:

A. Jeannie Pickens married Mitchell Whaley.

Children by the third wife are:

A. Douskah Pickens married Dr. Dugas. They had two children:

a. Lucy Dugas married B. R. Tillman, Jr.

b. Dolly Dugas married J. C. Sheppard, Jr.

2. Susan Pickens and husband, Jas. M. Calhoun, had the following children:

A. Andrew Calhoun.

B. Susan Calhoun.

C. Francis Calhoun.

D. Sarah Calhoun.

E. John Calhoun.

VII. Rebecca Pickens and husband, Wm. Noble, had the following children:

1. William Noble—married.

2. Andrew Noble—married.
3. Ezekiel Noble.
4. Samuel Noble
5. Joseph Noble.

VIII. Catherine Pickens and husband, Dr. John Hunter, had the following children:
1. Maria Hunter.
2. Margaret Hunter.
3. Eliza Hunter.
4. Andrew Hunter.
5. Ezekiel Hunter.
6. Joseph Hunter.

IX. Joseph Pickens and wife, Caroline (Henderson) Pickens, had the following children:
1. Sarah Pickens.
2. Rebecca Pickens.
3. Joseph Pickens.
4. Henderson Pickens.
5. Andrew Pickens.

OWEN FAMILY.

Obediah Owen married Patsy Ford and had the following children:
I. Nancy Owen married Dr. Estes (Micaja).
II. Kiszice Owen married Fant Forbes.
III. Cinthia Owen married Wm. Brewer.
IV. Jane Owen married Jesse Martin.
V. Lavisa Owen married John Banks.
VI. Elijah Owen married Patsy Kelly.
VII. Wm. Owen married Tabetha Brewer.
VIII. John Owen married Catherine Owen.
IX. Joshua Owen married Drucilla Watson.
IX. John Owen and wife, Catherine Owen, had no children.

John Owen married the second time, Judy R. Owen, and they had four children:

1. W. F. C. Owen married Miss Sharp.
2. E. Lee Owen married Miss Hammond.
3. Ada Owen married W. G. Wilson.
4. Theo. Owen married Augustus Mitchel.

1. W. F. C. Owen and wife, Miss Sharp, had the following children:

A. Raymond Owen.
B. Harrold Owen.
C. Ralph Owen.
D. Ruth Owen.
E. Vera Owen.
F. Fred Owen.

2. E. Lee Owen and wife, Miss Hammond, had the following children:

A. John Owen.
B. Clifton L. Owen.
C. Dessie R. Owen.
D. Meta Owen.
E. E. Lee Owen, Jr.

3. Ada Owen and husband, W. G. Wilson, have the following children:

A. O. E. Wilson.
B. James T. Wilson.
C. Wm. W. Wilson.
D. Lelia A. Wilson.
E. Wilton G. Wilson.
F. Eva D. Wilson.
G. Lawrence G. Wilson.
H. U. G. Wilson.

4. Theodocia Owen and husband, Augustus Mitchel, have the following children:

A. Olin O. Mitchel.
B. Jane A. Mitchel.

C.   Judy R. Mitchel.
D.   Percy A. Mitchel.
E.   Edna Mitchel.

MARTIN FAMILY.

Edmond Martin married Katherine Crenshaw and moved from Virginia, 1803, and settled on Six-and-Twenty-Mile Creek.   He had the following children:
I.   Johnson Martin married Polly Brewer.
II.   Jesse Martin married Jane Owen.
III.   Edmund Martin married Cynthia Robertson.
IV.   Anderson Martin married Lucinda Elliott.
V.   Stephen Martin married, first, Sophrony Ford; second, Rosa McKinney.
VI.   Mary Martin married Wm. Ford.
VII.   Jane Martin married B. F. Evatt.

II.   Jesse Martin and wife, Jane (Owen) Martin, had the following children:
1.   Warren J. Martin married, first, Mary J. Watkins; second, Sarah M. Reeves.
2.   N. E. Martin married Matthew Crenshaw.
3.   Martha C. Martin—never married.
4.   Newton T. Martin married Mary Lay.
5.   Martha C. Martin married W. C. Mullinix.
6.   Wm. A. Martin married Rebecca J. Fielding.
7.   Berry T. Martin married Mary McPhail.
8.   Lavisa Martin—never married.

1.   Warren J. Martin and wife, Mary J. (Watkins) Martin, have the following children:
A.   Ellen J. Martin married Marion W. Newton.
B.   Amanda Martin married James L. Crenshaw.
C.   Savilla J. Martin married James F. Lay.
D.   Georgia Ann Martin married W. A. Boggs.
E.   Holbert J. Martin—unmarried.
F.   Munro L. Martin married Della Hamilton.

G.   Felix B. Martin married Corry Webb.

A.   Ellen J. Martin and husband, Marion W. Newton, have twelve children as follows:
Oscar, Silas, Jane, Sarah, Clayton, Henry, Mary, Ruth, and others—names unknown.

B.   Amanda Martin and husband, Jas. L. Crenshaw, have the following children:
   a.   Rula Jane Crenshaw.
   b.   Jesse Crenshaw.
   c.   Martin L. Crenshaw.
   d.   Bluford Crenshaw.

C.   Savilla J. Martin and husband, James F. Lay, have the following children:
   a.   Mary E. Lay.
   b.   Birdie J. Lay.
   c.   Sallie Lay.
   d.   James F. Lay.

D.   Georgia Ann Martin and husband, W. A. Boggs, have the following children:
   a.   Claude Boggs.
   b.   Norman Boggs.

F.   Munro L. Martin and wife, Della (Hamilton) Martin, have the following children:
   a.   Edgar Martin.
   b.   Fanny Belle Martin.
   c.   Leonard Martin.

G.   Felix B. Martin and wife, Corry (Webb) Martin, have the following children:
   (No data).

2.   Nancy E. Martin and husband, Matthew Crenshaw, have the following children:
   A.   Lemuel Crenshaw married Mattie Boggs.
   B.   Lou Crenshaw married Samuel P. Hall.   (See Hall Family).

4. Newton T. Martin and wife, Mary (Lay) Martin, have the following children:
A. Charles Martin.
B. Jesse Martin.
C. Mary Martin.
D. Walter Martin.
E. James Martin.

5. Martha C. Martin and husband, W. C. Mullinix, have the following children:
A. James Mullinix.
B. William C. Mullinix.

7. Berry T. Martin and wife, Mary McPhail, have the following children:
A. Mac Martin.
B. Gus Martin.
C. William Martin.
D. Clarence Martin.
E. Lizzie Martin.
F. Melvina Martin.
G. Lois Martin.

6. Wm. A. Martin and wife, Rebecca (Fielding) Martin, had one child:
A. W. Henry Martin married Lula Newton.

TRESCOT.

William Henry Trescot was born on one of the islands on the coast of South Carolina and removed to Pendleton, where he died and was buried in the Episcopal churchyard in Pendleton. His father was Henry Trescot, and his mother was Sarah McCrady. He married Eliza N. Cuthbert, daughter of Thomas Heyward Cuthbert and his wife, Eliza N. Barnwell. Mr. Trescot was the Assistant Secretary of State under President Buchanan and was acting Secretary of State when South

Carolina seceded. He resigned his office and returned to South Carolina. He never sought office. He was an author of distinction and an international lawyer of reputation. He negotiated many valuable and important treaties and was the author of the inscription on the mon-- ument erected to the memory of the Confederate dead in Columbia, which beautifully describes the patriotic impulses that governed his faith and actions.

William Henry Trescot and his wife, Eliza N. (Cuthbert) Trescot, had seven children, namely:

I. Stephen Barnwell Trescot married Elizabeth Worthington.

II. Thomas Cuthbert Trescot—unmarried.

III. Henry S. Trescot married Ella Holmes.

IV. Wm. Bull Trescot—died unmarried.

V. Edward Amory Trescot—unmarried.

VI. Katherine B. Trescot—unmarried.

VII. Sarah McCrady Trescot—unmarried.

I. Stephen Barnwell Trescot and his wife, Elizabeth (Worthington) Trescot, had the following children :

1. Wm. Henry Trescot—died in infancy.

2. Bessie Trescot—unmarried.

3. Stephenena Trescot—unmarried.

III. Henry S. Trescot and his wife, Ella (Holmes) Trescot, have the following children:

1. Harry Trescot.

2. John Trescot.

3. Warley Trescot.

WARLEY FAMILY.

Jacob Warley married Sophia Fraser and had the following children:

I. Jacob Warley—died unmarried.

II. Capt. Alex. Warley married, first, Miss Emily Forrest; second, Miss Isabella Huger.

III.   Sophia Warley married F. D. Wagner—no issue.

IV.   Elizabeth Warley married, first Mr. Schuttz;
second, Mr. Bourne—no issue.

V.   Hamilton Warley—died unmarried.

VI.   Col. Frederick Warley married Miss Rowena
Law—no issue.   Killed in Confederate War.

VII.   Anna Warley married John H. Holmes.

VIII.   Ella Warley married T. D. Wagner.

IX.   Felix Warley—died unmarried.

II.   Capt. Alex. Warley and wife, Miss Huger, have
the following children:

1.   Allen Warley.

2.   Sophia Warley.

3.   Theodore Warley.

4.   Felix Warley.

VII.   Anna Warley and husband, John H. Holmes,
have the following children:

1.   Henry Holmes married Miss Gibbs—no issue.

2.   Edward Holmes—died unmarried.

3.   Ella Holmes married Henry S. Trescot.   (See
Trescot Family.)

4.   Emmie Holmes married Legare Walker.

5.   Felix Holmes married Miss Kate Bonneau—issue, three children.   Marie Anna Holmes; Felix Cheves
Holmes; Catherine Warley Holmes.

6.   Fredericka Holmes married Dr. A. C. Strick-
land—no issue.

7.   Wm. Holmes married Miss Sue Pope.

4.   Emmie Holmes and her husband, Legare Walker,
have the following children:

A.   Emily St. P. Walker.

B.   Ruth Holmes Walker.

7.   Wm. Holmes and wife, Sarah (Pope) Holmes,
have the following children:

A.   Susie Marian Holmes.

B. John H. Holmes.

C. Anna W. Holmes.

VIII. Ella Warley and her husband, T. D. Wagner, had the following children:

1. Anna Wagner married W. H. Talley.

2. Ella Wagner married Clayton Woods.

3. Dora Wagner married E. O. Woods.

STRIBLING FAMILY.

Thomas Stribling came to America in 1710 and set-tled in Stafford County, Virginia. Died 1755. In 1715 he married Elizabeth, a daughter of John Taliaferro and his wife, Sarah (Smith) Taliaferro. He had a number of children, but their names are unknown because of the loss of his will. Robert Taliaferro, Jr., a brother of Eliz-abeth, mentions her three eldest sons in his will, dated 1725 and probated 1726. The three sons named are Francis, William and Taliaferro Stribling, but there is no doubt but he had other children, one of whom was Thomas Stribling, the progenitor of the South Carolina Striblings.—McIlhany's Stribling Family, p. 86.

Francis Stribling married Dorothy ———— and re-mained in Virginia, and nothing is known of him.

William never married.

Taliaferro married Elizabeth ———— and had six children: Francis, Taliaferro, Ann, Thomas, William and John Stribling. Thomas Stribling, the progenitor of the South Carolina Striblings, son of Thomas and Elizabeth (Taliaferro) Stribling, was born in Prince William Coun-ty, Va., about 1730, and about 1750 moved to South Caro-lina, and settled on Seneca River, in old Pendleton Dis-trict, his home being in that part now Anderson County. He married Nancy Kinchelae and had four children:

I. Thomas Stribling married Elizabeth Haile.

II. Jesse Stribling married Elizabeth Sloan, daugh-ter of David Sloan and wife, Susan (Majors) Sloan.

III.   Lucy Stribling married ———— Trimmier.

IV.   Nancy Stribling married ———— Tate.

I.   Thomas Stribling and his wife, Elizabeth (Haile) Stribling, had seven children:

1.   Robert Stribling married Sabra Clark.

2.   Mark M. Stribling married—unknown.

3.   Benjamin H. Stribling married Ruth B. Greenwood.

4.   Cornelius Kinchelae Stribling married Helen M. Payne.

5.   Mary Stribling married Richard Rosamond.

6.   Frances Stribling married I. J. Foster.

7.   Maria Stribling married ———— Moreland.

4.   Cornelius Kinchelae Stribling was born a few miles from Pendleton in 1796, and when only a boy of fifteen years of age ran away from his home and walked to Charleston, S. C., and went to sea.   Entered U. S. Navy as midshipman in 1812, was lieutenant in 1818, commander in 1840, captain in Mexican War, superintendent of Naval Academy in Annapolis, Md., 1850 to 1853, Commodore in 1862 and Rear Admiral in 1866. He remained in the U. S. service during the Confederate War and died in 1880 at Martinsburg, W. Va., and was buried at Washington, D. C.   He married Helen Mary Payne, of Virginia, in 1820, and had five children:

A.   Elizabeth Stribling—unmarried.

B.   Louisa Stribling—unmarried.

C.   Mary Stribling—unmarried.

D.   Cornelius Kinchelae Stribling married first, Emma Nourse; second, Ann Riddle.

E.   John Maxwell Stribling was lieutenant in U. S. Navy, resigned and joined the Confederate Navy and served under Admiral Simms.   Died of yellow fever, aged 27 years.

II.   Jesse Stribling and his wife, Elizabeth (Sloan) Stribling, had the following children:

1.   Thomas M. Stribling married Mary Jones.

2. Mary S. Stribling married Hartwell Jones.

3. William Harrison Stribling married Jane B. McKindly.

4. Rebecca C. Stribling married B. F. Kilpatrick.

5. Robt. Stribling married Ruth P. Bruce.

6. David Sloan Stribling married Anna C. Hodges.

7. Susan A. Stribling married Thomas R. Shelor.

8. M. Stokes Stribling married Anna M. Verner.

9. Nancy Trimmier Stribling married Henry N. White.

10. Elizabeth C. Stribling married Josiah Harkey.

11. Warren Webb Stribling married Emily R. Dendy.

1. Thomas M. Stribling and wife, Mary (Jones) Stribling, had the following children:

A. Jones H. Stribling—killed July 7, 1862, Confederate Army.

B. Wm. E. Stribling—killed July 6, 1862, Confederate Army.

C. Thomas J. Stribling—killed April 25, 1865, Confederate Army.

D. Martha H. Stribling married Alexander Ramsey.

E. Jesse Cornelius Stribling married Virginia Hunter.

F. Mary E. Stribling married C. L. Reid.

G. Sloan Y. Stribling married Ida Sligh.

H. Roxie A. Stribling married C. S. Reid.

I. Llewellen Stribling married Mrs. Ida Finconnon.

E. Jesse Cornelius Stribling and wife, Virginia (Hunter) Stribling, have the following children:

a. Harry L. Stribling married Ella Osborne.

b. Jesse C. Stribling, Jr., married Meta Henshall.

c. James Hunter Stribling.

d. Mary Eliza Stribling.

e. Thomas Eugene Stribling—died 1894.
f. Elizabeth Stribling.
g. Roxie Alice Stribling.

STEEL FAMILY.

William Steel, son of Aaron and Violet (Alexander) Steel, was born in North Carolina and was a soldier in the Revolutionary War. He, after the war, clerked for Gen. Andrew Pickens in his store near Cherry's Bridge on Seneca River, and afterwards became a partner of General Pickens. He married Esther Love of Augusta County, Virginia. They had the following children:

I. Mary Love Steel married Gresham (Joseph.)
II. Elizabeth Steel married Elijah Alexander.
III. Aaron Steel married Nancy H. Davis
IV. William Steel married Margaret Guyton.
V. Joseph Steel—unmarried.
VI. James Steel married, first, Elizabeth Bruce; second, Sarah Davis.

I. Mary Love Steel and her husband, Joseph Gresham, had the following children:
1. William Steel Gresham.
2. Elizabeth Gresham married Joseph E. Brown, Ex-Governor and Senator of Georgia.

2. Elizabeth Gresham and her husband, Joseph E. Brown, had the following children:
A. Julius L. Brown married Fannie Fort.
B. Mary V. Brown married Dr. E. L. Connally.
C. Joseph M. Brown married Cora McCord.
D. Franklin P. Brown.
E. Elijah A. Brown married, first, Miss McBride; second, Miss Johnson.
F. Charles Brown.
G. Miss Sarah E. Brown.
H. George M. Brown married Carrie Hoyt.

II.   Elizabeth Steel and her husband, Elijah Alexander, had one daughter, Mary, now the wife of Dr. J. H. Maxwell, of Greenville, S. C.—no issue.

III.   Aaron Steel and wife, Nancy H. (Davis) Steel, had the following children:

1.   Robert A. Steel.

2.   William Davis Steel married Margaret McElroy.

IV.   William Steel and Margaret Guyton had the following children:

1.   Lou Alice Steel married Jackson, of Mississippi.

2.   Sue Steel married Evans Norris.

3.   Rebecca Steel married William Norris.

4.   Joseph Steel married Mattie Alexander.

5.   Dr. William Steel married Agnes Forbes.

6.   John Steel married Annie Owen.

7.   Anna Steel married James Miller.

8.   Myra Steel married Prof. Eli Doyle.

9.   Margaret Steel married William Harper; second, Hughes.

William Steel was a soldier in the War of 1812, was with Perry in his great victory, afterwards was taken prisoner and was carried to England.

VI.   James Steel and wife, Elizabeth (Bruce) Steel had the following children:

1.   Esther Love Steel married Rev. Joseph B. Hillhouse.

2.   James T. Steel married, first, Antoinette Dickson; second, Laura Alexander.

3.   Martha Steel married William C. Hillhouse.

4.   Robert E. Steel married, first, Eliza J. McElroy; second, Georgia Miller.

5.   Charles S. Steel married Harriett Brewster.

6.   William Love Steel married Rebecca Shelor.

VI.   James Steel and his second wife, Sarah C. Davis, had one child, Richard Henry Steel who married Nannie Gresham.

1. Esther Love Steel and husband, Rev. Joseph B Hillhouse, had the following children:
  A. Rev. James Steel Hillhouse married Belle Boaz.
  B. Idilette Hillhouse.
  C. Louis D. Hillhouse married Tessie Van Buren.
  D. William Laurens Hillhouse.
  E. Rev. Joseph B. Hillhouse, Jr.
  F. ————— married Alfred Bowden.
2. James T. Steel and second wife, Laura Alexander, had the following children:
  A. Esther Love Steel married Edwin L. C. Terrie and had one child, Harry Steel Terrie.
  B. John McN. Steel.
  C. James A. Steel married Lillian Hall.
  D. Charles M. Steel married Fannie Flint.
  E. Harry Steel.
3. Martha Steel and her husband, Wm. C. Hillhouse, had the following children:
  A. Martha A. Hillhouse married Albert W. Anderson.
  B. Wm. C. Hillhouse married Nell Thomas.
4. Robert E. Steel and wife, Eliza J. (McElroy) Steel, had one child:
  A. Elizabeth Steel married Reese Bowen.

WATKINS FAMILY.

Three brothers came from Virginia and settled on Therre-and-Twenty-Mile Creek early in 1800. I do not know their names, but one of them had Baylis Watkins, Felix Watkins, David Watkins; John and Willis went west long ago.
  I. Baylis Watkins married ————— Martin and had the following children:
    1. Jeptha Watkins.
    2. Willis Watkins married Lucinda Traynham.

3. Enoch Watkins married Martha Smith.
4. Warren Watkins—never married.
5. Chesley Watkins—never married.
6. Hester J. Watkins married Munro Smith. (See Smith Family.)
7. Tempy Ann Watkins married, first, Smith; second, Sanford Martin.

II. Joseph Watkins married a Passmore and had the following children:
1. William (called Billy) Watkins—never married.
2. David Watkins married a Martin.
3. Elliot Watkins—never married.
4. Alfred Watkins—never married.
5. Joseph Watkins—never married.
6. Annie Watkins married Zeffie Smith.
7. Rebecca Watkins—never married.
8. Jane Watkins—never married.
9. Elizabeth Watkins married James G. Douthit. (See Douthit Family.)

III. Felix Watkins married Ellen Robinson and had the following children:
1. Col. Thomas C. Watkins married Margaret Smith.
2. Baylis Watkins—never married.
3. William Watkins—never married.
4. Mary J. Watkins married Warren J. Martin. (See Martin Family.)
5. Tempy Ann Watkins married John Calvin Boggs.
6. Maudy Watkins married W. H. McMurtry.

1. Col. Thomas C. Watkins was a gallant soldier in the Confederate War and was killed in battle in Virginia. He and his wife, Margaret (Smith) Watkins, had the following children:
A. John C. Watkins married his cousin, Lizzie Smith.

B.   William W. Watkins married Margaret Garlington Simpson—no issue.

C.   Felix E. Watkins married Miss Mattison.

D.   Luther Watkins married Harriet Whitten.

E.   Mary Watkins married J. B. Douthit.

F.   Carry Watkins married J. D. McElroy—no
issue.

G.   Margaret Watkins married J. Reed Garrison.

A.   John C. Watkins, Clerk of Court for Anderson
County several years, married Elizabeth J. Smith and
they have the following children:

a.   Thos. Franklin Watkins married Miss Law.

b.   Ernest Monroe Watkins—unmarried.

c.   W. Paul Watkins—unmarried.

d.   Nellie Watkins married A. C. Lee.

e.   Ruth Watkins—unmarried.

f.   Harold Watkins—unmarried.

g.   John C. Watkins, Jr.—unmarried.

h.   W. W. Watkins, Jr.

i.   Helen Watkins.

C.   Felix E. Watkins married Miss Mattison and
has the following children:

a.   F. E. Watkins, Jr., married Miss Stephens.

b.   Charles Watkins—unmarried.

c.   Mary Stark Watkins—unmarried.

d.   Luther Watkins—unmarried.

D.   Luther Watkins married Harriet Whitten, died
about 1888, leaving the following children:

a.   Ralph Watkins—unmarried.

b.   Thos. G. Watkins—unmarried.

c.   Christopher Watkins—unmarried.

E.   Mary Watkins married J. B. Douthit and has
the following children:

a.   Maud Douthit married Joe Bell.

b.   Claude Douthit—unmarried.

c. Leora Douthit married Charles Manship of Mississippi.

d. Carrie Douthit—unmarried.

e. Gertrude Douthit—unmarried.

f. J. B. Douthit, Jr.—unmarried.

G. Margaret Watkins married J. R. Garrison and they have eight children.

McELHENNY.

Rev. James McElhenny built the four main rooms of the residence of John C. Calhoun on Fort Hill, which residence was known at the time it was purchased by Mrs. Calhoun, the widow of John Ewing Calhoun and given by her to her daughter, Mrs. John C. Calhoun, as Clergy Hall.

I. Rev. James McElhenny married Jane Moore first and had one daughter, Jane McElhenny.

I. Rev. James McElhenny married second time Mrs. Wilkinson, of John's Island, who was originally a Miss Smith. Mrs. Wilkinson by her first marriage had one daughter, Susan Wilkinson, who married Gov. Andrew Pickens, son of Gen. Andrew Pickens, who had a son, Gov. F. W. Pickens.

Rev. James McElhenny and his wife, Mrs. Wilkinson, had a daughter and a son:

1. Emily McElhenny married Lieut. Hamilton Hayne, U. S. N. Their son was Paul Hamilton Hayne, the poet.

2. Moreton McElhenny married and left two daughters:

A. Ada McElhenny.

B. Susan McElhenny—never married.

A. Ada McElhenny was talented and went upon the stage, married a foreigner and was lost at sea.

GAILLARD.

Charles Gaillard came from Charleston and settled near the place afterwards known as the R. C. L. Gaillard old home place. He married Sarah Du Pree. They had the following children:

I. Ann Gaillard married Peyton Holleman.

II. C. L. Gaillard married, first, Ann Gaillard: second, Elizabeth Dart; third, Alethia Hammond.

III. Rebecca Gaillard married Elijah Webb.

IV. Cornelius D. Gaillard married Satterfield.

V. Sarah S. Gaillard married Whitefield Holleman; second, A. D. Gaillard.

II. C. L. Gaillard and his first wife, Ann (Gaillard) Gaillard, had the following children:

1. Marian Gaillard married, first, J. E. Allen; second, R. S. Hill.

2. Charlotte Gaillard—died unmarried.

3. Scotti Gaillard married Samuel Brown.

4. Charles David Gaillard married Miss Silcox.

1. Marian Gaillard and her first husband, J. E. Allen, had the following children:

A. J. E. Allen, Jr., married Miss Aldrich.

B. Pet Allen married Dr. S. M. Orr.

1. Marian Gaillard and her second husband, R. S. Hill, had one child:

A. Ena Hill married ———— Gray.

4. Charles David Gaillard married Miss Silcox, had one child and was blown up in the Petersburg mine.

II. C. L. Gaillard and his second wife, Elizabeth (Dart) Gaillard, had one child:

1. Motte Gaillard who died unmarried.

II. C. L. Gaillard and his third wife, Alethia (Hammond) Gaillard, had the following children:

1. L. L. Gaillard married Miss Hammond.

2. Ann Gaillard married R. M. Jenkins.

3. Lena Gaillard.
4. Jane Gaillard married Robinson.
5. Lou Gaillard married Osborne.
6. Palma Gaillard—never married.
7. Hammond Gaillard.
8. William Gaillard married Sue Pickens, daughter of Dr. T. J. Pickens.

III. Rebecca Gaillard married Elijah Webb and had one child, Rebecca. She married James A. Hoyt.

V. Sarah S. Gaillard by her first husband, White-field Holleman, had three children:
1. J. W. Holleman and two others who died in infancy.

Sarah S. Gaillard and her second husband, A. D. Gaillard, had two children.

1. J. W. Holleman married Sarah S. Sharpe and had the following children:
A. J. T. Holleman married Sallie Ramsey.
B. Frank S. Holleman married Grace Thompson.
C. Lee G. Holleman.
D. Hugh S. Holleman—never married.
E. Kate Holleman married J. M. Moss.
F. Henrietta Holleman married N. W. Macauley.
G. Gussy Holleman married George Seaborn.

BLASSINGAME.

General Blassingame married Miss Easley, sister of Colonel Easley. They had the following children:
1. Polly Blassingame married ———— Cleveland.
2. Esther Blassingame married Berry Benson. (See Benson Family.)
3. Eliza Blassingame married Dr. John Robinson.
4. Nancy Blassingame married Thomas Sloan.
5. Daughter married William Wickliffe.
6. William Blassingame—unknown.

7. John Blassingame married Sallie Sloan.

3. Eliza Blassingame married Dr. Robinson and had the following children:
A. Elizabeth Robinson married Earle Holcomb.
B. Ann Robinson married Alex. Briggs.
C. Esther Robinson married James Hagood.
D. Mary Robinson—unmarried.
E. Jane Robinson married Sam Owen.
F. Sallie Robinson married John Partlou.
G. Julia Robinson married William Lee.
H. John Robinson married an Alabama lady.
I. William Robinson married Myra Hagood.

A. Elizabeth Robinson and husband, Earle Holcomb, had the following children:
a. Henry Holcomb.
b. Eliza Holcomb married Dr. Tom Evins.

B. Ann Robinson and husband, Alex. Briggs, had the following children:
a. Henry Briggs married Lula McBee.
b. Miller Briggs married Rosa Nearn.
c. George Briggs married Miss Reynolds.
d. Myra Briggs—unmarried.
e. Mary Briggs married Baxter Carpenter.
f. James Briggs—unmarried.

C. Esther Robinson and husband, James Hagood, had the following children:
a. Mary Hagood married Mac Bruce.
b. Benjamin Hagood—unmarried.
c. James Hagood married Miss Folger.
d. William Hagood married Kate Cleveland.
e. Lucy Hagood.
f. ———— Hagood married J. T. Mauldin.

F. Sallie Robinson married John Partlou and had the following children:
a. Mamie Partlou married Sam Craig.

b. Lizzie Partlou married Louis Sharpe.

c. Sallie Partlou married John O'Donnell.

a. Mamie Partlou married Sam Craig and had the following children:

Sam Craig—unmarried.

Jim Craig married Lucy Barton.

Mamie Craig—unmarried.

Marshall Craig—unmarried.

b. Lizzie Partlou married Louis Sharpe and had the following children:

Lizzie Sharpe—married.

c. Sallie Partlou married John O'Donnell and had the following children:

Cecelia O'Donnell—unmarried.

Aline O'Donnell—unmarried.

Louise O'Donnell—unmarried.

G. Julia Robinson married William Lee and had one son:

a. William Lee.

I. William Robinson married Myra Hagood and had the following children:

a. John Robinson.

b. Ed Robinson.

c. Benjamin Robinson. ---

Major Hamilton married ——————————— and had the following children:

a. Emeline Hamilton married Rev. B. F. Mauldin.

b. ——————————— married Leverett Osborne.

c. Mary Hamilton married Washington Archer.

d. ——————————— married Shumate.

e. Col. Andrew Hamilton married Miss Stokes.

a. Emeline Hamilton married Rev. B. F. Mauldin and had the following children:

1a. B. F. Mauldin married Mamie Reed.

2a. W. H. Mauldin.

3a. Joe Mauldin married, first ——————;
second, Rosa Story.

4a. Mamie Mauldin married Tribble—no issue.

5a. Maggie Mauldin married Rev. West Sadler
—no issue.

6a. Addie Mauldin—unmarried.

1a. B. F. Mauldin married Mamie Reed and had
the following children:

1b. Elise Mauldin married J. M. Paget.

2b. Ellen Mauldin—unmarried.

3b. Cora Mauldin married Prue Clinkscales.

3a. Joe Mauldin married —————————— and
had one son, Guy Mauldin.

3a. Joe Mauldin and his second wife, Miss Story,
had the following children:

1b. Charlie Mauldin.

2b. Frank Mauldin.

3b. Lawrence Mauldin.

e. Col. Andrew Hamilton married Miss Stokes and
had the following children:

1a. Edward Hamilton—unmarried.

2a. Mary Hamilton married Robert Hill.

————————

BENSON.

————

B. E. Benson and Jack Benson were brothers. Their
parents were from Virginia.

1. Berry E. Benson married Esther Blassingame,
daughter of General Blassingame, and had the following
children:

1. Eliza Ann Benson married John T. Sloan. (See
Sloan Family).

2. Amanda Benson married Dr. James Earle.

3. Mary Benson married Gen. James Harrison.

4. John Benson married Lizzie Norton.

5. Esther Benson married Hewlet Moore.

6. Rebecca Benson married Frank Sloan. (See Sloan Family.)

7. Tom Benson—unmarried—died in war.

2. Amanda Benson married Dr. James Earle, and had the following children:

A. Eugenia Earle married Ed Bomar.

B. Alice Earle married Tom Russell.

C. Dr. George Earle married Jeanette Breazeale.

D. Berry Earle married Miss Baker.

E. Mattie Earle married O'Neal.

F. Emmie Earle married Professor Austin.

II. Jack Benson married Kittie Sloan and had the following children:

1. Evelyn Benson married Baylis Crayton.

2. Rebecca Benson married Cunningham.

3. Sue Benson married Alex. Weir.

4. Sloan Benson married Sallie Miller.

5. Prue Benson married ———— McGee.

6. Nannie Benson married Tom White.

7. Mollie Benson married Berry E. Sloan.

1. Evelyn Benson married B. F. Crayton and had the following children:

A. Kate Crayton married Sloan Maxwell.

B. Sam Crayton married Sallie Nevitt.

C. Frank Crayton married Mary Broyles.

B. Sam Crayton married Sallie Nevitt and they had the following children:

a. Maxwell Crayton married Lizzie McBee.

b. Blair Crayton married Sue Gilmer.

c. Bessie Crayton—unmarried.

C. Frank Crayton married Mary Broyles and they had the following children:

a. Lizzie Crayton married Clarence Prevost.

b. Eugene Crayton married ———— Thompson.

c. Frank Crayton—unmarried.

SITTON FAMILY.

I. John Sitton came from England about the time of the Restoration.

II. John Sitton, Jr., born in North Carolina, moved to South. Carolina.

III. Phillip Sitton, father of John B. Sitton, born in Pendleton District, now Pickens County, South Carolina.

IV. John B. Sitton, born in Pendleton District, now Pickens County, on George's Creek, near the present Town of Easley, November 28, 1810. Came to Pendleton March 4, 1829, walking the whole distance carrying his entire possessions in a pocket handkerchief package.

IV. John B. Sitton married (1832) Celena J.. daughter of Col. Jeptha Norton, of Pickens County, South Carolina, by whom he had the following children:

1. Augustus J. Sitton married Miss L. E. Aull.

2. Emma C. Sitton—never married.

3. Alice E. Sitton married Maj. S. P. Dendy, Walhalla, S. C.

4. Frank L. Sitton married Miss Leila Jones, of Georgia.

5. M. Janie Sitton married W. W. Russell, Anderson, S. C.

6. Miles N. Sitton married Lillian Holland, Anderson County, South Carolina.

7. Henry P. Sitton married Amy J. Wilkinson, Adams Run, S. C.

8. Joseph J. Sitton married Sue H. Gaillard, Pendleton, S. C.

James E. Sitton—died in infancy.

1. Augustus J. Sitton, President and sole owner of Pendleton Manufacturing Company, Autun, S. C.,

married Miss L. E. Aull, by whom he had the following children:

 A. Aug. J. Sitton, Jr.—died in 1900.

 B. Cema Sitton—unmarried.

 C. Eugene N. Sitton—unmarried.

 2. Emma C. Sitton—unmarried, and still living in Pendleton at the old homestead.

 3. Alice E. Sitton married Maj. S. P. Dendy, a prominent attorney of Walhalla, S. C., and had the following children (two children died in infancy):

 A. Marie Dendy married Louis W. Barr, of Greenville, S. C.

 B. Sue M. Dendy married Dr. Charles W. Gentry, of Spartanburg, S. C.

 C. J. B. S. Dendy—unmarried—attorney, Walhalla, S. C.

 4. Frank L. Sitton married Leila Jones by whom he had the following children:

 A. Gussie Sitton married Ramsey O. Doyle, of Seneca, S. C.

 B. James E. Sitton married Mrs. Mamie Bostic. deceased; second time, Miss Emma Lay, of Oconee.

 C. John B. Sitton, unmarried—Oconee County.

Macie Sitton—deceased.

 D. Lee Sitton—unmarried.

 E. Janie Sitton married Jos. Lawrence now of Toccoa, Ga.

 F. Claude Sitton—unmarried—Oconee County.

 5. M. Janie Sitton married Walker W. Russell now of Anderson, S. C., and have the following children:

 A. Wade H. Russell—moved to Mississippi—married and died there a few years ago.

 B. Robert M. Russell married Miss A. B. Aull of Newberry, S. C.—lived for years at Autun, S. C., and died a few years ago.

 C. J. B. S. Russell—died out west.

D.   Lena J. Russell married J. D. Smith, a successful dairyman, of Autun, S. C.

E.   Daisy H. Russell married Winslow P. Sloan, merchant of Clemson College, S. C.

F.   Hal P. Russell married Leila Harris, daughter of Bonneau Harris, Pendleton.

6.   Miles N. Sitton married Lillian Holland, a daughter of Berry Holland—no children.

7.   Henry P. Sitton married Miss Amy Wilkinson, of Adams Run, S. C., by whom he had the following children:

A.   James M. Sitton—unmarried.

B.   C. Vedder Sitton—unmarried.

C.   H. P. Sitton, Jr.—unmarried.

D.   Ella H. Sitton—unmarried.

Alice Sitton—died in childhood.

8.   Joseph J. Sitton, organizer and cashier of the Bank of Pendleton for eighteen years, married Miss Sue H., daughter of W. H. D. Gaillard, of Pendleton, S. C., by whom he had the following children:

A.   Emma A. Sitton—unmarried.

B.   Henrietta Sitton married B. M. Aull, manager of Pendleton Manufacturing Co., Autun, S. C.

C.   Arthur M. Sitton—unmarried—secretary Pendleton Cotton Mill.

D.   Louis S. Sitton—unmarried.

E.   John B. Sitton—unmarried.

H. P. Sitton—died in infancy.

F.   Jos. J. Sitton, Jr.,—unmarried.

G.   Ben G. Sitton—unmarried.

COL. ROBERT ANDERSON THOMPSON.

The great grand-father, James Thompson, and great grand-mother of Colonel Thompson were born in Ireland. They came to America in 1776 and landed in New York

City, from whence they made their way over land to South Carolina, and settled in Union County and at once heartily aligned themselves with the Whig or patriot cause. His grand-father, William Thompson, was born in Union County, but afterwards he removed to Pendleton District and settled on Twelve-Mile River, about eight miles north of Pendleton village, where his father, Charles Thompson, was born, reared and died. Charles Thompson intermarried with Mahala Gaines, and their son, Col. Robt. A. Thompson, is the subject of this sketch. The Gaines family were from Virginia, and descendants here have exhibited within themselves the character and attainments of that distinguished family. Charles Thompson and his wife, Mahala (Gaines) Thompson had seven children, all of whom are dead, except Col. Robt. A. Thompson and his youngest brother, Rev. George McDuffie Thompson, who resides in Texas. Col. Robt. A. Thompson married Miss V. Rose Starritt, of Clarksville, Georgia, in 1858. From this union seven children were born, viz: Robert S. Thompson, Lizzie R. Thompson, Mahala Thompson, Charles J. Thompson, Isabella Thompson, Pickens R. Thompson and one died in infancy.

Robert A. Thompson was born in Pickens District, South Carolina, on the 13th day of June, 1828. His education was much neglected in his youth on account of the poor facilities for schools in the section in which he resided. At an early age he entered the printing office of Messrs. Symmes & Bridwell, the owners and publishers of The Pendleton Messenger, printed at Pendleton, S. C. After completing his services with this paper, he was employed with The Laurensville Herald, at Laurens, S. C. In 1849, with Hon. Frank Burt, he edited and published The Pendleton Messenger for nearly three years.

In 1853, he purchased The Keowee Courier, at Pickens Court House, S. C., with which paper at Pickens and Walhalla, to which latter place it was removed, after the division of Pickens District, he continued principally as owner and editor for forty-five consecutive years.

In 1853, he was appointed by the Governor Commissioner in Equity for Pickens District, to fill a vacancy; and was afterwards re-elected to the same office by the Legislature, every four years, until the office was merged into the Court of Common Pleas in 1870.

Anterior to the war, Colonel Thompson was elected by the Legislature for a number of years one of the Commissioners of Free Schools, and also Commissioner of Public Buildings. Positions of honor without compensation.

In 1860, he was elected a member of the Secession Convention from Pickens District, and voted for the Ordinance of Secession. As soon as the Convention adjourned, he raised a company of infantry for the war in the service of the Confederate States. This company formed part of the Second Regiment of Rifles, Col. John V. Moore, Commanding, and was attached to Jenkin's Brigade, Longstreet's Corps. Mr. James W. Crawford, of Cold Spring, Pickens District, contributed most cheerfully one thousand dollars to uniform and equip this gallant company. After the second battle of Manassas, he was promoted to the rank of lieutenant-colonel of his regiment, in which position he continued to serve until his health gave way during the latter part of the war, and he was compelled to retire from active service. He continued, however, to serve the government of the Confederate States in various capacities until the war closed.

After the war he was admitted to the Bar by Judge James L. Orr, of the Circuit Court, and practiced his profession successfully with Gen. Samuel McGowan, James L. Orr, Judge Earle and others.

Colonel Thompson was appointed Commissioner of the United States and continued in office for several years immediately after the war. He was also appointed Register and Referee in Bankruptcy for Oconee County.

In 1900, Colonel Thompson was elected a member of the General Assembly of the State, in which position he rendered valuable service.

Colonel Thompson has been an active member of the Presbyterian Church for many years, and has represented his church in Presbytery and for two sessions in the General Assembly.

Colonel Thompson has been actively engaged in politics since 1853, and well and faithfully has he represented the best interests of the people of his county and State. Now, in the evening of a well-spent life, he can look back over the rough and rugged road that he has had to travel and hold up his head and look into the faces of his fellowmen and say he has injured no man and has labored always to help and lift up and advance the interests of all he came in contact with. Many years of his youth and early manhood he was a struggling printer. Nearly four years of his life spent in war, and eight years more spent in Reconstruction—even more than war. Surely no man could do more.

Colonel Thompson, during all the exciting periods through which he has gone, has occupied a conspicuous position in the State, especially in the Piedmont section. He is a fluent writer, a close thinker, and ever expressed his views clearly and forcibly, whereby through the medium of his paper he exercised a powerful influence in the State. His life has been spent in stormy times, a bright example to the youth of the State, as to what position of prominence a man can rise to by energy, honesty, and intelligence properly used. May God grant that his latest years may be spent in the enjoyment of perfect peace and happiness, and in the consciousness of a life well spent for God and his fellowman.

R. W. SIMPSON.

INDEX

This index lists every name in the historical part (pages 5-68) and the buried names in the genealogical part (pages 69-223) of this book. Thus, if you are researching the Adams family, look first in the Adams family article (pages 142 and 143) and then check the individual names found elsewhere in the book.

BELL (continued)
Maud 210
BELLOTTE, Family 71-72
BELOTTE, Michael A 43 William M 43
BENSON, 17 35 family 216 217
Amanda 130 Berry 213
Catherine 107 Catherine E 95
E B 23 42 117 130 173 Eliza
95 Esther 173 213 Gertrude 112
Jno P 95 John P 107 Mamie
148 149 Mary 95 96 173 Miss
85 Prue 112 Rebecca 99 102
BERWICK, Simon 11
BETHEL, Florida 125
BEVERLEY, Annie 106 Bradshaw
106 Janie 96
BEVERLY, Annie 177 Benjamin
Sloan 177 Bradshaw 177 Janie
95
BILLINGS, Miss 41
BIRNIE, Miss 168
BISHOP, Dorcas 76 Jane 76 Mr 76
Nicholas 76
BISSELL, H E 57 Kate 178 179
BLACKMAN, Miss 84
BLAKE, A L 122 J R 177 Mary B
122 Mary E 177
BLAKENEY, J C 57
BLASINGAMES, General 40
BLASINGHAM, John 95 Nancy 95
104 Sallie 95
BLASSINGAME, family 213-216
Eliza 85 Esther 216 General 85
216
BLECKLEY, Alice Gertrude 93
John N 93
BLUE, J G 58
BOATWRIGHT, Florence 167
BOAZ, Belle 208
BOBO, Miss 155
BOGGS, Alice 186 Annie 186 187
Annie Lee 187 C J 186 187
Claude 199 DeWitt 187 F E 93
G W 117 Georgia Ann 198 199
John Calvin 209 Louisa A 117
Mary 186 187 Mattie 199 Norman 199 Ruth 187 Tempy Ann
209 W A 198 199
BOLT, L M 43
BOMAR, Annie 97 Berry 97 David
S 97 Ed 217 Edward D 97

BOMAR (continued)
Eli Geddings 97 Emily 95 97
Emma 97 Eugenia 97 217
Fanny 97 G W 95 97 George 97
Henry 97 John 95 Julia 97
Landrum 97 Mary 97 Robert 97
Sallie 95 97 William 97
BONNEAU, Elizabeth 190 191
Floride 191 Kate 202
BOON, 16 Mary 194
BOONE, Mary 192
BOSTIC, C V 118 J V 118 Mamie
118 219
BOSTICK, Mary H 127 Wm Mann
127
BOURNE, Elizabeth 202 Mr 202
BOWDEN, Alfred 208 Annie 91
Samuel L 43
BOWEN, family 124 125
Elizabeth 208 John 13 Mary 76
Reese 208 Thomas 76
BOWIE, 15 George 191 195
Louisa 195 Margaret 191 195
BOYD, Charles 6 Dr 134 Laura
134 Robert W 6 Sarah 134
BRADFIELD, Mary Caldwell 137
138
BRADFORD, Charles 105 Fanny
105
BRADLEY, D F 58 61 W K 57
BRANDON, Thomas 11
BREAZEALE, 35 Adda 72
Jeanette 217 John E 72 Mary
72 Oliver 72
BREWER, Cinthia 196 Ellen 187
Polly 198 Tabetha 196 Wm
196
BREWSTER, Harriett 207
BRICE, Mary 148 149
BRIDWELL, 221
BRIGGS, Alex 85 214 Ann 85 214
George 214 Henry 214 James
214 Lula 214 Mary 214 Miller
214 Myra 214 Rosa 214 Ruth
93
BROOKS, John 43
BROWN, Amelia 84 Annie 84
Carrie 206 Charles 206 Cora
206 Elijah 83 84 Elijah A 206
Elizabeth 206 Ella 118 Ernest
83 Eula 84 Fannie 206 Feaster
83 Franklin P 206 Geo M 206

BROWN (continued)
Georgia 83 Hattie 83 Irene V
118 Joel E 118 John 83 Joseph
12 Joseph E 17 40 206 Joseph
M 206 Julius L 206 Marie 84
Mary 83 Mary V 206 Olive 180
Ralph 84 Samuel 212 Sarah E
206 Scotti 212 W C 57 Wil-
liam 83 Wm S 118
BROWNING, Newton J 43
BROWNLEE, Hattie 83 Sam 83
BROYLES, family 133-135
Elizabeth 83 173 John 83 Mar-
garet C 109 Mary 217 O R 118
133 Sarah A 133 Thomas T 173
BRUCE, Elizabeth 206 207 Har-
riet 115 116 Mac 214 Mary 214
Robert 94 Ruth P 205 Susan 94
BRUNELL, Nancy 105
BRYAN, Eliza North 75 John F O
75 L D 57
BURCHMYER, Miss 178 179
BURKHEAD, A L (Mrs) 180
BURNS, Family 84
BURRISS, Mary 70 W Rufus 70
BURT, 17 24 family 76 77 Armis-
tead 36 Armisted 117 Frances
23 158 Francis 39 157 Frank
36 76 221
BURTON, John 13
BUTLER, M C 66
BYERS, W B 58
BYNUM, 36 Turner 35
CALDWELL, Martha 140 141
CALHOUN, 17 35 136 family
140-144 A P 30 Andrew 195
Andrew P 29 146 Angie 146
Capt 19 Catherine 192 Ezekiel
190 192 Floride 28 191 Francis
195 James M 195 John 40 195
John C 25 28 29 37-40 42 146
191 211 John C (Mrs) 29 84
124 144 211 John C Jr 146
John E 23 144 John Ewing 190
191 211 Joseph 37 Martha 76
144 Mary 111 Mr 19 24 35 111
Mrs 211 Pat 40 Patrick 190
Rebecca 190 192 Susan 195 W
Ransom 36
CALLISON, James 58
CAMDEN, Lord 161 162
CAMERON, Duncan 12

CAMINADE, John C 43
CAMPBELL, 16 A C 36 146
Elizabeth 146 Jasper 146 Lord
159 160 162
CANNON, Eleanor 111 Ruth 70
CAPERS, Frank 177 John G 177
Mary 79 William 79
CARLISLE, Alice 92 Annie 91 92
Charles E 92 Charles H 91 92
Edwin Sharpe 91 Eliza 91
Eliza Allen 92 Elizabeth 91
157 164 Emma 91 Francis M
92 Gladys 91 James A 92
James B 91 James H 5 John
91 John E 91 John M 91 92 157
164 Lilly 92 Marcus L 91 92
Mary R 91 Sarah 91 Susan
Elizabeth 91 92 William 91
Wm A 92 Wm Mayson 91
CARNE, Eliza Frances 92 Esther
Mary 92
CARPENTER, Baxter 214 Ellen S
115 166 J Lee 115 166 John
Lewis 166 Lewis 115 Mary 214
Nina 115 Nina Hunter 166
Sallie 96 Sue Ellen 115 166
CARROLL, N Pickens 43
CARSON, Florrie 186
CARTER, Hannah 132 John 132
Margaret Chew 132 133 135
CATER, Lavinia 83
CHAMBERLAIN, 53 61 65 66 D H
45 46 59 Gov 51 Mr 54
CHAPPEL, Sarah 122
CHAPPELL, Congressman 142
Eugenia 142
CHASTAIN, Joseph N 43
CHATHAM, Lord 162
CHERRY, 17 34 Annie Reese 89
Carolina 89 Charles Henry 89
David 23 90 David E 89 Ed-
monia 89 Edward B 89 Edwin
Augustus 89 Evylin Judith 127
Fannie Lewis 167 Fanny
Lewis 90 George Reese 90
James Alvin 89 Jane Adelaide
89 John C 43 89 Kate 89 Laura
89 Lillie B 89 Lorty 89 Mary E
89 Mary George 90 Mary Lor-
ton 167 Mary Reese 89 Mary
Story 89 90 Minnie 90
Nathaniel H 89 Robert M 89

CHERRY (continued)
Samuel 23 88 167 Samuel D 90
Samuel Sidney 89 Sarah 89 90
167 Sarah Ann 89 Sid 42
Thomas R 89 Thomas Reese
89 William B 89 167
CHEVER, 16
CHEVES, Langdon 40
CHEW, Hannah 132
CHILDS, Sarah 86
CHISHOLM, Alexander 102
Caspar 102 Esteria 102 Felicia
101 102 Felix 102 Harry 102
Sue 102 Tudor Hall 102 Wm B
101 102
CHOICE, 15
CHRISTIAN, Sanders 156 Tommy
42
CHURCH, Annie P 171 172 Sarah
170
CLARK, Elizabeth 119 Henry 12
John 134 Rebecca 134 Sabra
204
CLARKE, Jonathan 12 Miss 127
CLAYTON, Carter 182 Lawrence
82 Miss 86 Sarah Ann 182
CLEMENT, Lucia 113 Mary 115
Moultrie 113
CLEMSON, Anna M 142-144
Calhoun 144 Colonel 26 27
Floride 28 29 144 John C 29 30
Mr 30 Mrs 30 Thomas G 25 26
29 31 Thos G 7 22 142-144 146
Thos G (Mrs) 146
CLEVELAND, Benj 12 Benjamin
15 Kate 214 Polly 213
CLIFFORD, Patrick 43
CLINKSCALES, Cora 216 Prue
216
COBB, Howell 170 Martha 170
171 T R R 170
COIT, J C 57
COLLINS, McKenzie 23
COMPTON, W P 58
CONNALLY, E L 206 Mary V 206
CONNER, James 52
CONNOR, F A 57 Miss 173
COOK, Thompson H 59
COOLEY, Dr 132
COOPER, Brooks 121 Florence
121 J R 57
CORBIN, 117

CORNISH, Family 146
CORROUTH, Louisa 178 Mary
178 Mr 178
CORRUTH, Mary 175 Mr 175
COX, Ella 81 John W 43 Miss 86
CRAIG, family 93 94 Agnes 174
179 Jim 215 Lucy 215 Mamie
214 215 Marshall 215 Sam 214
215
CRAWFORD, 35 Andrew 101 102
Andrew Jr 102 Annie 176 B C
99 104 B C Jr 99 Daniel 102
Eliza 99 101 102 Eliza Earle
102 Fanny 105 Frank 99 176
Henry 99 J B E 102 J W 104
141 James 99 James W 22 129
222 John 102 Kate Lorraine
102 Lucia 105 Mary 181 Mary
Bell 99 Nannie S 104 Nanny
128 129 Paul 99 Rebecca 99
104 Sloan 105 Stateria 102 Sue
99 Susan 102 Susan M 104 Wm
Hall 102
CRAYTON, B F 217 Baylis 217
Bessie 217 Blair 217 Eugene
217 Evelyn 217 Frank 217
Julian 106 Lizeve 106 Lizzie
217 Mary 217 Maxwell 106 217
Nancy 104 106 Sallie 217 Sam
217 Sue 217 T S 104 106
CRENSHAW, Amanda 120 198
199 Bluford 199 Carolina 89
Emma 153 Henry 153 James L
198 Jas L 199 Jesse 199
Katherine 198 Lemuel 199 Lou
120 121 199 Martin L 199 Mary
E 88 Matthew 198 199 Mattie
199 N E 198 Nancy E 199 Rula
Jane 199
CRESWELL, Sarah 90
CROCKER, Joseph A 43
CROMER, Samuel H 43
CROW, Roberta 105 Thomas 43
CUDWORTH, Edmund 176 Kate
176
CUMMINGS, J M 57
CUMNOCK, Eva Sloan 98 Mr 98
CUNNINGHAM, Anna Ross 174
Frank Harrison 173 Jennie E
174 Joseph G 173 Joseph G Jr
174 Martha 173 Rebecca 217
Sallie A 174 Sarah 173

CUNNINGHAM (continued)
Thomas Harrison 174
CURETON, Miss 86
CUTHBERT, 16 Anna 113 Eliza N
200 201 Thomas Heyward 200
DANDRIDGE, Alexander
Spotswood 124 Jane Pendleton
124
DANIELS, Capt 19 Columbus A
43 John W 43
DARBY, B D 173 Ida 173 Meta
173
DARRICOTT, Theodore 43
DART, 16 Dr 75 76 92 Elizabeth
212 Mary 92 Thomas L 23
DAVANT, family 127 128 Chas
192 Mary 192
DAVENPORT, James 13
DAVIS, Family 144 Fannie Lewis
168 Fanny Lewis 90 J P 58
Martha 140 141 Nancy H 206
207 President 29 143 Sarah 206
Sarah C 207 Warren R 14 23 37
38 40 90 141 168
DAWSON, Georgia 77 Wm 77
DAY, Alice 186
DEAL, J A 58
DEAN, Hamilton Symmes 156 J H
156 J Harry 156 Mary 156
DEARING, Marion 195
DENDY, Alice E 218 219 Emily R
205 J B S 219 Marie 219 S P
218 219 Sue M 219
DERIT, Florence 105 Harry 105
DEYAMPERT, Lou 112 Mary
Rosa 112 Rebecca 112
DICKINSON, family 114-116 Ada
122 Carrie C 166
DICKSON, 17 33-35 family 69-73
Antoinette 207 Benjamin 23 Dr
42 James L 43 Sarah 71 T E
69 Thomas 76 Widow 185
DIXON, John 13
DODD, George W 43
DONNALD, J F 57
DOUTHIT, Carrie 211 Claude 210
Elizabeth 209 Gertrude 211 J B
210 J B Jr 211 James G 209
Leora 211 Mary 210 Maud 210
DOWDLE, Robert 12
DOYLE, 35 Eli 207 Gussie 219
Julia 169 Leah 84 Myra 207

DOYLE (continued)
Ramsey O 219
DRAYTON, Eliza Elliot 73
Elizabeth 73 General 73
DUGAS, Dolly 195 Douskah 195
Dr 195 Lucy 195
DUKE, James (Mrs) 157 James M
43 Mrs 164
DUNHAM, Marie 150
DUPRE, Benjamin Sr 23
DUPREE, 16 Family 92 Ben 76
Daniel 79 Helen 79 Sarah 212
Susanna 71
DUVAL, Miss 171
DWIGHT, Lieut 102 Sue 102
DYE, Fannie 97
EARLE, 17 40 Family 129-132
Alice 217 Amanda 216 217 Ann
Berry 165 Antoinette 173 B J
14 Baylis 175 177 Berry 217
Dock 83 E Preston 173 Eleanor
165 Elias 37 172 Eliza C 95 99
Elizabeth 175 Emmie 217
Eugenia 97 217 Frances Wil-
ton 172 Geo W 14 15 George
217 Hannah 173 Harriet 175
177 Hattie 83 J B 23 J Baylis
146 James 216 217 Joe Berry
95 104 John B 37 150 165 John
Baylis 111 165 Joseph B 23
Joseph J 105 Judge 222 Lucia
105 Maria 85 169 Mary E 99
101 Mary Prince 175 177
Mattie 217 Miriam 147 Miss
146 Rebecca 95 104 Sam 147
Samuel 15 23 36 175 Sarah 172
Sarah Ann 150 T J 15 Theron
177 Washington 85 165
EARLY, Hallie 110
EASLEY, Carlus 105 Carrie 104
105 Colonel 213 Elizabeth 104
105 Florence 105 John 104 105
Loula 104 105 Mamie 105
Mary 104 105 Miss 213 Nancy
105 Nannie 105 Ogier 105
Robert 105 Roberta 105 Samuel
104 105 South Carolina 105 T
M Sloan 105 Thrace 105 W K
104 105
EDENS, T N 58
EDWARDS, Amelia 84 Rev Mr 84
ELFORD, Sallie 97

ELLIOTT, 16 Catherine Ann 169
  J H 169 Lucinda 198
ELLIS, Miss 186
ELLISON, Sarah E 123
EMBREE, James 13
ERSKINE, Ida 153 Jefferson 153
  Joseph 153 Maria 153 Martha
  153 Mary 153 Sarah 153
ERWIN, J B 57
ESKEW, Jacob 43 S L 154
ESTES, Micaja 196 Nancy 196
EUBANKS, John L 171
EVATT, B F 198 J W 186 Jane
  198 Matilda 186 Miss 121
  Olivia 186
EVERS, Rowena Lee 147
EVINS, Eliza 214 Tom 214
EWING, Jane 140 John 37
FANT, Edward 43
FARIS, James 23
FARMER, Agnes L 181 182 Alice
  105 182 Andrew E 182 Annie
  Hunter 182 Cathline B 182 E B
  181 182 Edwin 182 J L 181 182
  James L 182 Joseph Simpson
  182 Lewis Hunter 182 Louise
  182 Mary 105 Mary Alice 181
  182 Mary Hunter 182 Mary
  Reamer 182 Nathaniel 182
  Nina Lewis 182 Robert 182 W
  Frank 182 Wm Anderson 182
FARRAR, 14 T 23 T W 23
FARROW, Cornelia 171 H P 171
  Lidie 171
FERGUSON, Fannie 176
FERRELL, Charlotte M 127 Jane
  K 127 Jane Keith 127 John B
  127 Louis O 127 Martha Ogier
  127
FIELDING, Frances 165 Rebecca
  200 Rebecca J 198
FINCONNON, Ida 205
FINDLEY, Lydie 88 Mr 88
FINLEY, Susan 80
FITZGERALD, Martha 84 151
FLEMING, Jane E 123
FLINT, Fannie 208
FOLGER, Miss 214
FOLK, Sarah 181 182
FOOTMAN, Mary 108
FORBES, Agnes 207 Fant 196
  Kiszice 196

FORD, John 13 Mary 198 Patsy
  196 Sophrony 198 Wm 198
FORREST, 134 Emily 201
FORSYTH, Mary 185 Warren 185
FORT, Fannie 206
FORT HILL GUARDS, 42
FOSTER, Augusta 139 Frances
  204 Garland 139 I J 204
FOWLER, J S 132
FOX, Mr 162
FRAME, Nancy 105
FRANKS, Marvin 120 Mary G 120
FRASER, Sophia 201
FRIERSON, Dr 34
FRIPP, Cuthbert 114 Sue 114
GAILLARD, family 212 213 Ann
  126 Anna R 126 Benj 99
  Charles 23 Elisha 13 Eliza 99
  Eliza Earle 183 Elizabeth 115
  116 Eoline 99 101 Henrietta 99
  100 Irene 100 James Culbraith
  101 Jane H 125 Jas H 127 John
  23 37 38 Josias 23 Julia 193
  Lawrence 116 Lena 99 100
  Margaret 100 P C Jr 101 P
  Cordes 99 101 Pauline 99 100
  183 184 Perkins Green 100
  Prioleau 116 Rebecca 99 104
  Sallie T 99 Sue H 218 220
  Susan 99 100 Susan Gourdin
  116 Susan M 127 Theodore 23
  116 W H D 99 100 220 Wil-
  liam 193 Wm 116 Wm D 115
  116 Wm H D 42 Wm H D Jr 99
  100
GAINES, Ann 81 Barnard 80
  Capers 81 Elizabeth 81 Ella 81
  Emma 81 Frances 165 George
  81 Helen 81 Jane 81 Joe 81
  Louisa 81 Mahala 221 Mar-
  garet 80 Mary 81 Sue 167 168
  Walker 81
GAMBRELL, Charles E 156
  Daisy 156 Jane Anne 156
GANTT, John C 43
GARLINGTON, Capt 19 John 136
  Maria Louise 8 136 Susan
  Washington 136
GARRISON, J R 211 J Reed 210
  Margaret 210 211
GARVIN, Thomas 12
GARY, M W 7

230

GASSAWAY, Ann 81 Samuel 23
GASTON, Mr 72 Mrs 72 William
   23
GATES, James 12
GENTRY, Charles W 219 Sue M
   219
GEORGE III king of England, 159
   161
GERARD, Thomas H 43
GIBB, 16
GIBBES, Cynthia 96
GIBBS, Cynthia 97 Dr 87 Mary 87
   Miss 202
GILFILLIN, Emma 97 James 97
GILKERSON, Addie A 70 An-
   toinette 70 John L 70
GILKIE, Sarah 180
GILLIAM, General 178 Louisa
   178 Mrs 95
GILMAN, 17
GILMER, Sue 217
GILMORE, Lollie J 118
GLENN, Amanda 82 Carrie 82
   Corrie 82 F M 82 J M 82 J P
   82 Miss 83 T S 116
GLOVER, Elizabeth Toccoa 171
   Thos J 171
GLYN, Sergeant 159
GRAHAM, Bertie 140 Bessie 140
   David 140 Genella 140 Mary J
   139 140 William 139 William
   W 43 Wm 140
GRANT, Colonel 189 May 115 Mr
   115 President 64 65 William
   13
GRAY, Ena 212 J W 57
GREEN, Charles 115 Duff 142
   James F 114 Jas F 115 John
   23 Lawrence Lee 115 Lena 100
   Margaret 142 Mary 115 May
   115 Rachel K 114 115
GREENE, Lena 99
GREENWOOD, Ruth B 204
GRESHAM, 35 Elizabeth 206 G T
   107 J T 104 Joseph 206 Julia
   107 Lucilla 104 Lucilla Sep-
   tima 107 Mary Love 206
   Nannie 207 William S 42 Wil-
   liam Steel 206
GREY, Clelia 155 Dora 155 G
   Thomisena 155 Jacob T 155
   Thomas Eugene 155

GRIFFIN, James 69 80 86 James
   C 23 72 Martha 80 Mary 165
   166 Narcissa 69 Rebecca W 86
   Sarah Ann 86
GRISHAM, John Sr 13 Joseph 23
GROGAN, Sarah 84 William 84
GRUBBS, Richard W 43 W
   Thompson 43
GUERARD, Benjamin 163
GUIGNARD, John G 57
GUYTON, Margaret 206 207
HACKET, Covie 87 Ida 86 87
   John R 87 John T 86 87
HACKETT, Eliza 95 107 Robert
   43
HADDON, Eala 93 Mr 93
HAGOOD, Benjamin 214 Elvira 85
   Esther 85 214 James 214
   James E 85 Johnson 52 Kate
   214 Lucy 214 Mary 214 Miss
   169 Myra 214 215 William 214
HAILE, Elizabeth 203 204
HALBERT, John 23 William 12
   Wm 12
HALCOMB, Earle 85 Elizabeth 85
HALL, Family 120 121 Dr 75 76
   Edward 77 Edward M 43 Eliza
   101 102 Felicia 101 102
   Floride 102 Georgiana 76
   Henry G 102 John 23 Lawrence
   Orr 102 Lillian 208 Lou 199
   Samuel P 199 Susan 99 101
   Tudor 102 Wm P 99 101 102
   Wm P Jr 102
HALLUM, Emily 183 John 13
HALLWOOD, Lillian 138
HALSEY, Caroline 178 179 John
   179 Leroy 178 179 Leroy (2)
   179 Lucy 179 Martha 179
   Samuel Pickens 179
HAMER, P M 58
HAMILTON, 16 63 Family 116
   117 Andrew 79 215 216 David
   12 David K 23 40 Della 198
   199 Edward 216 Emeline 215
   James 13 Leonard S 43 Major
   215 Mary 215 216 Paul 73 80
   87 Sarah 79 Widow 80 William
   W 43
HAMMOND, Alethia 212 J B 23
   Miss 157 197
HAMPTON, Eliz 172 Gen 54 55

HAMPTON (continued)
Gov 7 61 64 66 67 Wade 7 52
144
HANCKEL, Family 119 120 C 145
170
HARDIN, Josephine 108 Mr 108
HARKEY, Elizabeth C 205 Josiah
205
HARPER, Margaret 207 William
207
HARRELL, Susan 91
HARRIS, 35 Andrew 191 Ann 178
Benjamin 191 Bonneau 220
Della 187 Eliza 191 Ezekiel
191 Jane 87 John 190 191 John
A 43 Jos Pickens 178 Joseph
191 Leila 220 Mary 190 191
Mary Reese 89 Nathaniel 191
Rebecca 88 191 Robt 87
Thomas 191
HARRISON, 14 17 Family 172–
174 Anna E 184 Benjamin 154
Bettie 134 135 Elizabeth
Hampton 170 171 F E 131
Frank E 184 Harriet 130 J W
109 James 13 131 216 Laurie
Hardee 110 Mary 216 Nettie
131 Nina 109 Richard 23 Sarah
131 Thos 131
HASKEL, 16
HASKELL, Alex 60 Judge 61
HASTIE, John 149 150 William
149
HAWKINS, Philemon 13
HAYES, President 67
HAYNE, 16 40 Family 145 Emily
211 Fanny 91 Governor 157 164
Hamilton 211 Paul Hamilton
211 R Y 167 Robert Y 91
HAYNSWORTH, Miss 131
HAYS, President 7
HEMPHILL, R R 57
HENDERSON, Caroline 191 196
HENRY, 35 Beverly A 167 Julia K
168 Mary 167 Overton 168
HENSHALL, Meta 183 205
HEYWARD, Ellineta 113 Helen
Taylor 113 Taliaferro Taylor
113 Thomas 156 163 Wm
Henry 113
HILL, Ena 212 Josephine 93
Marian 212 Mary 216

HILL (continued)
Miss 77 78 R S 212 Robert 216
HILLHOUSE, Belle 208 Esther
Love 207 208 Idilette 208 J
Waddill 43 James 23 James
Steel 208 Joseph B 207 208
Joseph B Jr 208 Louis 208
Martha 207 208 Martha A 208
Nell 208 S Porter 43 Tessie
208 William C 207 208 Wil-
liam Laurens 208 Wm C 208
HINTON, John 185 Mary 185
HIX, C R 43
HOBBS, Ellen Mildred 148 John D
148 Josepha 148
HODGES, Anna C 205
HOKE, Frances Burton 110 Laurie
Hardee 110 Lydia M 110 Lydia
Maverick 110 Michael 110 R F
110 Van Wyck 110
HOLBROOK, E 130
HOLCOMB, Earle 214 Eliza 214
Elizabeth 214 Henry 214
HOLCOMBE, Lucy 195 Virginia
112
HOLLAND, Berry 220 Lillian 218
220
HOLLEMAN, Ann 212 Frank S
213 Grace 213 Gussie 150
Henrietta 213 Hugh S 213 J T
213 J W 213 Kate 213 Lee G
213 Peyton 212 Sallie 213
Sarah S 212 213 Whitefield 212
213
HOLLINGSWORTH, Miss 82
HOLMES, A G (Mrs) 8 Alester G
137 Alester G Jr 137 Alister G
137 Anna 202 Anna W 203
Annie Ball 137 Catherine War-
ley 202 Edward 202 Ella 201
202 Emmie 202 Felix 202
Feliz Cheves 202 Fredericka
202 Henry 202 J W 57 John H
202 203 Kate 202 Louise Garlington 137 Marie Anna 202
Mrs 148 Sue 202 Susie Marian
202 Wm 202
HOOD, Wm 57
HOOK, J N 138 Ressie E 138
HOPKINS, John W 43
HORSCE, Benjamin 12
HOUSTON, 107 Bryan 108

PICKENS (continued)
178 213 Thomas J 128 Thos J
87 176 Tom 42 William P 178
PICKERELL, W R 43
PIKE, Family 84 151 152
PILGRIM, William 13
PINCKNEY, 16 40 Family 145
Roger 43 Thomas Jr 23
PINKHIND, Nettie 183
POE, Family 128 129 Azalia
Josepha 147 Baylis 103 Dora
102 103 Ellen 103 147 155 El-
len C 112 Ellen Matilda 155
Frank 103 H T 102 Harry T Jr
103 Nancy 95 96 Nannie S 104
Nelson 104 Thomas 103 Wil-
liam 147 155 Wm 112
POLK, Susan 87 88 90
POLLUCK, John 12
POOSER, Benjamin 117 Matilda
117
POPE, Miss 168 Sue 202
PORCHER, 16 Anna 168 Hess 102
103
PORTER, C J 127 128 Charles
128 Clarence 128 Evylin
Cherry 127 128 Henrietta P 75
James 128 May 128 Richard Y
75 Samuel 13
POTTER, 16 Rev Mr 80 87
POWERS, Lucy 120 Till 120
PRESSLEY, Louise 74 75
PREVOST, Clarence 217 Leila
114 Lizzie 217 Stephen 114
PRICE, J T 185 Miss 177
PRINCE, Miss 130
PRUITT, David 13
PURVIS, Mary 130
PUTNAM, Miss 142 143
PYLES, Alice 92
RAINEY, Mary 134
RAINY, Mary 135
RAMSAY, 35
RAMSEY, Alexander 13 205 Mar-
tha H 205 Sallie 213
RANDELL, Family 145
RANDOLPH, Elizabeth 171 Jane
171
RAST, Annie 92
RAVENEL, 16
REAMS, Miss 69 William 43

RECONSTRUCTION IN SOUTH
CAROLINA, 87
REDFEARN, D T 57
REED, Clifton 148 Cora S 148
Helen 148 149 Jacob P 42
Joseph 23 Lucy 148 Mamie
215 216
REEDER, Mary 95 98
REEDISH, W H 58
REESE, 17 34 Family 87-90 Ed-
win 167 Flora 151 George Jr 23
George Sr 23 Mary 84 Milton
84 Miss 111 Sarah Ann 167
Thomas 34
REEVES, Lillie 186 Sarah M 198
REID, C L 205 C S 205 Crayton L
43 Mary E 205 R H (Mrs) 180
Roxie A 205 Samuel (Mrs) 25
REYNOLDS, Miss 214
RHETT, Colonel 36 R B 141
RICE, Maggie 96
RICHARDS, Gregg G 150 Mattie
150
RICHARDSON, A N 75 Effie 187
Henry 187 M B 75 186 187
Sallie 187 Sarah R 186 187
RICHMOND, Duke of 162
RIDDLE, Andrew 13 Ann 204
ROBERTSON, Cynthia 198 Horse
Shoe 15
ROBINN, Ellen 209
ROBINSON, Family 84-87 Ann
214 Benjamin 215 Dr 214 Ed
215 Eliza 213 214 Elizabeth
214 Esther 214 Frances Melton
131 Frances Wilton 172 Jane
213 John 213-215 Julia 214
215 Myra 214 215 Sallie 214
Virginia 169 William 169 214
215 Wm 130
ROCHESTER, Leah 94
RODDY, Catherine 172
ROGERS, Alma 112 R H 58 W A
179
ROLAND, Kate 91
ROOT, James 105 South Carolina
105
ROSAMOND, Mary 204 Richard
204
ROSS, 17 35 Family 184 185 A W
173 Anna 173 Anthony W 170

ROSS (continued)
Elizabeth 170 173
ROUNTREE, M A 57
ROWE, Andrew 12
ROWLAND, Flora 88 Kate 72 Mr
88
RUCKER, Bessie 114 E Marion
171 Elbert M 171 Elizabeth
171 172 Guy 172 James H 171
Joseph N 171 Sarah F 171
RUGER, Gen 59 61 64
RUSK, 35 General 40 John R 34
Thos J 34
RUSSELL, A B 219 Alice 217
Benjamin F 117 D H 117 Daisy
96 Daisy H 220 David H 117 Dr
78 Edw A 117 Emma 117
Florence Scott 70 Geo W 117
George 70 Hal P 220 J B S 219
John A 117 Leila 220 Lena J
118 220 Louisa A 117 M Janie
218 219 Marion Augustus 117
Martha Jane 117 Mary 78 117
Matilda A 117 Robert 219
Thomas H 117 Thomas W 117
Thos H 117 Tom 217 W W 218
Wade H 219 Walker W 219
William W 117
RUTHERFORD, Gen 90
RUTLEDGE, Edward 156 163
SADLER, Catherine Ann 169
Maggie 216 West 216
SALLEY, Miss 84 Captain 194
Rebecca 194
SANDERS, Martha 156
SATTERFIELD, 212
SAWYER, C E 57
SAXON, 15
SCHILLE, Hallie 134
SCHOEN, Allen M 141 Edward
141 Sarah 141 Sarah L 141
SCHULL, Edmonia 89
SCHUTTZ, Elizabeth 202 Mr 202
SCOTT, A E 69 James G 69 Jane
88 Joseph D 69 Julia K 69
Nancy Young 69 Narcissa 69
W W 88 William 69
SEABORN, 17 Family 150 151
George 24 42 213 Gussy 213
SEABORNE, George 130 Mollie
99 101 Sallie 95 97 Sarah 130

SEABROOK, Edward 100 Eliza 73
Gov 73 Henrietta 99 100 Mary
73 P C 100 William 100 Wm
99 Wm Jr 100
SEARS, George P 43
SECESSION CONVENTION,
MEMBERS OF 42
SEIBELS, Louise Caroline 148
SHACKELFORD, Elizabeth 170
SHANKLIN, 15 17 Family 168 169
Capt 19 E H 86 J A 78 Joseph
V 23 Julius A 193 Julius L 43
Sue Conyers 193 Van 86 Vir-
ginia 86
SHARP, Miss 197
SHARPE, 35 Family 90-92 Edwin
164 Elam 23 157 164 Elizabeth
157 164 Lizzie 215 Louis 215
Marcus 157 Marcus L 164
Martha R 167 Sarah S 213
SHAW, Family 152-154 H A 58
Jane 175 Mr 175
SHELDON, Maud 176
SHELOR, Rebecca 207 Susan A
205 Thomas R 205
SHELTON, Maud 176
SHEPPARD, Dolly 195 J C 58 J C
Jr 195 Mr 60
SHILLITO, Sarah W 93
SHREWSBURY, Elzabeth K 123
SHUFORD, Lydia Maverick 109 T
S 109
SHUMATE, 215
SILCOX, Miss 212
SIMMS, Admiral 204
SIMONS, James 193 Mary 193
SIMPKINS, Arthur 11 Eliza 195
SIMPSON, 17 Family 135-140
Andrew 194 Ann 190 194
Caroline Virginia 138 Chair-
man 7 Colonel 7 8 31 Cornelia
171 Dick 5 Ezekiel 194 J G 8 J
Richard 43 Jane 194 John 190
194 Leah 194 Leonard 23 Lt
Gov 66 M L 8 Margaret 5 Mar-
garet Garlington 210 Margaret
M 133 Maria L 103 Maria
Louise 8 Mary 181 Mary Mar-
garet 133 135 R F 22 133 R W
22 26 57 103 R W Jr 8
Rebecca 194 Richard F 5 38 42

239

SIMPSON (continued)
133 135 Richard Wright 5-9
Susan James 103 T N 6 T S 8
W D 52 W W 138
SIMS, Julia 97 R M 52 R W 43 44
SITTON, 17 Family 218-220 A J
41 Arthur 100 Augustus J 43
Ben Gaillard 100 Emma 100
Glennella 118 H P 87 Henrietta
100 Henry 100 J E 118 John 42
100 Joseph 100 Joseph J 99
100 Louis 100 Macie 118
Mamie 118 Susan 99 100
SKELTON, J O 43
SKINNER, Kate 184 Miss 100
SLIGH, Ida 205
SLOAN, 17 35 Family 94-107
Annie 176 177 B F 41 130 131
B Frank 58 129 137 166 Benj
22 Benjamin 176 177 Berry E
217 D B 128 D Jr 23 Daisy H
220 David 111 203 Dora 129
Elise M 118 Eliza 130 131
Eliza Ann 216 Eliza Earle 137
Elizabeth 203 204 Ella Max-
well 137 Ellen M 166 Esther
171 Frank 217 Harry A 118
Harry A Jr 118 Hattie 118 J B
E 150 Jean Conway 137 Joe
Berry 131 132 John T 216 John
T Sr 59 Kate 176 Kittie 217
Lucy 175 Lucy Maxwell 137
Margaret Taliaferro 137 Maria
Louise Garlington 137 Mary
126 131 132 Mary Richard 137
Mollie 217 Mollie S 150 Nancy
111 128 213 Nanny T 128 P H
E Jr 136 137 P H E Jr (Mrs) 8
Paul Earle 118 Paul H E Jr
137 R E 145 Rebecca 217
Sallie 214 Sallie Taylor 150
Sunie M 118 Susan 167 168 203
Susan James 136 137 Susan
Simpson 137 Susanah 111
Thomas 23 213 Thos 176 Thos
J 150 Winslow P 220
SMITH, 16 17 Family 73-76
Aaron 94 Amanda 82 Ann 152
181 Anna 168 Benjamin 23
Benjamin Savage 73 Carrie 82
Catherine 94 Chess 82
Elizabeth 82 Elizabeth J 210

SMITH (continued)
Harriet 88 Hattie 103 Herbert 82
Hester J 209 Ida N 180 J D 180
220 J Laurens N 43 J P 82
James 82 James L 43 John 89
Joseph N 94 Judge 111 Lena L
220 Lizzie 209 Lois 82 Mar-
garet 209 Maria 152-154 Mar-
tha 209 Mary 111 Mary Eliza
73 Matilda 152 153 Miss 211
Mr 82 Munro 82 209 O 13 Pearl
82 R Frank 82 Ruth 94 Sarah
85 203 Sarah Ann 89 Sarah
North 73 Tempy Ann 209
Thomas 152 W 88 Walter 82
83 William 152 153 William C
43 Wm Cutino 74 Zeffie 209
SMYTH, Margaret M 123 Thos M
123
SMYTHE, A T 123 124 145 El-
lison A 123 Margaret M 123
SNODDY, Elizabeth 139
SORRELL, Ann 130 131
SPANN, Miss 170
SPICU, Sarah 185
STARKE, Elizabeth 90 R 90
STARRITT, V Rose 221
STEEL, Family 206-208
STEELE, 35 Charles S 43 Wil-
liam 13 23 43
STEPHENS, Andrew 84 152 Angie
152 Daniel 152 Dora 152 Ed-
ward B 43 Hampton 152 Hayne
152 J Stewart 152 Lelitia 152
Lucretia 84 Miss 210 Samuel
152 Zeruah 152
STEVEN, 16
STEVENS, Family 78 79 Ann 78
Carrie 127 Chauncy 127 Cle-
ment 40 78 Elizabeth 127 Ella
127 Janie 127 Kate 127 Lucius
127 Martha Ogier 127 Mattie
127 Peter 40 Sarah 127
Thomas 127 William 127
STEVENSON, Robert 13 William
H 43
STEWART, Dr 87
STILES, Miss 145
STOKES, Miss 215 216
STONY, Charles 23
STOREY, 35
STORY, Anna 90 Rosa 216

240

TURPIN, Catherine 108 Joseph 108 Lydia 108 Mary 108 William 108
TWEETY, John 13
TWITCHELL, Albert 97 Mary 97
TYMOTHY, 163
VANBUREN, Tessie 208
VANCE, Jacob 13
VANDIVER, H R 57
VANSHANKLIN, Ann Elvira 167 Joseph 167
VANSWEARENGER, Hannah 110 111 Mr 111
VANWYCK, 17 Ann Early 110 Augustus 109 110 Benjamain Stephens 109 Elizabeth Hale 109 Grace 109 Hallie 110 Leila 110 Leila Gray 110 Lillie 109 Lydia Ann 109 110 134 Lydia Maverick 109 110 Maggie May 109 Margaret C 109 Margaret Caroline 134 Mary 109 Mary Battle 110 Mary Elizabeth 109 Maverick 109 Nina 109 173 Nina Harrison 109 Oze 109 Oze B 109 134 Oze Keith 109 Robert Anderson 109 110 Sallie Ann 109 Sam 134 Sam M 134 Sam Maverick 134 Samuel M 109 173 Samuel Maverick 109 William 109 110 Wm 134 Wm Overman 109 Zeruah 109 110
VERNER, 61 Anna M 205 J S 58 60
VRAYTON, Kate 217
VROOMAN, Luve 96 97
WADDELL, Mahala 82 83
WAGNER, Anna 203 Dora 203 Ella 202 203 F D 202 Sophia 202 T D 202 203
WALDEN, 103
WALKER, 35 Annie 134 Edith E 138 Emily St P 202 Emmie 202 Jane E 116 Legare 202 Ruth Holmes 202
WALLACE, Judge 62 Speaker 65 W H 58 59
WALON, 42
WALTON, E 147
WARING, Annie 193 194 Frank 192 193 Kizzie 192 193
WARLEY, 16 17 Family 201 203

WARREN, Col 33 40 Elizabeth Taylor 178 Jane 123 124 John 32 Maria Louisa 177 Mary 193 194 Mary Earle 178 Robert Maxwell 178 Samuel 15 23 32 36 Samuel Fenner 31 32 Sarah E 123 Thos J 177 William Dalton 123 124
WASHINGTON, Bertie 165 Col 69 Elizabeth A 131 General 164 George 131 165
WATERS, Philemon 11
WATKINS, Family 208-211 Baylis 82 Carolina 70 Elizabeth 82 Esther 82 J C 82 Margaret Garlington 136 Mary J 198 W W 136 W W (Mrs) 8
WATSON, Allen 153 Drucilla 153 196 Elizabeth 153 Emma 153 Ferdinand 153 Ida 153 Jane 153 154 Joseph N 153 Louisa 153 Maria 153 154 Matilda 153 Sarah 153 Thomas 153 William 153
WATT, Rebecca 85
WATTS, J W 58
WAYMON, Emily 176 177 Joe 176 Joseph 177 Josephine 177 Samuel 177
WEBB, Corry 199 Elijah 212 213 Lydia M 110 Rebecca 212 213
WEIR, Alex 217 Sue 217
WELBORN, Ruth 185 186
WELLS, David A 44 Mary 136
WERNER, P Edward 44
WESTBERRY, J H 58
WESTMORELAND, J L 57
WEYMAN, Augustus Maverick 108 Catherine 108 Edward 108 Eliza Houston 108 Emmala 108 Joseph B 108 Joseph T 108 Josephine 108 Mary 108 Mary Elizabeth 108 Robert 108 Samuel T 108
WHALEY, Jeannie 195 Mitchell 195
WHITE, A Frank 44 Alice 96 Anna E 120 Arna E 120 Elias 44 Henry N 205 James 44 Nancy Trimmier 205 Nannie 217 Tom 217
WHITFIELD, 14 Family 80-82

WHITFIELD (continued)
J T 23 John T 36
WHITNER, 15 17 34 Family
170-172 Amanda 79 80
Elizabeth 184 Elizabeth
Hampton 172 Essie M 95
Frank 79 J N 79 Jos N 172
Joseph 23 73 155 184 Joseph N
42 117 155 184 Sarah 155 Wm
H 95
WHITTEN, A L 151 152 Alice
151 152 Allie 188 Baylis 151
Clyde 151 Colin 151 Edith 151
Ernest 152 Eugene 151 Floyd
151 Furman 152 George 151
Green 152 Harriet 210 John 152
Lewis 152 Mamie 152 Mary
151 152 187 May 188 Norman
151 Ressie 152 S E 187 188
Thelma 188 Walter 152
WICKLIFFE, William 213
WILBANKS, Louis 105 Mamie
105
WILCOX, Daniel 105 Mary 105
WILHITE, J O 97 98 Meta 97 98
WILKINS, Leila 110
WILKINSON, Amy 220 Amy J 218
Maggie 166 Mrs 211 Susan 191
195 211
WILLIAMS, Anna Simpson 138
Eliza Snead 138 Frances 153
George W 142 Hannah 110
John Q 135 Lucian 135 Mar-
garet 135 Maria Louise 138
Mary 136 138 Minnie 135 Miss
171 Mr 153 Richard Franklin
138 Sallie 142 143 Sarah Ann
134 135 Thos Lanier 136 138
Wm D 134 135 Wm D Jr 135
138 Zae 135
WILSON, 16 Ada 197 Eliza North
75 Elizabeth 75 Eva D 197
Henrietta P 75 Isaac Hume 75
J Edward 44 James T 197 John
12 Laura B 75 Lawrence G 197
Lelia A 197 Mary 83 Mary
Hume 75 Mrs 164 O E 197
Richard (Mrs) 157 Sarah Annie
75 Sarah Elizabeth 75 Stephen
75 Stephen Mazyck 75 U G 197
W G 197 Wilton G 197 Wm
Cuttino 75 Wm W 197

WITTE, Alice 101
WOFFORD, Florence A 126 J E
126 J W 58 John E Jr 126 Wm
Jenkins 126
WOODFALL, 159 160 162 Henry
Sampson 158
WOODS, Clayton 203 Dora 203 E
O 203 Ella 203
WOODWARD, J J 57
WORTHINGTON, Elizabeth 201
WRIGHT, Anna M 177 Annie
Hampton 139 Harriet 130 John
D 177 Maria Louisa 177
Richard M 177
YANCEY, 14 15
YANCY, W L 130 Wm L 132
YATES, William McCharles 12
YORK, Richard 13
YOUMANS, L W 57

243